PRAISE FOR

THE TEMPLE REVEALED

"*The Temple Revealed* is absolutely fascinating! Christian Widener's writing style draws the reader into a captivating adventure to uncover secrets 'hidden in plain sight' for centuries! With an impressive engineering background, Dr. Widener presents the research with unquestionable logic while reference to biblical citations adds academic and prophetic gravitas. The site of the Temple in Jerusalem is without a doubt the most important piece of real estate on the planet, and Christian Widener's *The Temple Revealed* unveils so many important clues as to its true location. It is not just reading a book, it is an exciting journey of discovery!"

—WILLIAM J. FEDERER, SPEAKER, BESTSELLING AUTHOR, AND AMERICAN HISTORIAN, PRESIDENT, AMERISEARCH, INC., AMERICANMINUTE.COM

"A must read for students of biblical prophecy. Christian Widener's exploration of the location of the Jewish Temple is a very important contribution to this ongoing debate. He has done an excellent job examining the relevant biblical and historical data. His arguments should be carefully considered by everyone interested in this momentous subject."

—JOEL RICHARDSON, *NEW YORK TIMES* BESTSELLING AUTHOR, AND INTERNATIONALLY RECOGNIZED PROPHECY TEACHER

"Well written and thoroughly researched, Dr. Widener has provided a valuable contribution to the larger issue of the Temple's location."

—DR. RANDALL J. PRICE, DISTINGUISHED RESEARCH PROFESSOR OF BIBLICAL AND JUDAIC STUDIES, LIBERTY UNIVERSITY

"Astonishing and a great read! I encourage any Christian interested in prophecies of Christ's return to read this book. Dr. Widener has a great love for Israel and a deep interest in biblical prophecy. Believing that Scripture predicts not only the reestablishment of the State of Israel (which occurred in 1948) and the return of Jerusalem to Israeli control (which occurred in 1967) but also that the Jewish Temple must be rebuilt on Temple Mount before Jesus returns, he has set himself to examine how this could possibly happen, given the fact that the Mosque of Omar and the Dome of the Rock dominate the site. No one believes the Islamists will voluntarily surrender this territory, and any attempt to seize it would clearly result in bloody violence. Dr. Widener examines the historical and archaeological record carefully, as well as the geography of Temple Mount, and he demonstrates that the Third Temple (of Herod's day) actually stood north of the Dome of the Rock. Therefore the Jewish Temple can be rebuilt on its original site without the risk of war, and he strongly believes it will be. While the details regarding the future Temple may still be debatable, what is clear and certain is where the former temples used to sit and that Christ will come again to rule and reign from Jerusalem."

—DR. MICHAEL P. ANDRUS, LEAD PASTOR, RETIRED, FIRST EVANGELICAL FREE CHURCH, WICHITA, KS

THE
TEMPLE
REVEALED

CHRISTIAN WIDENER, PH.D.

Foreword by JOSH MCDOWELL

THE
TEMPLE
REVEALED

THE TRUE LOCATION OF *THE JEWISH TEMPLE* HIDDEN IN PLAIN SIGHT

The Temple Revealed

Cover photo: The unoccupied northern portion of the Temple Mount platform. The picture was taken standing directly east of the Dome of the Spirits and looking east towards the Golden Gate and the Mount of Olives. (Author's photo)

Hardcover ISBN: 978-0-578748-82-5
Paperback ISBN: 978-0-578749-87-7
Ebook ISBN: 978-0-578748-84-9

Book designed by Mark Karis
Published by End Times Berean, LLC
Visit www.EndTimesBerean.com

THIS BOOK IS DEDICATED to the One who has chosen Jerusalem as his possession and the site of the temple as the place for the soles of his feet and for his throne. To my Lord and Savior, Jesus Christ, who is the great High Priest, the King of kings, the Son of the living God, and the only Mediator for humankind to God, offering salvation to everyone who believes and follows after him.

I would like to thank my wife, Consuelo, and our four children, Elena, Corban, Noah, and Eva, for going along with me on this journey. I am also grateful for the encouragement of all the friends and godly people who have helped me along the way.

To the only God our Savior be glory, majesty, power and authority, through Jesus Christ our Lord, before all ages, now and forevermore! Amen.
JUDE 25

CONTENTS

FOREWORD

THE FIRST TIME I MET CHRISTIAN WIDENER was in 2013 when I invited him to come put his engineering skills to work on a project I was leading called Discover the Evidence in Plano, Texas. I knew right away that he was a young man who had a heart for God and that he was just as passionate as I am about demonstrating the reliability of the Scriptures.

When Christian first started describing his thoughts about the temple to me a few years ago, I thought, well, just maybe he has stumbled onto something. But when he told me he had finished the book and would like me to take a look at it and consider writing the foreword, I immediately wanted to know what kind of scholarly support he had for his research. I told him I thought he should get reviews by some top archaeological scholars if he wanted his work to be taken seriously. It's just too technical and too controversial a subject to try and address without getting real scholarly review. I have been researching and writing books for sixty years and have learned if you really want to prove something, you have to face your toughest critics, the top scholars, and the most respected people in the field and get an honest fact-based review of your arguments.

I believe strongly in *The Temple Revealed* for two reasons. First of all, this book demonstrates the reliability of the Scriptures, which is something I'm more than just passionate about. It's one of the things that brought me to faith from my own disbelief. The second reason is because of the *strength of the scholarship*. He went out and did what I asked. He contacted the most well-respected scholars in this area for comment and has cited and referenced his findings more than what you will find in most PhD dissertations. Now the fact that these findings are still not fully embraced by modern scholarship will give some readers pause, but I encourage you to read this book and see for yourself how strong the case really is. *The implications of his findings are nothing short of world-changing*, and I think he's correct that it is time for the Church to give its support to Israel for rebuilding the temple to make it "a house of prayer for all nations" (Is. 56:7).

I was just a boy when Israel became a nation, but I've been watching it struggle my whole life. To think that there is now in my lifetime a real chance for peace and the fulfillment of biblical prophecy to prepare the way for the Lord's return by rebuilding the temple, is just too powerful for words!

This is one book you won't ever forget reading. I encourage every Christian believer who supports Israel and is excited about seeing the return of Jesus Christ to read this book and share these exciting insights with your unbelieving friends, because the time is near!

TILL THE WHOLE WORLD HEARS,

JOSH D. MCDOWELL

PREFACE

THE PURPOSE OF THIS BOOK is to attempt to settle the question of the location of the Jewish temple through a multidisciplinary approach that includes religious and prophetic reasoning. In the past, this question has been mainly addressed with either: (1) simply less information than what is currently available today, or (2) by using a disciplined approach with purely historical or archaeological evidences. In either case, definitively substantiating the precise location of the temple before it was destroyed in AD 70 has proven intractable.

I have been studying this question for more than a decade because of its prophetic implications and because I think it is a key to achieving lasting peace in Israel. Many would challenge the latter statement and assert that it is exactly the temple that presents the greatest risk to peace. But that idea is deeply flawed because it assumes that it is possible that in some future state the Jewish people will finally forget about the temple. But we have almost two thousand years of observational data that argue quite convincingly to me that this is not true. It is like a piece of shrapnel embedded near the Jewish heart or the proverbial thorn in the lion's paw. In both cases, the offense must be removed, i.e., by rebuilding the temple, in order for true peace to be achieved.

The other reason that this issue matters is that support from the U.S., fueled by the Christian community, is the key to Israel being able to establish sufficient sovereignty over the Temple Mount in order to allow them to begin rebuilding the temple. Some might chafe at this comment as well, but the truth is that it was the support of the U.S. that tipped the balance to approve the establishment of statehood by Israel in the first place. The U.S. has also played a significant role in the defense and continued existence of Israel as a nation. It was the acknowledgment of the U.S. that Jerusalem is the capital of Israel that finally made it a reality for the world to just accept. The U.S. also first approved the annexation of the Golan Heights, which afterwards was approved by the Israeli Knesset and annexed. Therefore, it is not mere fanciful imagination to expect that finally allowing full and equal access to the Temple Mount and the rebuilding of the Jewish temple will also first require American support.

And the more I studied the issue, the more I became convinced that a comprehensive multidisciplinary approach could definitively identify the precise temple location. What I didn't know was whether or not it could be satisfactorily proven. But that's what you are here to find out. Is the question truly solvable at this point in time? I believe it is. There is a difference between speculation (the forming of a theory or conjecture without firm evidence) and deduction (the inference of facts by logical consideration of other known facts, natural laws, or universal principles). This book is a case to prove, beyond a reasonable doubt, where the holy temple stood before its destruction in AD 70, using secular and religious lines of reasoning to make logical deductions and inferences from the things we know are true about the site. This book is written for the average person, not the scholar, but references are heavily cited within the text to support the arguments presented.

I understand that these are bold claims, especially since I am neither an archaeologist, nor am I known in the field. But I have a proven track record in multidisciplinary investigations that cut across diverse fields, including materials, manufacturing, mechanical engineering design, nanoscience, and electrochemistry. I have a PhD in mechanical engineering with an emphasis in materials science and manufacturing, I am well published in these areas, and I was formerly a tenured university professor at the South Dakota School of Mines and Technology. As an associate professor, I directed an active research program that was awarded more than $10 million in competitively funded, cutting-edge advanced materials manufacturing and repair research. I am also a successful entrepreneur and cofounded a high-tech start-up that made the Inc. 500 list in 2017. So, what does that tell you? Just that while I'm not an archaeologist or historian per se, I am a competent researcher in an advanced engineering field who knows the difference between conjecture and proof. And when you have correctly answered a seemingly intractable problem, it should be like solving a Rubik's Cube*—Even though it may seem difficult, or even impossible, to solve, when you finally arrive at the correct solution it should be obvious to others as well.

My first experience applying my engineering expertise to biblical archaeology was in 2013, when I was invited to be involved in Discover the Evidence with Josh McDowell, a unique event centered around the discovery of first- and second-century papyrus texts in Egyptian cartonnage masks. Looking back, that event, and things it set in motion, changed my life. But even before that, I had been studying about Israel and the temple since 2007. As I did, I noticed that much of what is believed about the archaeology of the Holy Land, and the Temple Mount in particular, is based on consensus around interpretations of the data rather than hard facts alone. Actually, most people probably realize and acknowledge this but still generally trust the consensus—rely on it, in fact. That is how certainty is achieved in fields where it is very difficult to be certain about anything (like trying to determine how events happened thousands of years ago) particularly, when very little evidence remains on which to base our conclusions. Consequently, we seek consensus, which gives us the feeling of settled truth, even if it is not. In engineering, that is not generally how we arrive at certainty, though. We are dealing with the present. So, rather than relying on consensus of opinion, we achieve certainty through repeated testing until we are sure that we have characterized the variability of a system and have obtained results that can be repeated by someone else. Nevertheless, in any scientific discipline, once an idea becomes consensus, it is very difficult to change. The burden of proof becomes even higher than it was when it became the collective opinion in the first place. But what is more important: to achieve consensus or to discover the truth?

The Bible records that Pontius Pilate once asked Jesus a very important philosophical question, "What is truth?" (John 18:38). In today's postmodern world, there is a cancer of logical thought, called *relativism*. Relativism is defined as "the doctrine that knowledge, truth, and morality exist in relation to culture, society, or historical context and are not absolute."[1] But Pilate's question proves that this idea isn't new. It was probably already an old idea when Pilate asked Jesus the question. Asking that question reveals an understanding that in a subjective world without objective references, everything is subject to someone's opinion, and truth cannot be established absolutely. Am I saying, then, that relativism is correct? No, absolute truth logically has to exist. So, relativism as an ideology is bankrupt, a cancer of reason. What, then, is our source of objective truth? For the Christian and the religious Jew, objective truth regarding the things that can't simply be observed or tested and repeated scientifically can only be known through divine revelation, i.e. the Bible. Some objective external source of authority outside of ourselves is needed on which we can base our understanding of absolute reality. The secularist answer to understanding absolute reality is purely science and consensus—science for things that are measurable and repeatable, and consensus for those that are not, such as moral truth, theories about origins, and other hypotheses that cannot be directly tested and proven. This is a convenient solution to the dilemma of how we determine truth without God, but it fails to arrive at universal truth, which by definition must be true across all spheres of science, philosophy, and religion and not subject to someone's opinion. But even if we agree that there is a necessity for divinely revealed truth, which book do we go by? This is where the secularist throws up his hands and says, "See? It's all relative!"

But the answer is not abandonment of the Holy Scriptures, particularly for answering questions of both a religious and a historic nature. I find both the Old and New Testaments to be true revelations of God, which have been tested more rigorously than any other book in history, and can be considered reliable, even in areas that we have not yet been able to substantiate with archaeological evidence. That is why, when I read historic accounts in the Bible, I expect that there is some evidence left behind of the events described. There is probably not as much as we'd like to find, but I presume that things can be found to give confidence in the reality of what was recorded. In fact, that is why people originally went looking for many of the biblical places that we have already found, and as a result, the modern field of archaeology was born. And who were the people that founded modern archaeology? They were biblical scholars, experts in various technical fields, clergymen, university professors, and Orientalists, the majority of whom were Christians or who at least considered the historical accounts of the Scriptures as credible.

Therefore, I want to acknowledge that this book is the work of a Christian who loves Israel and the Jewish people. I also fully believe that the Word of God is accurate and authoritative, and therefore it can be tested and used as a guide when looking for the truth. In my research, I have used the Bible as a GPS to help me solve the enigma of the temple. But when you follow it and arrive at your destination, as with a GPS, it is obvious whether or not it guided you correctly. I believe that the evidence presented in this book is sound and objective, despite starting with a faith-based hypothesis. In fact, all hypotheses are ultimately faith based because they have their origins in the beliefs and understandings of their author but have yet to be proven. The evidence I present, though, mostly comes from external sources that cannot reflect any biases of my own. Furthermore, the conclusions I draw and the logic I used to arrive there are explained so that you can evaluate my conclusions based on the reasoning presented. I have made my best effort to present the information in this book in a straightforward and objective manner and to separate facts from opinions and inferences. Finally, the only firmly held views I have brought to this investigation are simply that there was formerly a Jewish temple in Jerusalem and that it will be rebuilt someday. All other assertions presented in the book are my conclusions based on the evidence I collected, logical deduction, and inference.

To that point, this book is a serious investigation into the history and archaeology of the Temple Mount, and it depends on the invaluable work of a multitude of incredible archaeologists and historians, without which this book would not have been possible. Deprived of the testimonies of people such as Flavius Josephus, Tacitus, Eusebius, Procopius, al-Tabari, the faithful pilgrims, the generations of rabbis who left reliable histories in antiquity, and the great modern-day archaeologists, scholars, and historians, such as Charles Warren, F. E. Peters, Dr. Leen Ritmeyer, and Dr. Asher Kaufmann, I wouldn't have been able to write this book. But the reality is that all of this information comes on top of a great deal of tradition and popular belief, and it is all generally interpreted through the author's viewpoint when it was reported. The great volume of work done in the Middle East has come from a broad range of personal worldviews, which affects how people interpret the data that has been collected. Plus, the interpretation of each work represents the views and beliefs of the author only at the time it was written, after which it becomes frozen in time, like words spoken that cannot be taken back. Furthermore, those interpretations have often been made without the benefit of knowing about finds that would come later that might have changed their interpretation. The most obvious consequence of this is that the literature is full of conclusions about the data that are no longer valid but continue to muddy the water because they have been cited, accepted, and made a part of popular belief. And this is where the work of an outsider can be very helpful. An outsider can provide a fresh perspective. The purpose of this book is to sift through the data and primary sources available on the historical and archaeological past of the temple, and then pull out the facts so that anyone interested in the truth can see what has been hidden in plain sight, namely, the proper location of the Jewish temple.

Through wisdom and careful examination, I believe it is possible for all to know with certainty where the temple was located. As an example, there was a seemingly impossible case brought to King Solomon three thousand years ago by two women. One woman's baby had died; the other's was alive and healthy. So, the first woman stole the living child, and now, *both* women stood before the king, claiming the living child. Who could know which one was the real mother? The problem couldn't be solved using the conventional wisdom of the day. There was no method at the time to test the truth, and they couldn't wait three thousand years for a DNA test. So, using his God-given wisdom, Solomon invented his own test to effectively deduce which woman was the child's mother.

> Then the king said, "Bring me a sword." So they brought a sword for the king. He then gave an order: "Cut the living child in two and give half to one and half to the other."
>
> The woman whose son was alive was deeply moved out of love for her son and said to the king, "Please, my lord, give her the living baby! Don't kill him!"
>
> But the other said, "Neither I nor you shall have him. Cut him in two!"
>
> Then the king gave his ruling: "Give the living baby to the first woman. Do not kill him; she is his mother."

With this test, Solomon was able to separate truth from fiction, and everyone present could as well.

We find ourselves in a similar situation today concerning the true location of the ancient temple. Like Solomon, we are missing the kind of indisputable proof that we'd like to have (such as photographs, detailed construction drawings, or epigraphic proof carved onto the foundation stone of the Holy of Holies, or Most Holy Place). However, through wisdom and sound reasoning, a reliable determination can be made. I believe the way to do it is to collect all of the relevant literature and then present the information in a way that helps the reader confidently sort through it. Only then is it possible to see what can be reliably known and stated about the history and archaeology of the temple, and to clearly delineate fact from speculation.

Another thing that must be done to solve the mystery of the temple location is to talk about what is probable and what is highly improbable. Just like a jury determining the truth in a court case, we can judge what is true beyond a reasonable doubt. And as those acquainted with the law or who have ever served on a jury know, reasonable doubt does not mean beyond any possibility of an alternate explanation. Because two thousand years after the fact, without the benefit of living eyewitnesses, photographs, or videos, we have to make some judgments with imperfect information. But if this book achieves its purpose, you will be able to understand the data and come to a confident verdict about the temple location.

I hope you will go on this journey with me to find the true location of the Jewish temple that was destroyed in AD 70. As you read, be prepared to reevaluate what most of the modern world has accepted as true—the assumption that the Dome of the Rock would have to be destroyed in order to rebuild the holy temple. This book reveals what has been hidden in plain sight using engineering, forensics, and logic to sift through historical records and archaeological findings to develop new insights. It is the testimony of historians and archaeologists, alongside logical deduction and reason, that should convince you of the truth. My job with this book is just to present things in a way that makes that easier. If this book is successful in illuminating the truth, it will be for God's glory, not mine.

I would also like to include a comment about the historic quotations that I have included in this book. Language is always somewhat inherently imprecise in that words out of context or unclearly written can often be taken multiple ways, particularly when people are writing about events and places that they have seen. From the writers' perspective, they were reporting what they saw, and the language they chose was intended to communicate, in their estimation, what they observed. However, the early witnesses were not writing with this present generation in mind. Neither did they consider the changes to Jerusalem and its environs that they would never see but of which we are very much aware. Therefore, it is important to include as much of the surrounding context with their comments as is practical and elucidating. Therefore, I ask your indulgence in some cases where it might seem that I have included too much of a particular quotation. I've done this on purpose so that you can judge for yourself if I have correctly interpreted their comments. In far too many of the works on the Temple Mount, where the authors' assertions about the temple rely on historic testimony, quotations have been misunderstood or misused to support a particular point of view. It happens so often, in fact, that I am also concerned about being accused of misinterpreting or taking liberties with the text myself—that is, seeing what I want to see. The best way to guard against this is to include more of the passage, so the legitimacy of the interpretation is protected by including its proper context, particularly since during my investigation, I found many places where others have used portions of text out of context to imply something very different from what I think was there. The same thing goes for the many scriptural quotations and even modern quotations in this text.

And one final note: I have chosen intentionally to refer to dates in this book using the old convention of *BC* (before Christ) and *AD* (*Anno Domini*, "in the year of the Lord"), rather than *BCE* (before the Common Era) and *CE* (Common Era), a dating convention that is still indexed by the birth of Jesus Christ. It's what I grew up with, and I don't believe there is a need to change it, though the use of *BCE* and

CE has become conventional in academic circles over the past fifteen years or so. In a recent trip through the Louvre in Paris, I noticed that the French have also remained with the old convention, albeit in their format, *av. J.-C.* (before Jesus Christ) and *ap. J.-C.* (after Jesus Christ), for which I applaud them.

It is the glory of God to conceal a matter, to search out a matter is the glory of kings.

(PROVERBS 25:2)

A key landmark of the temple, the messianic Golden Gate (Eastern Gate) of the Temple Mount in Jerusalem, which has been walled up with stone. Islamic tombs surround the gate and most of the Eastern Wall. [Author's photo]

INTRODUCTION

I WANT TO THANK YOU for picking up this book and engaging in one of the most significant debates regarding Jerusalem—something even more controversial than the decision to recognize Jerusalem as the capital of the State of Israel.[1] The issue revolves around the rebuilding of the Jewish temple, which has lain in ruins since AD 70 and is the next prophetic piece in Israel's restoration. Of course, that necessitates determining precisely where it should be located when it is rebuilt. For many Christians the rebuilding of the temple signifies the final steps before the physical return of Jesus Christ to the earth. For Jews, it will mean an answer to almost two thousand years of prayer and also the near return of the Messiah. For Muslims seeking peace it may signal a hopeful future of tolerance, but for others in the Middle East, it will be a sign of defeat, a signal of the strength of Israel, and the reality of Israel's indefinite presence in the land. Since it is widely believed that the Dome of the Rock would have to be demolished to rebuild the temple, for many there is a very real fear that it would cause a terrible war. For all of those reasons, the rebuilding of the temple remains, for now, only a dream.

Theologians, archaeologists, and scholars have earnestly debated the proper location of the temple for over two centuries, and all the more so since Israel became a nation again in 1948.[2] Those debates are still going on today.[3] In recent years, some have even denied that the temple ever existed and are trying to use historical revisionism (denialism) to retell the history of the Temple Mount.[4] And yet, with no Jewish temple to point to and no consensus even on its exact former location, it is no wonder that denialists are attempting to erase any trace of a Jewish presence or claim on the Temple Mount and rewrite its history.[5] However, the problem of locating the true placement of the temple is not so much a lack of archaeological evidence, but more a problem of properly identifying and understanding what we do have that is known and visible. And no wonder it is difficult, when there are so many accounts, histories, and conflicting reports that have to be sifted through to find the truth. It also doesn't help that everyone who has tried has had a different opinion.

In fact, by my count, there have been at least forty-seven people who have published views regarding exactly where the temple used to be located, from the seventeenth century to the present (see the appendix for a full list). Many of those ideas overlap, though, and can be condensed into just four primary views. In this book I will propose my own view, which is essentially a modification of Asher Kaufman's proposal, which located the Temple in the northern portion of the Temple Mount, with the exception that it must also be in line with the Golden Gate. I will present information and reasoning to demonstrate, beyond a reasonable doubt, why this is the proper location, and also expose why other views are simply untenable in light of the archaeological evidence and weight of historical testimony. By using the reliable testimony of Scripture along with the testimonies of Jewish rabbis, historians, visitors, and pilgrims to the region; archaeological assessments; and logical inference, it is possible to establish once and for all where the temple was located. It is also important to remember that, as noted by the well-known archaeologist Eilat Mazar, archaeological work is divided into two parts: the things that are fixed (the documented excavation data such as the location and depth of an artifact) and those that can vary (the analyses, interpretations, and corresponding conclusions that are drawn from the excavated data).[6] As she admits, the latter, the conclusions derived from archaeological analysis, "will hold until better ones come along and replace them." I am hopeful that by assembling all of the information presented here in this book, it will be possible to arrive at a new and better understanding of the temple location.

I first started thinking about writing a book on this subject more than ten years ago, after doing some initial research on the Temple Mount, and coming across some verses in the book of Ezekiel.

> Then the man brought me back to the outer gate of the sanctuary, the one facing east, and it was shut. The LORD said to me, "This gate is to remain shut. It must not be opened; no one may enter through it. It is to remain shut because the LORD, the God of Israel, has entered through it." (Ezekiel 44:1–2)

Since you've picked up this book, you may know about the Golden Gate of Jerusalem's Temple Mount, the gate that faces east, and its messianic connection. The gate is prominently observed when viewed from the east while standing on the Mount of Olives, as seen in Figure 1. The tradition probably comes from the book of Ezekiel, and people have been talking about his prophetic words since he wrote them, more than twenty-five hundred years ago, because the gate was already an important part of temple service at that time. In fact, there has been a gate in the Eastern Wall of the Temple Mount since it was first constructed, about three thousand years ago. But the key thing to know about the Golden Gate is that it has been shut for most of the last two thousand years (as seen in the photo at the beginning of this introduction). To make sure it could never be opened again, the Ottoman sultan Suleiman the Magnificent had it walled up in stone in 1541.[7] It is reported that he sought to prevent the messiah of the Jews and Christians from ever entering through the gate. Even before that time, however, Muslims were placing their burial tombs in front of the gate and along the Eastern Wall of the Temple Mount, as reported by Santo Brasca in AD 1458.[8] Traditionally, it is thought that this was done to defile the coming messiah by blocking the entrance with corpses. Whether or not this is the true reason for the cemetery, when I read that Ezekiel had prophesied that the Eastern Gate would be shut and "is to remain shut," and I see that the gate is permanently closed . . . that makes me pay attention.

Figure 1: View of the Temple Mount in Jerusalem, viewed from the Mount of Olives to the east. *[Author's photo]*

And that isn't the only fulfilled prophecy in the passage. Today, because the site is under the control of the Islamic Waqf of Jordan, it is freely used as an Islamic holy site, but there are severe restrictions for access to non-Muslims, particularly Jews, who are not even allowed to pray openly on the Temple Mount. Logically, this is somewhat of a mystery since Israel now controls all of Jerusalem, and the Temple

Mount is the holiest site in Judaism, but it makes sense biblically and prophetically because of Ezekiel 44:8:

> And you have not kept charge of My holy things yourselves, but you have set foreigners to keep charge of My sanctuary. (NASB)

Now, when I first read that, my eyes nearly popped out of my head! If you don't know the history of the Temple Mount, then you might not be aware that the government of Israel, right after regaining control of the eastern part of Jerusalem, including the Temple Mount, in the Six-Day War (June 5–10, 1967), immediately surrendered control of the Temple Mount (*Al-Haram ash-Sharif*) back to the Islamic Waqf of Jordan, who had previously been in control of the haram, or sacred place. The gesture was part of securing a lasting peace to the short-lived war. And I understand that to a point. But seriously?! Why would they give the control of their holiest site on earth back to a country that had just attacked them and tried to wipe them out and was actively working to erase all traces of a Jewish presence there? That makes absolutely NO sense to me. However, in light of God's Word, through his prophet Ezekiel, we can have confidence that it did not take God by surprise! In fact, it's exactly what He said would happen. Now, if that doesn't make the hair on the back of your neck stand up, you probably aren't too sure about this prophecy stuff and may just think it's a matter of seeing whatever one wants to see. Well, hold on. That's not all. As I continued to read Ezekiel 43–44, looking a little closer, I started seeing a multitude of other modern fulfillments of prophecy in those same chapters. One possible fulfillment alone could be argued as coincidental, but the more unlikely events you have in one passage, the more convincing the case is that prophecy is not only real, but is being fulfilled before our eyes!

> He said to me, "Son of man, *this is the place of My throne and the place of the soles of My feet*, where I will dwell among the sons of Israel forever. And the house of Israel will not again defile My holy name, neither they nor their kings, by their harlotry and *by the corpses of their kings* when they die, *by setting their threshold by My threshold and*

their doorpost beside My doorpost, with only the wall between Me and them. And they have defiled My holy name by their abominations which they have committed. So I have consumed them in My anger. Now let them put away their *harlotry and the corpses of their kings far from Me*; and I will dwell among them forever." (Ezekiel 43:7–9 NASB, emphasis added)

Perhaps at this time it would be good to review why Jerusalem is such a special place. Where Ezekiel wrote, "the place of My throne and place of the soles of My feet," God was talking about the temple, and we are immediately directed to the area of the Temple Mount, and to Jerusalem in general. This is the only place on the planet that God has called his own, in writing. This makes Jerusalem holy to everyone who believes the Scriptures, Jews and Christians. Muslims also regard Jerusalem as their third most holy site. And by calling it a "holy" site, it means that it is entirely separate from other places. It's odd, then, that we read of the defilement of God's holy temple "by the corpses of . . . kings." It would have been such an abomination to have people actually buried on the Temple Mount that we don't expect it to be possible. So, *are* there corpses of kings buried on the Temple Mount? Have there ever been? Or is that a mistranslation of the text? These are important questions.

But some readers would jump in here saying that the translation should read "lifeless idols" and not "corpses of their kings," but let's just acknowledge that the meaning of the Hebrew in this passage is debated. To the English mind it may be hard to understand why the translation could vary so much, but it's just that the more literal meaning is "corpses of their kings" and a more idiomatic or figurative translation would be "lifeless idols." An example of this might be "kill the lights" meaning "turn off the lights" rather than "destroy the lights." Properly translating this passage depends on our understanding of what Ezekiel was talking about. We know what it says literally in Hebrew, but what did it mean? Well, frankly, I would never have lost any sleep over this question had I not watched a video tour of the Temple Mount, posted by Rabbi Chaim

Richman, the former international director of the Temple Institute in Israel. While making his way around the Temple Mount, talking about various features and points of interest, he mentioned that there was a king buried right on the Temple Mount, not far from where the Holy of Holies, or Most Holy Place (NIV), used to be, and he mentioned what a desecration it was to have dead people buried in this holy site. So when I read this passage and remembered what he said, again I couldn't believe my eyes! So, I had to check it out for myself. And sure enough, Hussein ibn Ali al-Hashimi (or Ḥusayn ibn ʿAlī), king of Hejaz, who died June 4, 1931, is buried on the Temple Mount,[9] near the Gate of the Cotton Merchants, on the northwest interior of the Temple Mount. A picture of his tomb is shown in Figure 2. That's amazing! Until watching that video I didn't know that there are actual burial tombs in the northwest corner of the complex. The words of Ezekiel, written between 593 and 571 BC, were fulfilled less than a century ago.

Now, someone might say that's a coincidence, and it could happen anywhere, if you wait long enough. But of the 15.7 billion acres of land on the earth, few have any kings buried on them, and the 36 acres of the Temple Mount are expressly forbidden to have anyone buried there in the first place. According to public sources on Wikipedia, about 287 different monarchies have existed around the world since the early Bronze Age.[10] Recognizing that kings are often buried together or in close proximity for a given monarchy, we can estimate that up to 5,000 acres of land may entomb all of the world's kings from the early Bronze Age until now. That means the odds of having a king buried on the Temple Mount by accident is 1 in 87,222 (a 0.001 percent chance). If you don't like that estimate because people only inhabit about 10 percent of the land on the planet, and if you'd like to double the number of acres globally that contain buried kings for good measure to account for unknown kings, then the odds are still fewer than 1 in 4,361 (a 0.02 percent chance) that a king would be buried in the 36 acres of the Temple Mount by happenstance. That means it's not just a coincidence, and it's a very unlikely thing to predict, without divine inspiration.

Figure 2: Burial site of Hussein ibn Ali al-Hashimi, King of Hejaz. He died on June 4, 1931 and was buried inside the Temple Mount. His tomb is shown here and lies near the Cotton Merchants Gate, in partial fulfillment of Ezekiel 43:7. *[Author's photo]*

Without that information, you can abstractly debate the proper meaning, but when you find out that the event described actually happened . . . literally . . . then this should settle the question of whether or not it is just a figurative reference. And you could certainly make the argument that it is both figurative *and* literal, without causing a contradiction, because both lifeless idols and kings' corpses have been found on the Temple Mount over that past twenty-six hundred years or so. But one interpretation is general, and the other is extremely specific and timely (within the last century and continuing to the present day).

Looking back at Ezekiel 43:8, we see that the phrase "setting their threshold by My threshold and their door post beside My door post, with only the wall between Me and them" has also been fulfilled. That is the core reason I'm writing this book. When I first started reading about the Temple Mount and the Dome of the Rock, I immediately accepted the idea that the Dome of the Rock was sitting on the exact location of the former Jewish temple. But later, as I explored further, I became less sure—particularly as I realized that this verse was telling us there would be a foreign temple on the Temple Mount sitting right next to God's house! I thought, *If that is the case, then there must be the evidence to prove it.*

In the pages ahead the entire case is laid out, with the evidence to prove, beyond a reasonable doubt, that the famed Golden Gate is the true eastern gate of the First and Second Temples and marks the east-west line of where the temple should be rebuilt. It will also be shown that the Dome of the Spirits covers the remains of the threshing floor of Araunah, which gives us the precise location of the Holy of Holies of the temple. Using these two landmarks, which are validated using historic testimonies, recent and not-so-recent archaeological finds, logical deduction, and God's Word, we can now confidently proclaim the correct location to begin rebuilding the temple. Answering anything definitively about Jerusalem is like trying to untangle a knotted fishing line, but with a little patience and persistence, we can separate a lot of fact from fiction. This book will start with the accounts recorded in the Bible and will then use historic testimony and archaeological evidence to discover the true location of the Jewish temple from before AD 70. Then perhaps, after almost two thousand years, the temple can be rebuilt in its proper location in the northern portion of the Temple Mount, which is free and clear of any obstructions that might otherwise prevent its immediate construction.

Maranatha!

PART I

DISCOVERING WHAT HAS BEEN HIDING IN PLAIN SIGHT

"Call to me and I will answer you, and will tell you great and hidden things that you have not known."
(JEREMIAH 33:3 ESV)

Aerial view of the Temple Mount *[Photo by Andrew Shiva]*[1]

1

HIDDEN IN PLAIN SIGHT

TO SOLVE ANY MYSTERY, a detective must uncover clues that others have missed. Sometimes that comes from returning to the scene of the crime and seeing something that was there but wasn't noticed before. Other times it comes from looking again at the same evidence but seeing something new. We can miss things when we become comfortable with an idea that blinds us to the obvious. Here's an example. I want you to repeat a word for me. Ready? The word is *silk*. Say it out loud three times: Silk. Silk. Silk.

Now, quick, answer me out loud: What do cows drink?

(I bet you said, "Milk.")

Now, I know that this is an extremely juvenile example, but hopefully it illustrates the point. But if that doesn't seem relevant for understanding how something being repeated multiple times can misdirect us, let me try another example.

In 1983, David Copperfield performed a famous illusion in front of a live audience. Right before their eyes, he made the Statue of Liberty vanish and then later reappear. He accomplished this feat by seating the entire audience and his own stage on a very slowly rotating platform. He began his trick with the crowd facing Lady Liberty. Then he lowered a very large curtain behind the stage to obscure the statue. While he distracted the crowd with a variety of other entertainment, the stage slowly turned away from the statue, so slowly that no one noticed the motion. Then he raised the curtain to show the crowd that the statue had vanished, then closed the curtain and entertained them with loud music until the platform had returned to its original position. Finally, he removed the curtain to show them that all was right again in the world and that our liberties, so hard-won in our country, were still secure. By misdirection, he had hidden something so enormous in plain sight.

If we look up the Webster definition of the word *hidden*, we find that it doesn't just mean buried and out of sight. It can simply be that it is obscured or made difficult to understand or perceive.

> **hidden** adjective | \ ˈhi-dᵊn
> 1 : being out of sight or not readily apparent : concealed
> 2 : obscure, unexplained, undisclosed[2]

How could something as important as the temple be hidden in plain sight? Simply by misdirection and mislabeling of the things that have been found. Certainly, there have been many attempts over the millennia to deliberately destroy Jerusalem, the Temple Mount, and any evidence of the Jewish presence there, but it can also happen innocently. In attempts to be conservative and try to avoid potential bias, archaeologists prefer to take their stand on more defensible positions, which favor younger dating assertions over older ones. Furthermore, none of the work is free of bias or religious implication, not when we are speaking about Jerusalem and the lands of the Bible. Plus, we are also talking about things pertaining to God; so, I think God could have intentionally concealed this truth until it was the proper time. And it wouldn't be the first time God has hidden things in plain sight. For example, one day, Jesus was speaking with the Pharisees and the Sadducees on the Temple Mount, and he was speaking to them very bluntly, which angered them and made them want to stone him. I will reproduce the whole passage here because I think it bears reading. After you read it, you will understand how miraculous it was that these religious leaders were not able to stone Jesus at that very moment:

> When Jesus spoke again to the people, he said, "I am the light of the world. Whoever follows me will never walk in darkness but will have the light of life."
>
> The Pharisees challenged him, "Here you are, appearing as your own witness; your testimony is not valid."
>
> Jesus answered, "Even if I testify on my own behalf, my testimony is valid, for I know where I came from and where I am going. But you have no idea where I come from or where I am going. You judge by human standards; I pass judgment on no one. But if I do judge, my decisions are true, because I am not alone. I stand with the Father, who sent me. In your own Law it is written that the testimony of two witnesses is true. I am one who testifies for myself; my other witness is the Father, who sent me."
>
> Then they asked him, "Where is your father?"
>
> "You do not know me or my Father," Jesus replied. "If you knew me, you would know my Father also." He spoke these words while teaching in the temple courts near the place where the offerings were put. Yet no one seized him, because his hour had not yet come.
>
> Once more Jesus said to them, "I am going away, and you will look for me, and you will die in your sin. Where I go, you cannot come."
>
> This made the Jews ask, "Will he kill himself? Is that why he says, 'Where I go, you cannot come'?"
>
> But he continued, "You are from below; I am from above. You are of this world; I am not of this world. I told you that you would die in your sins; if you do not believe that I am he, you will indeed die in your sins."
>
> "Who are you?" they asked.

"Just what I have been telling you from the beginning," Jesus replied. "I have much to say in judgment of you. But he who sent me is trustworthy, and what I have heard from him I tell the world."

They did not understand that he was telling them about his Father. So Jesus said, "When you have lifted up the Son of Man, then you will know that I am he and that I do nothing on my own but speak just what the Father has taught me. The one who sent me is with me; he has not left me alone, for I always do what pleases him." Even as he spoke, many believed in him.

To the Jews who had believed him, Jesus said, "If you hold to my teaching, you are really my disciples. Then you will know the truth, and the truth will set you free."

They answered him, "We are Abraham's descendants and have never been slaves of anyone. How can you say that we shall be set free?"

Jesus replied, "Very truly I tell you, everyone who sins is a slave to sin. Now a slave has no permanent place in the family, but a son belongs to it forever. So if the Son sets you free, you will be free indeed. I know that you are Abraham's descendants. Yet you are looking for a way to kill me, because you have no room for my word. I am telling you what I have seen in the Father's presence, and you are doing what you have heard from your father."

"Abraham is our father," they answered.

"If you were Abraham's children," said Jesus, "then you would do what Abraham did. As it is, you are looking for a way to kill me, a man who has told you the truth that I heard from God. Abraham did not do such things. You are doing the works of your own father."

"We are not illegitimate children," they protested. "The only Father we have is God himself."

Jesus said to them, "If God were your Father, you would love me, for I have come here from God. I have not come on my own; God sent me. Why is my language not clear to you? Because you are unable to hear what I say. You belong to your father, the devil, and you want to carry out your father's desires. He was a murderer from the beginning, not holding to the truth, for there is no truth in him. When he lies, he speaks his native language, for he is a liar and the father of lies. Yet because I tell the truth, you do not believe me! Can any of you prove me guilty of sin? If I am telling the truth, why don't you believe me? Whoever belongs to God hears what God says. The reason you do not hear is that you do not belong to God."

The Jews answered him, "Aren't we right in saying that you are a Samaritan and demon-possessed?"

"I am not possessed by a demon," said Jesus, "but I honor my Father and you dishonor me. I am not seeking glory for myself; but there is one who seeks it, and he is the judge. Very truly I tell you, whoever obeys my word will never see death."

At this they exclaimed, "Now we know that you are demon-possessed! Abraham died and so did the prophets, yet you say that whoever obeys your word will never taste death. Are you greater than our father Abraham? He died, and so did the prophets. Who do you think you are?"

Jesus replied, "If I glorify myself, my glory means nothing. My Father, whom you claim as your God, is the one who glorifies me. Though you do not know him, I know him. If I said I did not, I would be a liar like you, but I do know him and obey his word. Your father Abraham rejoiced at the thought of seeing my day; he saw it and was glad."

"You are not yet fifty years old," they said to him, "and you have seen Abraham!"

"Very truly I tell you," Jesus answered, "before Abraham was born, I am!" At this, they picked up stones to stone him, but Jesus hid himself, slipping away from the temple grounds. (John 8:12–59)

Jesus was equating himself with God and claiming to be his Son, which the Pharisees were not willing to accept and considered blasphemy. So needless to say, they were more than a little upset. Slipping away from this angry crowd in broad daylight on the Temple Mount appears to me to be much more of a miraculous event than what one might get from a casual reading of the text. How did he hide himself and slip away right in front of everyone? It should have been very easy to apprehend Jesus in a crowd when both Scripture and history indicate that he was a gentle and calm man. I don't think anyone can imagine Jesus as an Olympic athlete and parkour runner pulling some ninja move and vanishing by virtue of his physical prowess. And clearly, an angry crowd intent on stoning him would not just let him waltz away. So how did he do it? I think he simply confused their minds and made them unable to perceive him, and then he calmly walked away. A very similar thing happened in the days of Elisha the prophet when he prayed for God to blind the eyes of the army of Aram who had come to capture him.

> As the enemy came down toward him, Elisha prayed to the LORD, "Strike this army with blindness." *So he struck them with blindness, as Elisha had asked. Elisha told them,* "This is not the road and this is not the city. *Follow me, and I will lead you* to the man you are looking for." And he led them to Samaria. After they entered the city, Elisha said, "LORD, open the eyes of these men so they can see." Then the LORD opened their eyes and they looked, and there they were, inside Samaria. When the king of Israel saw them, he asked Elisha, "Shall I kill them, my father? Shall I kill them?"
>
> "Do not kill them," he answered. "Would you kill those you have captured with your own sword or bow? Set food and water before them so that they may eat and drink and then go back to their master." So he prepared a great feast for them, and after they had finished eating and drinking, he sent them away, and they returned to their master. So the bands from Aram stopped raiding Israel's territory. (2 Kings 6:18–23, emphasis added)

In this passage, we see that God also blinded the eyes of the army of Aram so that they would not recognize Elisha and kill him. While we don't know exactly how God did it, we can conclude that it is possible for something to be hidden by God in plain sight, even though it may seem unlikely or even impossible.

I'm bringing this up because it is perhaps the best explanation for how the temple location has remained obscured up to the present time. Hopefully, after reading this book, the truth will become obvious. The reason it isn't obvious is that there are too many wrong ideas and presumptions that have been accepted as facts. In reality, what is thought to be true is generally based on the work of a limited number of scholars who are trusted to have arrived at the proper conclusion. After all, how many people have months, even years of their life to dedicate to understanding the full history of the Temple Mount and all the associated archaeological findings, and then reassembling all the evidence into the correct picture of what happened? It's like trying to piece Humpty Dumpty back together again (which couldn't be done with "all the kings' horses and all the kings' men"[3]). As a result, we have dozens of different pictures of Humpty Dumpty, but none that are completely convincing—so, many have concluded it is simply not possible to be sure at this point in time. Why? Because the strength of modern consensus has made it difficult to recognize any reliable landmarks to show us the true location of the Jewish temple.

However, there are current landmarks, preserved to this day, that show us the true temple location. But to identify them, it is necessary to sift through the historical records and separate common beliefs from historical facts. The most important of these is finding and properly identifying the threshing floor, which was how the temple site was chosen/located in the first place. This will be discussed in the next chapter. But the landmark that is key to unlocking it all is the Eastern Gate, also known as the Shushan Gate or Golden Gate of the Temple Mount, which is discussed in detail in chapter 3, "The East Gate Points the Way."

There are four main viewpoints about where the First and Second Temples of Israel could have been located, shown in Figure 3. For purposes of orientation, the temple faced east. The Dome of the Rock today sits near the central portion of the rectangular Temple Mount (point b).

The City of David is directly south and begins where the map is ending and is also an area thought to have possibly housed the Temple (point d). The northern location supported in this book (point a) and the general area for southern locations (point c) are also shown on the map.

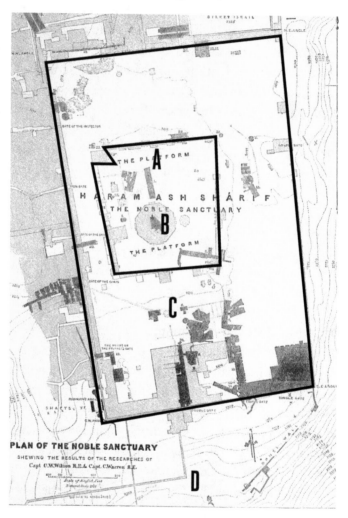

Figure 3: Plan of the Temple Mount (Noble Sanctuary) showing (a) the northern temple placement view, (b) on the Dome of the Rock view, (c) a southern view with a location near al-Aqsa Mosque, and (d) the view that the temple was located in or near the City of David to the south. Charles Warren (1871). *The Recovery of Jerusalem*. New York: D. Appleton with author additions.

Following are the principal viewpoints on the former location of the Jewish temple in Jerusalem:

a. North of the Dome of the Rock—firmly placed on the original bedrock of Mount Moriah, directly over the Dome of the Spirits as identified by Asher Kaufmann, and in line with the Eastern Gate (the position presented in this book).[4]

b. Near the middle of the Temple Mount platform—in the same place where the Dome of the Rock is located today. This view enjoys the majority of popular opinion.[5]

c. All areas proposed south of the Dome of the Rock—including areas near al-Aqsa mosque, aligned with the al-Kas fountain, and various other proposals.[6]

d. In the Ophel area south of the Temple Mount or in the City of David near the Gihon spring.[7]

By the end of this first section, I hope to have made the case clearly enough for all to see that the first location, north of the Dome of the Rock, is beyond a reasonable doubt the former location of the temple.

The Dome of the Spirits or Tablets, also called *Qubbat el-Arwah* [*Author's photo*]

2

THE THRESHING FLOOR IS THE DATUM

FOR NON-ENGINEERS, you may be asking, "What's a datum?" Well, it's not the singular of "data." Rather, "datum" in engineering speak is a term used to describe a point, surface, or axis on an object that can be measured against to locate other features on the part. In very simple terms it is a marker from which measurements can be made to locate something. This is a very important concept to me—probably because I am an engineer, and one of the principal areas of my research has been the repair of very expensive precision machined parts. When a part is damaged and you want to restore it, you need a way to not only add metal back onto the part, but also to re-machine the part back to its original dimensions and tolerances. If you don't have any reference points (datums) to measure against, it's challenging, or impossible in some cases, to properly re-machine a part, even if you can add the metal back where it is needed. Consequently, when I started thinking about where the temple was located, the first thing I wanted to do was find any true fixed reference points that could be reliably used to locate the temple. Without them it is challenging or even impossible to be precise in determining its former location. Therefore, the opening question to ask is, How was the temple site identified in the first place? What are the landmarks given in Scripture for its location? First Chronicles tells us the answer. It was built on the site of the threshing floor of Araunah.

> So the LORD sent a plague on Israel, and seventy thousand men of Israel fell dead. And God sent an angel to destroy Jerusalem. But as the angel was doing so, the LORD saw it and relented concerning the disaster and said to the angel who was destroying the people, "Enough! Withdraw your hand." The angel of the LORD was then standing at the threshing floor of Araunah the Jebusite.
>
> David looked up and saw the angel of the LORD standing between heaven and earth, with a drawn sword in his hand extended over Jerusalem. Then David and the elders, clothed in sackcloth, fell facedown.
>
> David said to God, "Was it not I who ordered the fighting men to be counted? I, the shepherd, have sinned and done wrong. These are but sheep. What have they done? LORD my God, let your hand fall on me and my family, but do not let this plague remain on your people."
>
> Then the angel of the LORD ordered Gad to tell David to go up and build an altar to the LORD on the threshing floor of Araunah the Jebusite. So David went up in obedience to the word that Gad had spoken in the name of the LORD.
>
> While Araunah was threshing wheat, he turned and saw the angel; his four sons who were with him hid themselves. Then David approached, and when Araunah looked and saw him, he left the threshing floor and bowed down before David with his face to the ground.
>
> David said to him, "Let me have the site of your threshing floor so I can build an altar to the LORD, that the plague on the people may be stopped. Sell it to me at the full price."
>
> Araunah said to David, "Take it! Let my lord the king do whatever

pleases him. Look, I will give the oxen for the burnt offerings, the threshing sledges for the wood, and the wheat for the grain offering. I will give all this."

But King David replied to Araunah, "No, I insist on paying the full price. I will not take for the LORD what is yours, or sacrifice a burnt offering that costs me nothing."

So, David paid Araunah six hundred shekels of gold for the site. David built an altar to the LORD there and sacrificed burnt offerings and fellowship offerings. He called on the LORD, and the LORD answered him with fire from heaven on the altar of burnt offering.

Then the LORD spoke to the angel, and he put his sword back into its sheath. At that time, when David saw that the LORD had answered him on the threshing floor of Araunah the Jebusite, he offered sacrifices there. The tabernacle of the LORD, which Moses had made in the wilderness, and the altar of burnt offering were at that time on the high place at Gibeon. But David could not go before it to inquire of God, because he was afraid of the sword of the angel of the LORD.

Then David said, "The house of the LORD God is to be here, and also the altar of burnt offering for Israel." (1 Chronicles 21:14–22:1)

Hence, if Solomon depended on knowing the location of the threshing floor to build the temple approximately three thousand years ago, then we too should be looking for the threshing floor to reestablish its correct location. Amazingly, for the majority of the temple site viewpoints, the location of the threshing floor is treated as a minor or irrelevant issue in determining the temple's true former location. Instead, most scholars are forced to presume one existed and theorize about its former location but cannot point to a compelling physical object or area that is visible today. In their view, the threshing floor has been lost to history and cannot be found again without extensive archaeological excavations on the Temple Mount, or it has been so marred and changed over time that it no longer resembles a threshing floor surface.

Ironically, periodic excavations have gone on over the years in various locations sanctioned by the Islamic Waqf, but with no effort to find or preserve evidence of a former Jewish presence on the Temple Mount. In fact, in 1999 when the Northern Branch of the Islamic Movement conducted illegal renovations on the Temple Mount, they disposed of more than nine thousand tons of dirt mixed with invaluable archaeological artifacts. And while no Waqf-sponsored projects have ever found anything acknowledged to be associated with the Jewish temple, the Temple Mount Sifting Project has found a lot of evidence from both the First and Second Temple periods by sifting through the debris of those 1999 excavations.[1] And even this effort has been criticized by modern scholarship in an attempt to discredit the efforts to learn everything possible about the debris taken from the Temple Mount.[2]

Nevertheless, with the threshing floor being such an important landmark, it is difficult to understand why anyone would feel confident that the temple's true location had been found without it. And yet, an existing threshing floor candidate has been identified, but not enough attention has been paid to it, though it is completely in the open and visible for all to see. Today, the Dome of the Spirits covers this location, which is the only site that can still be seen to be a surface that could have credibly served as a threshing floor. The location was thoroughly analyzed and reported on by Dr. Asher Kaufman, a scientist and physics professor at the Hebrew University.[3] In response to his book *The Temple Mount: Where Is the Holy of Holies?* there have been some attempts to refute his findings.[4] But as I'll show in this chapter, his principal identification of the threshing floor was absolutely correct. And as I said earlier, most temple placement views do not even address the problem of not being able to identify a threshing floor. However, this should be the starting point for any temple location discussion.

If God designated the threshing floor of Araunah as the site of the temple, then it really should be the start of our search as well. So, the questions being answered in this chapter are, What exactly does the threshing floor show us the location of? And, Is the area under the Dome of the Spirits a viable candidate for the threshing floor of Araunah?

WAS IT THE TEMPLE, OR JUST THE ALTAR, THAT WAS BUILT ON THE THRESHING FLOOR?

If you look very far into this issue, you will find that there appears to be some confusion about whether it was the altar or the Holy of Holies that was located on top of the threshing floor. So to clear up this issue and make sure that we are all on the same page, the short answer is that it was the Holy of Holies of the Temple of Solomon that was located on the threshing floor. The confusion regarding this question understandably has to do with the fact that, first of all, the Scriptures say that David initially built an altar on the threshing floor, and in 1 Chronicles 22 it says that both the temple and the altar were to be there. There is also a desire to connect the location of the sacrificial site of Isaac with the threshing floor and the temple altar, although obviously, both the Holy of Holies and the altar cannot be in the exact same place. We have this confirmed in 2 Chronicles 3, where we read that it was the temple and not the altar that was built on the threshing floor and it served as the datum for the temple location.

> Then Solomon began to build the temple of the LORD in Jerusalem on Mount Moriah, where the LORD had appeared to his father David. It was on the threshing floor of Araunah the Jebusite, the place provided by David. He began building on the second day of the second month in the fourth year of his reign. (2 Chronicles 3:1–2)

Notice carefully here that the temple of the Lord was built "on" the threshing floor. The Scriptures do not say "near," "by," or "in front of" the threshing floor, but literally "on" it. This by itself should be enough to establish for certain that the threshing floor was the datum to locate the temple instead of the altar, but there are other reasons. For example, it was the mercy seat (the top of the ark of the covenant) that received the sprinkled blood of atonement once a year that sat on the foundation stone (threshing floor). So theologically, there is no conflict with the ark of the covenant being placed where Abraham offered up Isaac. We can also infer that it is was the temple and not the altar that had the most precisely fixed location based on a closer look at what the Scriptures say about the altar.

WHERE, THEN, WAS THE ALTAR LOCATED?

By answering this question, we can strengthen confidence in the position that it really was the Holy of Holies that was centered on the threshing floor, and not the altar. Let's look at what the Bible says about the altar's location, construction, and so on, to help us better understand the layout of the original temple. First, we read that the altar of Solomon was made of bronze and was twenty cubits square and ten cubits high. We are also told that the altar was located to the east of the temple and that it was in front of its gates (portico). Therefore, the altar was located directly in front of the temple and was on the east-west line of the temple and its gates.

> He made a bronze altar twenty cubits long, twenty cubits wide and ten cubits high. . . .
>
> The priests then withdrew from the Holy Place. All the priests who were there had consecrated themselves, regardless of their divisions. All the Levites who were musicians—Asaph, Heman, Jeduthun and their sons and relatives—*stood on the east side of the altar*, dressed in fine linen and playing cymbals, harps and lyres. . . .
>
> *On the altar of the LORD that he had built in front of the portico,* Solomon sacrificed burnt offerings to the LORD, according to the daily requirement for offerings commanded by Moses for the Sabbaths, the New Moons and the three annual festivals—the Festival of Unleavened Bread, the Festival of Weeks and the Festival of Tabernacles. (2 Chronicles 4:1; 5:11–12; 8:12–13, emphasis added)

We can also glean a few more important details from scripture. For starters, we know that the altar had several different locations from the time of Solomon up until the time of Ahaz, based on passages in 1 and 2 Kings and 2 Chronicles:

> Then Solomon said, "The LORD has said that he would dwell in a dark cloud; I have built a magnificent temple for you, a place for you to dwell forever."
>
> While the whole assembly of Israel was standing there, the king turned around and blessed them. . . .
>
> Then Solomon *stood before the altar* of the LORD in front of the whole assembly of Israel and spread out his hands. Now he had made a bronze platform, five cubits long, five cubits wide and three cubits high, and had placed it *in the center* of the outer court. He stood on the platform and then knelt down before the whole assembly of Israel and spread out his hands toward heaven. (2 Chronicles 6:1–3, 12–13)

> On that same day the king consecrated the middle part of the courtyard in front of the temple of the LORD, and there he offered burnt offerings, grain offerings and the fat of the fellowship offerings, because the bronze altar that stood before the LORD was too small to hold the burnt offerings, the grain offerings and the fat of the fellowship offerings. (1 Kings 8:64)

> So Uriah the priest built an altar in accordance with all the plans that King Ahaz had sent from Damascus and finished it before King Ahaz returned. When the king came back from Damascus and saw the altar, he approached it and presented offerings on it. He offered up his burnt offering and grain offering, poured out his drink offering, and splashed the blood of his fellowship offerings against the altar. As for the bronze altar that stood before the LORD, he brought it from the front of the temple—from between the new altar and the temple of the LORD—and put it on the north side of the new altar. (2 Kings 16:11–14)

Because of these accounts, we can see that the bronze altar was originally to the west of center, making it closer to the temple on the east-west axis. It was close enough so that the middle of the outer court was left open for a small platform and an expanded area in the middle of the court to temporarily accommodate the incredible number of sacrifices performed during the first two weeks of its consecration (1 Kings 8:65). Next, in the days of Ahaz, a new altar was made and set in place while the old bronze altar was still in use, and it was set on the same east-west line with the temple and its gates, but to the east of the bronze altar. The old bronze altar was then moved to the north of the new altar. This means that the new altar was more or less centered in the courtyard, where Solomon's overflow sacrifices had been performed, and the old bronze altar was then moved directly north of the center of the court and the new altar. Finally, sacrifices continued at both of the new altar locations. Therefore, we have at least three locations within the outer court where sacrifices were performed. This implies that the altar did not have a fixed foundation stone for its location, which further supports the conclusion that it was definitely the temple and not the altar that sat on the foundation stone. If we put all of these locations that we are given in Scripture together into a diagram, we get the layout shown in Figure 4. Point A shows the original altar location in front of the temple. We know it was offset as shown for two reasons: First, because Solomon consecrated the middle of the courtyard for the overflow sacrifices (1 Kings 8:64) as shown by the area encompassed with the dotted line and point B, where Solomon stood in front of the sacrifices and the people (2 Chronicles 6:12–13). If the altar was already in the middle, then it should have said something like "and he consecrated the area *all around the altar.*" Second, the new altar that Uriah built in the time of Ahaz was to the east (right) of the original altar, and it was built while the old altar was still in use (2 Kings 16:14). While point D doesn't have to be in the exact middle, as shown, the relative positioning is still valid and could not have been too much farther east in any event to allow room for the priests to work. Next, the original altar was moved to the north of the new altar to point C (top).

By doing this, we can clearly see that the altar occupied multiple locations within the inner court of the temple complex. However, the temple location, of course, remained fixed. This means that sacrifices were made in at least three different locations within the courtyard, in front of the temple.

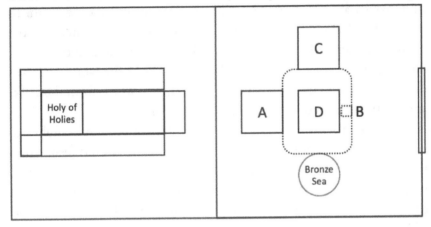

A – Original Bronze Altar Location
B – Solomon's Bronze Platform and Expanded Sacrificial Area
C – The New Location for the Bronze Altar by Ahaz
D– Ahaz's New Altar Location

Figure 4: Diagram of the Temple area and the approximate altar locations reported in 2 Chronicles and 1 and 2 Kings (the expanded sacrificial area of B is shown as a dotted line).

Since this was the case, we can be confident that the altar was not located by a fixed and immovable foundation stone or even a single location within the inner court. This does not mean that there is not one best and proper location for the altar, but since even Solomon sacrificed in multiple locations within the area, it was not fixed as tightly as the Holy of Holies, which is never reported to have moved anywhere. Therefore, the threshing floor located the temple, not the altar.

WHAT WAS A THRESHING FLOOR?

To even start looking for a threshing floor, we need to define what it is and what it may have looked like. We don't really use threshing floors anymore. As a result, we have somewhat lost touch with what they were, how they were used, and what exactly would identify one. Threshing is the act of separating the grains of wheat from the chaff and harvested stalks. This is generally accomplished on a threshing floor, which can be any hard, flat surface. Those surfaces can be smoothed rock, a tightly stone-paved area, a plastered claylike surface, or compacted earth. In ancient Israel, though, it was common to cut a large level area into the bedrock, either with or without a small wall around it, and to locate it on the outskirts of a settlement.[5] In most parts of the world, this was the common practice for separating the grains of wheat from the stalks and chaff, even up to the twentieth century or so.

To make a good threshing floor, a durable surface was desirable, to minimize contamination from dirt and debris that would result from beating or sledging the wheat stalks.[6] Beating and thrashing would have been accomplished with a flail, a long flexible stick, when smaller quantities were in question. In fact, the etymology for the word *thrashing*, which has come to mean getting a flogging or beating, is an Old English form of the word *thresh*, from threshing wheat. For larger amounts of grain, a sledge was used and dragged around in circle, as seen in Figure 5.

Figure 5: An example of ancient threshing using a sledge, which was still practiced up to modern times in Nazareth, Israel.[7]

A detailed description of a threshing sledge relates that they are generally of wood, with hundreds of small, jagged stones of a hard material, such as flint or quartz (protruding one-half to three-fourths of inch), which were dragged over the stalks of grain that were spread over the threshing floor. Sledges were often one and a half to two feet wide and up to five feet long and would be dragged in a circle over the grain by oxen. The sledge, by the cutting and grinding action of its teeth, separates the individual grains from the head and stalk.[8] An example of a threshing sledge from the Middle East is shown in Figure 6.

Figure 6: Example of a wooden threshing sledge on display in the Museum of the Bible (Washington, DC). *[Author's photo]*

The Bible is also an important source of information for understanding how threshing floors were used in ancient times in the land of Israel, especially if we want to get an idea of their size in those days. Of particular importance is understanding just how small a threshing floor could be. To that point, we find a story in the book of Judges about Gideon that can help set the lower end for the size of a threshing floor.

> The angel of the LORD came and sat down under the oak in Ophrah that belonged to Joash the Abiezrite, where his son Gideon was threshing wheat in a winepress to keep it from the Midianites. (Judges 6:11)

We know that this was a small threshing floor because it says that Gideon was threshing wheat in a winepress to avoid detection by the Midianites. There are many examples of winepresses from antiquity in the Middle East. A winepress is a kind of cistern that is usually cut out of solid rock, typically limestone, with an exit hole carved into the bottom for the pressed grape juice to flow out. Winepresses were generally large enough for two or more people to stand in while crushing the grapes with their feet and sometimes also included a press to squeeze even more liquid out of the grapes. While we can't know for sure how big the winepress was that Gideon was using, if we take cues from ancient winepresses found in Israel,[9] then an area six to nine feet (two to three meters) in diameter is possible as an area to clandestinely thresh wheat.

There is another account of threshing in the Bible found in the book of Ruth. It tells us that one person could thresh a bushel of grain in presumably a couple of hours, because the indication is that Ruth started late in the day but still returned home the same day, after gleaning and threshing. A bushel of barley would have sustained both Ruth and her mother-in-law, Naomi, for about a month (192 servings at approximately 193 calories per serving). Ruth would have also used the flail and thrash method, since she was a poor widow, and this was a relatively small amount of barley that she had gleaned by hand.

So Ruth gleaned in the field until evening. Then she threshed the barley she had gathered, and it amounted to about an ephah [about a bushel or six gallons]. (Ruth 2:17)

Therefore, the size of the threshing floor that we are looking for should be, for the present time at least, considered to be reasonably in the range of between five and fifty feet, square or round, and with a potential variety of hard, flat surfaces. One source suggests that in ancient Near Eastern agricultural practices, threshing floors were generally to be considered large, between forty and forty-six feet in diameter.[10] However, as shown above, no such precise dimension can be reliably ascribed to a threshing floor of antiquity.

WHAT KIND OF THRESHING FLOOR DID ARAUNAH USE?

Now that we have a common understanding of a threshing floor and enough basic information about them to align our thoughts, we can think about which type of threshing floor Araunah could have used. Should we be searching for a giant flattened stone, a stone paved area, a large plastered clay area, or an area of hard-packed dirt? Is it possible to be sure which type it was? The Bible does not tell us directly; however, it can be inferred from Scripture, rabbinic tradition, and historical testimony that we are looking for a threshing floor made from bedrock. The search for the biblical testimony about the temple location begins with Abraham and his offering of Isaac as a sacrifice in obedience to God, then, after that, to Jacob and his dream of a ladder up to heaven. And finally, we arrive at the site of Ornan (Araunah) the Jebusite's threshing floor.

Sometime later God tested Abraham. He said to him, "Abraham!"

"Here I am," he replied.

Then God said, "Take your son, your only son, whom you love—Isaac—and go to the region of Moriah. Sacrifice him there as a burnt offering on a mountain I will show you." Early the next morning Abraham got up and loaded his donkey. He took with him two of his servants and his son Isaac. When he had cut enough wood for the burnt offering, he set out for the place God had told him about. On the third day Abraham looked up and saw the place in the distance. He said to his servants, "Stay here with the donkey while I and the boy go over there. We will worship and then we will come back to you."

Abraham took the wood for the burnt offering and placed it on his son Isaac, and he himself carried the fire and the knife. As the two of them went on together, Isaac spoke up and said to his father Abraham, "Father?"

"Yes, my son?" Abraham replied.

"The fire and wood are here," Isaac said, "but where is the lamb for the burnt offering?"

Abraham answered, "God himself will provide the lamb for the burnt offering, my son." And the two of them went on together.

When they reached the place God had told him about, Abraham built an altar there and arranged the wood on it. He bound his son Isaac and laid him on the altar, on top of the wood. Then he reached out his hand and took the knife to slay his son. But the angel of the Lord called out to him from heaven, "Abraham! Abraham!"

"Here I am," he replied.

"Do not lay a hand on the boy," he said. "Do not do anything to him. Now I know that you fear God, because you have not withheld from me your son, your only son."

Abraham looked up and there in a thicket he saw a ram caught by its horns. He went over and took the ram and sacrificed it as a burnt offering instead of his son. So Abraham called that place The Lord Will Provide. And to this day it is said, "On the mountain of the Lord it will be provided."

The angel of the Lord called to Abraham from heaven a second time and said, "I swear by myself, declares the Lord, that because you have done this and have not withheld your son, your only son, I will surely bless you and make your descendants as numerous as the stars in the sky and as the sand on the seashore. Your descendants will take possession of the cities of their enemies, and through your offspring all nations on earth will be blessed, because you have obeyed me." (Genesis 22:1–18)

Now, in this passage we see that Abraham prepared to sacrifice Isaac in a place where they needed to bring the wood with them. It was sparse with vegetation, and he built the altar on the natural mountain, as he found it, when he was led there by God. We also identify the mountain from this passage as Mount Moriah. Then in a Midrash, we see that Rabbinic tradition surrounding Jacob (Yaakov) also supports the idea that the marker we are looking for, for the house of God, is a large, flat area of bedrock suitable for lying down and was considered the foundation stone of the earth.

Another version. The Rabbis said the minimum number that the word "stones" can refer to is two, and Yaakov woke up in the morning and found that they were one. He was in great fear and said "the house of the Holy One is in this place and I was not conscious of His Presence" as it says "And he was afraid and said, How dreadful is this place! *This is no other than the house of G-d"* {Genesis 28:17} From here they said that anyone who prays in Jerusalem is as if they pray before the Throne of Glory, because the gate of heaven is there; and an open door to hear prayer, as it says " . . . and this is the gate of heaven." (ibid.) Yaakov went back to gather the stones and he found that they were one stone. Yaakov took the stone and placed it as a monument in the midst of the place and oil descended from heaven for him and he poured it out on the stone, as it says ". . . and he poured oil on top of it." {Genesis 28:18} What did the Holy One do? He took its right foot, sank it to the deepest depths and made it a keystone for the earth, like a man who places a keystone in an arch. *Therefore it is called foundation stone,* because there is the navel of the world and from there the world was opened out. *And upon it is the palace of G-d, as it says "And this stone, which I have placed as a monument, shall be a house of God"* {Genesis 28:22} And Yaakov fell to the ground before the foundation stone, praying before the Holy One, and said "Master of the World! If you bring me back to this place in peace, then I will sacrifice before you whole offerings and thanksgiving offerings!" as it says, "And Jacob uttered a vow, saying, . . ." (Midrash Tehillim 91:5, emphasis added)

After the Ark was taken into exile, there was a rock in the Holy of Holies from the days of the early prophets, David and Samuel, who laid the groundwork for construction of the Temple, and this stone was called the foundation rock. It was three fingerbreadths higher than the ground, and the High Priest would place the incense on it. (Yoma 53b:10)

And according to the one who says it is referring to the Temple, the word hashatot is also clear, as we learned in a mishna {Yoma 53b:10}: There was a stone in the Holy of Holies from the days of the early prophets, David and Samuel, who laid the groundwork for construction of the Temple, and this stone was called the Foundation [shetiyya] Stone. (Sanhedrin 26b:5)

These rabbinic testimonies confirm that (1) the threshing floor was stone, and (2) that the foundation stone marked the temple and not the altar. Furthermore, we have the words of Scripture that speak of the durability and permanence of the foundations that God has chosen in Zion. When we think about the importance of a landmark for the location of God's house, it seems inconsistent with God's character to choose a location that could easily be lost with time. While Isaiah is not necessarily talking about the threshing floor of Araunah as the foundation stone "firmly placed," it still suggests that when God chooses a place for his foundations, they will not be lost and cannot be moved. I read this as a messianic prophecy referring to Jesus, but the verse also testifies in general to the durability of the things placed and chosen by God.

Therefore, thus says the Lord GOD, "Behold, I am laying in Zion a stone, a tested stone, a costly cornerstone for the foundation, firmly placed. He who believes in it will not be disturbed." (Isaiah 28:16 NASB)

So, if we want a permanent landmark, then the place that we are looking for should be a part of the original bedrock. The bedrock has been mapped on multiple occasions, initially by Charles Warren of the Palestine Exploration Fund in 1867–1870, and it was found to only be present in the northern two-thirds of the Temple Mount. He made a basic diagram of the original mountain slopes and bedrock, as shown in Figure 7.

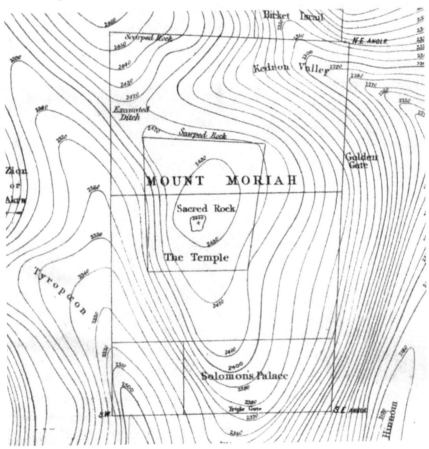

Figure 7: A section from Charles Warren's map of Mount Moriah and the Temple Mount area marking the original mountain slopes.[11]

Based on this map, we should be looking in the upper two-thirds of the current Temple Mount area, west of middle, where we know the bedrock exists. Furthermore, since we are looking for bedrock, we can also be sure that the area would have been part of the landscape four thousand years ago or so, when Abraham first visited Mount Moriah. Without identifying areas of the original mountain, there is no way to say that one has identified a legitimate location for the threshing floor of Araunah. Bedrock is in fact still visible at several locations. One of the locations where the visual evidence of the bedrock on the site still exists is seen in Figure 8. This tells us that while there have been many changes on the Temple Mount, the elevations in these locations are still basically unchanged from ancient times.

Figure 8: Evidence of the bedrock (white arrow) in a wall a little south of the Temple Mount platform. This bedrock is very near the southern end of the original mountain structure of Mount Moriah before it begins dropping off further south of this location. *[Author's photo]*

We also know that the threshing floor was large enough for a threshing sledge to be used because Araunah offered to give David his threshing sledges as fuel for the sacrificial fires since wood was still sparse or not available in the area.

Araunah said to David, "Let my lord the king take whatever he wishes and offer it up. Here are oxen for the burnt offering, and here are threshing sledges and ox yokes for the wood. Your Majesty, Araunah gives all this to the king." Araunah also said to him, "May the LORD your God accept you." (2 Samuel 24:22–23)

If sledges were used, we should be looking for an area that is ten feet in diameter or larger. This is about the smallest area that would be practical to use a sledge and oxen. In fact, one may even object to say that even ten feet in diameter is too small. However, if one needed to thresh wheat in an area greater than eighty square feet, I'm sure that oxen and a sledge would be faster than threshing by hand and would be greatly appreciated. There is also a surviving threshing floor hewn from solid bedrock at Deir Samaan in Samaria that is fourteen feet in diameter, as shown in Figure 9.[12] While the site remains largely unstudied, it is a good example of a smaller threshing floor that has been found in Israel.

Figure 9: The bedrock threshing floor at Deir Samaan in western Samaria. *[Photo courtesy of Biblewalks.com]*

Another rock-hewn threshing floor was discovered at Khirbet Mansur el-Aqab, near Caesarea, Israel, and it is a semicircular area measuring six by twenty-five feet, dated between the first century BC and the first century AD.[13] Consequently, based on these examples, I would argue that a flat area of bedrock as small as ten feet and up to fifty feet in diameter is in fact a reasonable estimate for threshing floors from antiquity in Israel.

IS THE DOME OF THE SPIRITS A VIABLE THRESHING FLOOR?

Considering that the large smooth stone that is level with the paving stones of the Temple Mount platform is underneath the Dome of the Spirits (also: Dome of the Tablets and Qubbat el-Arwah), some very important questions emerge. Is that stone the right size, shape, and appearance to be considered a good threshing floor candidate? Why was a dome built over it? And why is the entire platform leveled to a part of the bedrock?

Let's deal with the first question: The stone in the floor under the Dome of the Spirits measures roughly ten feet in diameter. As described above, a threshing floor could be from five to fifty feet in diameter (but more than ten feet to use a threshing sledge), so while this is on the lower end of that range, it meets that requirement.

> Additionally, what we see today could be smaller than what it was originally. Why? Because it is not inconceivable that during the destruction of the temple, parts of the temple could have fallen and damaged the bedrock of the threshing floor. In that case, what we see today could be just the portion that remained that was suitable for being incorporated into the Temple Mount platform. While that is conjecture on my part, it still means that any attempt to disqualify the Dome of the Spirits location based on its current size should be rejected, because it actually is big enough and could have been even larger in Araunah's time.

Figure 10: Use-wear polish observed on a Canaanean archaeological blade, related to cereal-harvesting [from Groman-Yaroslavski et al.—note 15].

Next, it was much better to have a solid area of hewn stone (bedrock) as a threshing floor, rather than an area of compressed dirt, hardened clay, or even paving stones, to minimize dirt and rocks among the grains after the stalks and chaff were liberated. Threshing sledges, as mentioned, need a hard surface against which to thresh the grains, without mixing in lots of other debris. Threshing floors were often both polished and pitted by the threshing sledges over time, because of the large number of jagged teeth in the bottom of the sledge and the repeated dragging of the sledge with weights or a person standing on it. As a result, the threshing floor would obtain a pockmarked but flat surface. This effect is admittedly not well reported in the literature for the floor itself, but wear on the stones of the threshing sledges has been thoroughly documented.[14] An example of the wear that can be caused by use with grain on an archaeological stone blade, related to cereal harvesting using a sickle, is shown in Figure 10.[15] The observed morphology of the wear on the stone is clearly at a finer scale than the wear observed on the threshing floor itself, but it exhibits the same basic pattern (like comparing a small crystal to a larger one of the same type). Stones like this used for harvesting grain as well as the stones of a threshing sledge and the stone floor beneath them are all under comparable wearing conditions and exhibit analogous wear patterns. Therefore, we would expect to see similar polishing of the threshing floor surface due to the repeated cutting action of the threshing sledge on a film of grain stalks. The pitting that is observed can occur naturally from defects in the stone and from periodic impacts of the sledge stones against the floor.

Consequently, the visible bedrock under the Dome of the Spirits, shown in Figure 11, is in agreement with what a threshing floor should look like. The stone area is large enough to be a threshing floor, and it is to this day in a state that proves it could have been useful in this capacity. In fact, if one were so inclined and the authorities did not interfere, one could thresh grain there today. The flat stone area was perhaps first modernly recognized for what it is by Rev. J. E. Hanauer (1926).[16] He noted that this stone would be "admirably suited for an oriental threshing floor such as was that of Ornan (Araunah)."

The pockmarked, flat stone underneath the Dome of the Spirits is also a logical match for the description given by the Bordeaux pilgrim in AD 333, who described a "perforated stone" (*lapis pertusis*) that the Jews would visit every year.

> And in the building (in aede) itself, where stood the temple which Solomon built, . . . there are two statues of Hadrian, and not far from the statues there is a perforated stone, to which the Jews come every year and anoint it, bewail themselves with groans, rend their garments, and so depart.[17]

This pitting in the stone could logically be described as perforated. In Latin, *lapis* means stone or rock, and *pertusis* can be pierced, leaky, bored through, or punched with holes. The stone underneath the Dome of the Spirits is both flat and smooth in its upper surface and at the same time heavily pitted. This is very consistent with and even characteristic of a surface that has had countless passes of a threshing sledge over its surface.

Figure 11: Bedrock underneath the Dome of the Spirits, the inside floor (left), and a close-up of the flat, pockmarked surface of the stone (right). *[Author's photos]*

It has been proposed, however, that this stone under the Dome of the Spirits is not bedrock but is in fact a megalithic paving stone.[18] There are several excellent counters to that assertion, however. First, if that were the case, it is the only megalithic paving stone inside the entire complex; so it would be entirely unique in this regard. Because of its huge size, the impracticality of this strains credulity. Second, it is highly irregular and therefore shows little resemblance to a quarried stone, in contrast to other paving stones, large or small, which are generally cut out of bedrock as blocks consisting of flat planes and right-angled corners. For instance, the rock under the Dome of the Spirits is considerably less square than the megalithic paving stones shown in Figure 12.

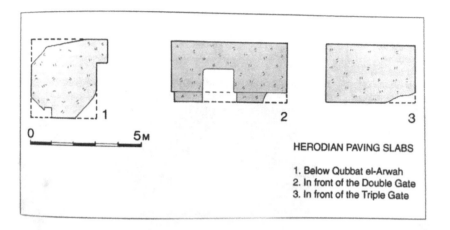

Figure 12: Proposed explanation for how the stone underneath the Qubbat el-Arwah (Dome of the Spirits) could be a paving stone and not a piece of worked bedrock.[19]

Clearly, examples 2 and 3, in contrast to stone 1, include mostly square corners with some modifications. That a paving stone would be so extensively cut from an even more massive rectangular block so that it could be placed inexplicably in the far corner of the platform, with nothing special to fit to, is not a tenable position. In fact, rather than being quarried, it shows evidence of being cut in situ, to accommodate the abutment of the other paving stones used to make the platform. This is strongly suggestive that the surrounding floor was fitted to it, not the other way around. Finally, there is no discernible purpose for deliberately placing a giant paving stone in this location. Even when paving stones of this magnitude are found, they are located in a structurally significant location, such as a principal gate entrance, and they are generally dual purpose—foundation blocks and paving surfaces. There is no reason to think that this was the case with the stone underneath the Dome of the Spirits. On the contrary, it shows every sign of being an original part of Mount Moriah since before the time of David.

There is also another requirement for threshing floors that bears mentioning. They were generally on an elevated place on a mountain or hillside,[20] where there was good amount of wind to carry away the chaff, but not at the very top, so as to get too much wind.[21] That being said, neither the Dome of the Spirits stone nor the al-Sakhra stone are at the very top of Mount Moriah; they are about ninety feet below it, so they both meet this condition.

Finally, recent archaeological reports confirm that the large, flattened stone under the Dome of the Spirits is part of the bedrock, as attested to by the survey reports of Charles Warren in 1884 and affirmed by members of the Israeli Antiquities Authority, the University of Haifa, and Tel Aviv University.[22] *We must not miss the significance of this:* leading Israeli authorities confirm that this is bedrock. They also confirm that it is not just their opinion either; evidence produced 135 years ago by Charles Warren during his survey of the Temple Mount also confirms this fact. In addition, for all of the reasons cited previously, this is also a logical conclusion from an examination of the site today.

Therefore, if we know it is bedrock, then we also know that it was there when Abraham first arrived at Mount Moriah, around 2000 BC. That means it was there when Araunah was looking for a good threshing floor location, too. We've already talked about the characteristics of a threshing floor, and this would have been as good as it gets. Consequently, there is no good reason not to at least consider this flattened rock as a candidate for the threshing floor of Araunah.

WHY IS THIS BEDROCK STONE LEVEL WITH THE PLATFORM?

This is an important question. And the answer is, *the entire platform was set to this stone.* How do we know the platform was built and leveled to this piece of bedrock? Because the bedrock is both (1) integral to the platform and (2) level with it. Therefore, this is not conjecture; it is simply fact. The platform could not have been built without leveling to it because the elevation of the bedrock is not adjustable, like paving stones. So, the real question is, When was the bedrock leveled? There are only two possible answers:

1. The bedrock was cut and leveled to build the platform.

2. The platform was set to an already flat and level threshing floor.

Consequently, we should ask which of those two possibilities is more reasonable and whether or not it is even possible to know. First of all, the randomized but relatively uniform pitted surface we see today is quite different from the surrounding paving stones (see Figure 13). If the bedrock was cut and leveled to be a reference point, then it would likely have some chisel marks still visible. All stone from this time was chiseled as a part of the quarrying or carving process. Examples of these marks are shown in Figure 14. Instead of seeing any of signs of chiseling, though, we see a very flat plane, with a polished top surface and lots of random pitting, as shown in Figure 15. Asher Kaufmann also reported a geological inspection by Dr. Hendrik J. Bruins wherein it was concluded that there are no signs of tool marks on the surface, and therefore it is likely that the rock is "naturally flat" rather than worked.[23] This, of course, does not preclude wear from threshing, but rather is a reference to the use of masonry tools to manually flatten the rock's surface for use as a paving stone.

Figure 13: Large paving stones in the immediate vicinity of the Dome of the Spirits. *[Author's photo]*

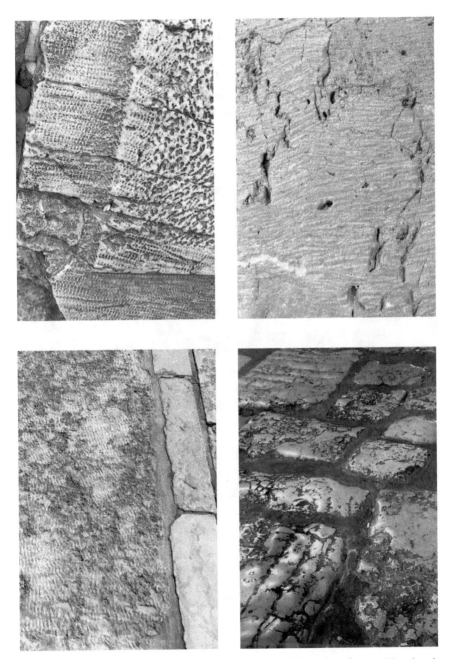

Figure 14: Chisel marks on a Western Wall ashlar (top left), chisel marks on a Nea church column from the sixth century (top right), chisel marks on a presumably more recent paving stone on the Temple Mount platform (bottom left), well-worn paving stones from the Old City along the Via Dolorosa where chiseled traction features are still visible (bottom right). *[Author's photos]*

Now, it could be argued that the chisel marks have simply been worn off, which is the case with many other highly worn paving stones all over Jerusalem. But I don't think that answers this problem so easily. For one, the stone is about eighty square feet in area, so that's a lot to erase. Second, the stone is amazingly plane, which wouldn't be the case from general foot traffic. It's like the difference between sanding something by hand versus using a sanding block. If we were talking about foot traffic, then the stone would be smooth, but not perfectly plane. The only other possibility is that it was planed flat after leveling it off to make it the reference point for building the platform; however, if that was the case, then the stone should be both plane and smooth, but not pockmarked. A similar surface, albeit less plane, can be seen in the stone threshing floor at Deir Samaan in western Samaria, as shown in Figure 16.

Figure 15: Full view of the bedrock under the Dome of the Spirits. *[Author's photo]*

Figure 16: Stone threshing floor surface at Deir Samaan in western Samaria. *[Photo courtesy of www.biblewalks.com]*

Therefore, the most logical deduction is that the bedrock was already level and pockmarked by Araunah using it as a threshing floor. Then, more than a thousand years later, the whole temple platform was leveled to that particular piece of bedrock because it made a ready reference point. To understand this line of reasoning, it helps to have experience building a brick patio or installing tile flooring. Imagine you are tasked with building a monumental platform on the Temple Mount after its destruction in AD 70, and it is literally strewn with debris everywhere. Where do you begin? And then, while you are clearing debris and trying to establish your foundations for the platform, you find a large, flat, and level portion of the bedrock in the northwest corner. Well, then you would have done what the ancient builder of the Temple Mount platform did. You would use that bedrock as your reference point for building the rest of the platform. Thus, this is the clear explanation for why the floor is level with the bedrock here. The bedrock stone under the Dome of the Spirits was used conveniently to set the elevation of the entire platform we see today, which, in its present form at least, is believed to be a post-Herodian construction. Therefore, the rock itself predates the current temple platform and is reasonably attributable to an earlier time period in temple history. Also, at this time the platform would have been built around al-Sakhra. It, too, is integral with the platform, but not level with it; however, it was deliberately left protruding from the platform—presumably because it was believed to have some significance or there was a desired use for it. It has large cuts in it, noted by Dr. Ritmeyer and others,[24] and therefore could have been left as foundation footing or a similar structural purpose. Bedrock was often used as the cornerstone of a building. The off-centered nature of the al-Sakhra stone to the trapezoidal platform is well placed as a cornerstone of a building that was built centered or otherwise geometrically aligned to the platform. This will be explored further in chapter 4, "Why It Wasn't at the Dome of the Rock."

This deduction about the present platform also solves a question raised by the Mishnah, which says the foundation stone (*shtiyah*) was "three fingerbreadths higher than the ground." The answer is that the Second Temple platform must have been three fingerbreadths lower than the current platform and probably did not cut into the *shtiyah* stone, as this would have been treated as holy. Logically, the builders of the platform post–AD 70 did not feel the stone was holy, but rather conveniently located for setting the level of their platform, and weren't afraid to carve into it.

WHY WAS THE DOME OF THE SPIRITS BUILT OVER THE STONE?

Another question that could be asked is why the Dome of the Spirits was built over this large flattened rock area in the first place. The simple answer is that we don't know. No historic record of its construction has been found. In fact, the earliest mention of the Dome of the Spirits (*Qubbat al-Arwah*) was in 1627, when Muhammad Agha wrote that money was to be appointed annually for the cost of lighting an oil lamp that hangs in the ceiling of the dome.[25] He recorded that it was to be lit every day throughout the year from sunset to sunrise, and that money was to be provided to furnish oil for the lamp and for a man to light the lamp and to serve it. One man was appointed for life, and then others were to be appointed in his place after him. So, we know that this place was considered important, but no mention is made of why. It is also speculated that the other name of this dome, the Dome of the Tablets, refers to Moses' Ten Commandments, and therefore the ark of the covenant, but again we don't really know.

We do know that the Dome was apparently not there yet in AD 985 because an Islamic pilgrim to the Temple Mount (*Haram*), named Muhammad Al Mukaddasi, reported only four domes standing on the platform of the *Haram* at that time, the Dome of the Chain, the Dome of the Ascension, the Dome of the Prophet, and the Dome of the Rock.[26] Obviously, this does not mean that the flattened bedrock beneath it was not there, but a cupola protecting this area was not reported. Therefore, the questions about who built it and why remain a mystery, unless other accounts are found, because it is not dated by any epigraphic texts in its construction or in any *waqf* documents that have been identified to date. We are left to speculate if perhaps this space was being protected and honored because of its association with the temple of Solomon, as we suspect, or for some other reason. Clearly, it may have been understood by someone in the past that it had been the place of the Holy of Holies, and so was covered to honor the site, but that cannot be proven. It certainly does not contradict that hypothesis, however. It has also effectively protected the site from heavy foot traffic since its construction, which must have been between four hundred and a thousand years ago, strengthening the argument that the smoothly worn surface is more likely from threshing than foot traffic.

COULD THE THRESHING FLOOR BE LOST TO TIME?

No other proposed alternate location for the Temple has a visible threshing floor to anchor its location. They all lack a viable threshing floor to use as a landmark and are forced to hypothesize where the threshing floor may have been located. In those cases, they must assume that the threshing floor used to be in a location that is now lost to time because it was destroyed or has been covered up such that it can't be seen or verified. Even in the case of those claiming that the al-Sakhra rock under the Dome of the Rock was the actual threshing floor, they are forced to imagine that it was radically different in the past and that massive amounts of stone have been removed to arrive at what we see today. While it is a historic fact that the crusaders quarried off parts of the al-Sakhra rock, it is hard to believe that so much was actually removed. In fact, a detailed inspection of the surface of the al-Sakhra rock shows that the vast majority of the visible surface is not quarried but contains natural formations consistent with an original rock surface. Where there are obvious cuts into the rock to remove stone, they are, well, obvious. There is no clear logical pathway to show how the stone that we see today was flat and level in the past, especially when it is speculated that the uppermost surface of the rock is the same as in Second Temple times, because it is claimed that a rectangular depression in the rock, which can still be seen today, was used to hold the ark of the covenant.[27] The arguments are all reasonable and logical, except for one critical flaw: the rock could not have been a threshing floor. Therefore, the careful observations made about the al-Sakhra stone are important for understanding the history of the stone and of the Dome of the Rock, but it tells us nothing about the temple itself because it does not meet the requirements for a threshing floor and therefore has nothing to do with where the temple was located.

Without real archaeological evidence of a threshing floor, any theory about where one could have been stands as an unprovable assumption and therefore a presumption in absentia (an assumption without evidence). This should raise serious questions about the viability of any such theory. Imagine if someone was trying to convict you of a crime, and even though no murder weapon had been found, it was assumed and proposed to the judge that one would someday be found with your fingerprints on it. Would that be admissible as evidence against you? *Without a credible threshing floor being presented, any assertion about the temple's location is of necessity substantially weakened.* Nevertheless, many views regarding the temple's former location have been presented, satisfied with this presumption that a threshing floor does not necessarily need to be found in order to locate the temple. After reviewing the principal opinions on this subject, I would say that, with the exception of Asher Kaufmann, the question of the threshing floor has not been properly addressed. This issue is incredibly significant and should not be ignored.

CHAPTER SUMMARY

The threshing floor was the original way that the temple location was identified. Therefore, the search for the threshing floor should be of prime importance in our quest for the original location of the temple sanctuary. Based on a review of biblical texts, we know that it was the temple and not the altar that was built directly on the threshing floor, for two reasons. First, this is indicated fairly explicitly in the texts, and second, the altar reportedly had several different locations in front of the temple. So logically, it was not at that time associated with a single fixed and immovable location. Furthermore, even though we do not find this explicitly stated in the biblical text, we can be confident that the threshing floor was at least primarily a large area of bedrock, rather than a makeshift area of paving stones or hardened clay that has been lost to time. Admittedly, this idea rests on inference and deduction and the patterns and nature of God that emerge in the Scriptures, which will be unacceptable reasoning for many scholars and skeptics. However, it is also consistent with Jewish rabbinic records that say that the Holy of Holies was placed on a foundation stone. We also know that the area of the threshing floor was in existence before the building of the sanctuary and surrounding retaining walls; therefore, the threshing floor has to be at the original ground level, squarely on the original structure of Mount Moriah. This knowledge, consequently, should focus our attention on the central and northern locations and mostly within the current trapezoidal temple platform, because it must be in an area that is not too close to either the eastern or western ends of the Temple Mount to allow space for the surrounding temple structures.

Within all of these stated and deduced criteria, the only visible candidates for a threshing floor are the al-Sakhra under the Dome of the Rock, and the large, flat, pockmarked stone underneath the Dome of the Spirits that is north and a little west of the Dome of the Rock. The al-Sakhra stone, while certainly being of an appropriate size, is not at all shaped to be a flat threshing floor. It is highly sloped and has many irregular cuts into its surface. Even though it is conceivable that today it is greatly modified from its original shape around the time of King David, it is extremely improbable that it was ever a large flattened area suitable for threshing grain. The stone underneath the Dome of the Spirits, on the other hand, while much smaller, is still large enough to be a threshing floor and is to this day in a state that proves it could have been useful in this capacity. This stone is also certainly bedrock and cannot be a megalithic paving stone as has been proposed. On the contrary, it shows every sign of being an original part of Mount Moriah since before the time of David, as does the al-Sakhra rock, but in a form for which even today we see clear support for its use in antiquity as a threshing floor. Thus, we have a viable threshing floor candidate that has received little attention, despite the fact that finding one should be at the core of a temple location argument, rather than a presumption in absentia. Hopefully, if this has not fully made the case, it at least raises the question to a higher level of plausibility and sparks the next question: Though it's possible that the Dome of the Spirits marks the ancient threshing floor of Araunah, how can we know for sure? Well, I'm glad I've got you thinking, because actually, the most compelling landmark is one that everyone knows about—it's the Golden Gate of the Temple Mount. The only problem is that it isn't recognized for what it truly is. In the next chapter we'll find out why.

The Golden Gate, East Gate, or Shushan Gate of the Temple Mount standing as an original landmark of the First and Second Temple periods. *[Author's photo]*

3

THE EAST GATE POINTS THE WAY

TODAY, MANY SCHOLARS AND RABBIS believe that the Golden Gate we see today was totally destroyed at some time in the past and was rebuilt in the wrong location. Some suppose this was done by Suleiman the Magnificent between 1538 and 1541, or possibly at some other time post–AD 70, by the Byzantines before the surrender of Jerusalem (c. AD 637–638) or the Umayyads after that. The principal reason for this belief is due to some early archaeological assessments of the age of the stonework of the gate and a failure to recognize historical testimonies regarding it. Another reason is the fact that the Golden Gate is not directly in front of the current Dome of the Rock, which from historic tradition is also believed to now rest on the former site of the Jewish temple. In this case, the logic is thus: if the Temple was where the Dome of the Rock is today and the Golden Gate is not directly in front of it, then the Golden Gate must be in the wrong location.[1] However, one must not forget the other possibility: that the Dome of the Rock is not the true location of the temple since it is not in front of the Golden Gate.

Now, to be sure, Suleiman definitely did make modifications to the gate. History records that he walled it up in stone,[2] which is obvious when looking at the stonework as it sits today, as shown in Figure 17. First, the stone was cut to fill the doorways, so it was installed after the doorways were completed. Also, both the apparent weathering age and the style of the stonework in the East Gate are different between the columns and arches of the gate and the stone raising its height and filling in its doorways. Therefore, the columns and arches are clearly older and were built at an earlier time. This stands as physical evidence that Suleiman did not move the gate; he only repaired and built it up and then walled it in. You see, if current landmarks have been moved, then obviously they no longer stand as landmarks, and we are forced to debate inferred evidence that can be interpreted in multiple ways, leaving us in the quandary in which we find ourselves today. But if they are still in their original location, then that is an entirely different matter.

Figure 17: Close-up pictures of the inside (left) and outside of the East Gate (right), showing clear demarcations of the later stonework to fill in the openings of the original stone gates, which were clearly not made at the same time as the rest of the gate, using stone which was obviously cut much later than the ancient stone of the columns and arches. *[Author's photos]*

In this chapter, we will explore the prophetic, historic, and archaeo-logical evidence that the East Gate—also called the Golden Gate or the Shushan Gate—is an original temple landmark. If it is a bona fide landmark, then it by definition marks the original location of the eastern gate of the temple and is therefore the key to finding its true location. It is also necessary to review the scriptural accounts and rabbinic testimonies about the East Gate to prove that it really can be used as a landmark for the temple. However, if ancient landmarks exist today from the temple that were never moved, then they quite simply, indisputably, and very reliably, show us exactly where the temple stood before it was destroyed in AD 70.

THE PROPHETIC CASE FOR THE EAST GATE AS A LANDMARK

The East Gate really is the key. The epiphany came for me back in 2008 after watching an online video tour of the Temple Mount led by Rabbi Chaim Richman of the Temple Institute.[3] First of all, I was shocked to learn that observant Jews were generally not encouraged to visit the Temple Mount at that time and in fact were also impeded from doing so by Israeli border police and Waqf officials. But right then I also began to realize how little work had been done archaeologically on the Temple Mount due to the political and religious sensitivities present at the site. Nevertheless, as Rabbi Richman was making his circuit around the mount and discussing the various points of interest, he came to the East Gate and mentioned that while this was the fabled Golden Gate, it was in the wrong location and had been mistakenly placed there by Suleiman the Magnificent when he rebuilt the walls of Jerusalem in the mid-1500s. He related that it was in the wrong location because in the times of the Holy Temple, it would have been directly in front of the temple. In other words, since the temple was believed to be where the Dome of the Rock sits today, then the gate had to be in the wrong location. Now, that logic makes perfect sense if we know with absolute certainty that the temple was formerly built directly over that location. But as I began to research the question, I realized that we actually don't have any proof or even solid evidence that the Dome of the Rock is sitting on top of the former site of the Second Temple. We have tradition, popular belief, and conjecture, but no solid evidence.

Then I came across Ezekiel 44, where it said that the outer gate facing east was to be shut and that it would remain shut. I remembered the walled-up East Gate of the Temple Mount from the video tour, and I thought it must be more than a coincidence. While it is well known that the East Gate is walled up (Figure 17), it is not as well known that this was prophesied by Ezekiel in the period from approximately 593 to 571 BC, before the destruction of the First Temple, and in the context of writing about a last-days temple in the messianic era. And so, I made the obvious connection that the East Gate is also shut, walled up in stone, in fact. If Ezekiel prophesied that the East Gate would be shut, then this certainly looked like a fulfillment of that verse.

> Then the man brought me back to the outer gate of the sanctuary, *the one facing east, and it was shut.* The LORD said to me, "This gate is to remain shut. It must not be opened; no one may enter through it. *It is to remain shut* because the LORD, the God of Israel, has entered through it." (Ezekiel 44:1–2, emphasis added)

Then it hit me like a ton of bricks! Jesus could have ridden into Jerusalem on a donkey through *that* gate, back around AD 33. So now, I really started to consider that this was a fulfillment of prophecy when, after almost two thousand years, the gate was still shut, and it was probably the gate through which Jesus actually entered into the temple area.

But at this point, some would say there are problems with that view—first, that this is a mistaken application of that passage because it refers only to Ezekiel's future temple, not the Second Temple,[4] so any resemblance with current events is solely coincidental. Such an objection errs for at least two reasons. For one, a thorough study of the way prophetic passages are recorded as fulfilled in the New Testament should be enough to demonstrate that this objection is baseless. For example, Luke 4 records Jesus referencing a prophecy from Isaiah 61 where he only applied the first verse and part of the second, but left the remainder of the passage unquoted because it was not meant for that time. It was for a future day.

> He went to Nazareth, where he had been brought up, and on the Sabbath day he went into the synagogue, as was his custom. He stood up to read, and the scroll of the prophet Isaiah was handed to him. Unrolling it, he found the place where it is written:

> "The Spirit of the Lord is on me,
>   because he has anointed me
>   to proclaim good news to the poor.
> He has sent me to proclaim freedom for the prisoners
>   and recovery of sight for the blind,
>   to set the oppressed free,
>   to proclaim the year of the Lord's favor."

> Then he rolled up the scroll, gave it back to the attendant and sat down. The eyes of everyone in the synagogue were fastened on him. He began by saying to them, "Today this scripture is fulfilled in your hearing." (Luke 4:16–21)

> The Spirit of the Sovereign LORD is on me,
>   because the LORD has anointed me
>   to proclaim good news to the poor.
> He has sent me to bind up the brokenhearted,
>   to proclaim freedom for the captives
>   and release from darkness for the prisoners,
>   to proclaim the year of the LORD's favor
>   and the day of vengeance of our God,
>   to comfort all who mourn. (Isaiah 61:1–2)

Matthew also affirms that Hosea 11:1 referred to Jesus, but other parts of the Hosea passage obviously do not. The same is true for numerous passages in the Old Testament that are referenced as fulfillments in the New Testament.

So [Joseph] got up, took the child and his mother during the night and left for Egypt, where he stayed until the death of Herod. And so was fulfilled what the Lord had said through the prophet: "Out of Egypt I called my son." (Matthew 2:14–15)

When Israel was a child, I loved him, and out of Egypt I called my son. But the more they were called, the more they went away from me. They sacrificed to the Baals and they burned incense to images. (Hosea 11:1–2)

This certainly creates more degrees of freedom for the interpretation of prophecy, which will cause some to scoff, but it is fully within the bounds of how prophecy is interpreted within the Scriptures themselves. Additionally, even if one proposes that these prophecies were fulfilled by random chance over time, they are still fulfillments that were extremely improbable. For example, that drought and famine will occur in a certain place is fairly probable over the course of time. But to say that the drought will last seven years and will be preceded by seven years of plenty that will begin soon, as in the story of Joseph in Egypt (Genesis 41:28–32), makes it very improbable to predict without true supernatural revelation. The point is that when we find agreement between real events and otherwise unlikely events predicted in Scripture, like the closing of the East Gate, it should be recognized as a fulfillment of scriptural prophecy, or at least a possible fulfillment, unless one lacks a belief in the divine inspiration of the Bible and is thus unwilling to acknowledge any fulfillment of scripture at any time. Therefore, the sealing off of the East Gate with stone is another evidence that it is in fact the correct gate, not just because it *must* be to prove Bible prophecy, but because it is more reasonable to assume that God fulfilled his Word than that mere happenstance fulfilled it over time. I understand that for some to believe that God is in control of world events and human affairs is anathema, but the God-fearing man or woman must believe and accept that this is indeed the truth because it is the testimony of Scripture. The Bible clearly declares that God is in charge of human

events, that he tells us in advance what will happen, and that everything
he says will come to pass.

> Remember this, keep it in mind, take it to heart, you rebels. Remember
> the former things, those of long ago; I am God, and there is no other;
> I am God, and there is none like me. I make known the end from
> the beginning, from ancient times, what is still to come. I say, "My
> purpose will stand, and I will do all that I please." (Isaiah 46:8–10)

The second reason that Ezekiel 44:1–2 does not apply to the third
temple but to the second is that first of all, there is no need for a gate
to be permanently shut in the third temple during the future messianic
reign, when all has been set right in the world as described in Isaiah 11.
So therefore, we are talking about a pre–messianic return prediction.

> Then a shoot will spring from the stem of Jesse,
>> And a branch from his roots will bear fruit.
> The Spirit of the LORD will rest on Him,
>> The spirit of wisdom and understanding,
>> The spirit of counsel and strength,
>> The spirit of knowledge and the fear of the LORD.
> And He will delight in the fear of the LORD,
>> And He will not judge by what His eyes see,
>> Nor make a decision by what His ears hear;
> But with righteousness He will judge the poor,
>> And decide with fairness for the afflicted of the earth;
> And He will strike the earth with the rod of His mouth,
>> And with the breath of His lips He will slay the wicked.
> Also righteousness will be the belt about His loins,
>> And faithfulness the belt about His waist.
> And the wolf will dwell with the lamb,
>> And the leopard will lie down with the young goat,
>> And the calf and the young lion and the fatling together;
> And a little boy will lead them.
> Also the cow and the bear will graze,

Their young will lie down together,
And the lion will eat straw like the ox.
The nursing child will play by the hole of the cobra,
And the weaned child will put his hand on the viper's den.
They will not hurt or destroy in all My holy mountain,
For the earth will be full of the knowledge of the LORD,
As the waters cover the sea.
Then in that day
The nations will resort to the root of Jesse,
Who will stand as a signal for the peoples;
And His resting place will be glorious.
(Isaiah 11:1–10 NASB)

The other likely objection is that Jesus could have ridden into Jerusalem from the Mount of Olives just as easily or more probably through the Sheep Gate into the city and not through the Golden Gate, and then entered directly into the Temple Mount enclosure from the north. The best response to this objection is to acknowledge that while we don't know explicitly which gate it was, and both gates were presumably operational and in the general area during the time of Christ, we can make some significant inferences. Both the East Gate entrance mentioned in Ezekiel 43 and the riding of the Messiah into Jerusalem on a donkey in Zechariah 9 were recognized as messianic prophecies.

Then the man brought me to the gate facing east, and I saw the glory of the God of Israel coming from the east. His voice was like the roar of rushing waters, and the land was radiant with his glory. The vision I saw was like the vision I had seen when he came to destroy the city and like the visions I had seen by the Kebar River, and I fell facedown. *The glory of the LORD entered the temple through the gate facing east.* Then the Spirit lifted me up and brought me into the inner court, *and the glory of the LORD filled the temple.* (Ezekiel 43:1–5, emphasis added)

As they approached Jerusalem and came to Bethphage on the Mount of Olives, Jesus sent two disciples, saying to them, "Go to the village ahead of you, and at once you will find a donkey tied there, with her colt by her. Untie them and bring them to me. If anyone says anything to you, say that the Lord needs them, and he will send them right away."

This took place to fulfill what was spoken through the prophet: "Say to Daughter Zion, 'See, your king comes to you, gentle and riding on a donkey, and on a colt, the foal of a donkey.'" (Zechariah 9:9)

The disciples went and did as Jesus had instructed them. They brought the donkey and the colt and placed their cloaks on them for Jesus to sit on. A very large crowd spread their cloaks on the road, while others cut branches from the trees and spread them on the road. The crowds that went ahead of him and those that followed shouted,

"Hosanna to the Son of David!"

"Blessed is he who comes in the name of the Lord!"

"Hosanna in the highest heaven!"

When Jesus entered Jerusalem, the whole city was stirred and asked, "Who is this?" The crowds answered, "This is Jesus, the prophet from Nazareth in Galilee." (Matthew 21:1–11)

Fulfilling either prophecy alone would not have caused people to proclaim Jesus as the Messiah as recorded in Matthew 21. Logically, he would have had to fulfill both at the same time in order to explain the recognition and exuberance of the people. Here's why: even today, it is widely believed by Muslims, Christians, and Jews alike that the Messiah will enter through the East Gate, and that was also the case back in the time of Jesus, most likely associated with Ezekiel 43:1–5. Although this was the people's expectation, he could not have just entered on foot through the Golden Gate and received recognition as the Messiah, because people often entered this gate on foot. Also, as recorded by Zechariah, they would not have easily recognized Jesus as Messiah simply by his entering the city on a donkey, through a gate where people regularly rode donkeys. He needed to simultaneously fulfill both prophecies, riding on a donkey, and entering the city through the Golden Gate, which was not a typical entrance for animals. Therefore, even though Jesus could have come through another gate, theoretically, it is unlikely that he would have gotten the recognition as Messiah and the response that it is recorded that he received.

Another point to consider is that the Golden Gate was the first of three eastern gates that one reached before entering the temple. Both Jews and Gentiles, Herod included, could enter this gate, but even Herod could not enter into the main courtyard gates of the temple enclosure located within the Temple Mount area. Based on the following report by Josephus, Jesus could have entered into the temple area through this outer eastern gate, or Golden Gate, of the Temple Mount into the Court of the Gentiles, which is the "first enclosure" referenced by Josephus. The next gate Josephus mentioned was the gate leading into the Court of the Women, where it was posted that no foreigner could enter. What this means is that the Golden Gate, while important and holy, was a gate that was generally accessible by all. It was not the gate that forbade the entrance of any non-Jew.

Thus was the first enclosure. In the midst of which, and not far from it, was the second, to be gone up to by a few steps; this was encompassed by a stone wall for a partition, with an inscription, which forbade any foreigner to go in, under pain of death. Now this inner enclosure had on its southern and northern quarters three gates [equally] distant from one another, but on the east quarter, towards the sunrising, there was one large gate through which such as were pure came in, together with their wives; but the temple farther inward in that gate was not allowed to the women; but still more inward was there a third [court of the] temple, whereunto it was not lawful for any but the priests alone to enter. The temple itself was within this; and before that temple was the altar, upon which we offer our sacrifices and burnt offerings to God. Into none of these three did King Herod enter, for he was forbidden, because he was not a priest. However, he took care of the cloisters and the outer enclosures; and these he built in eight years.[5]

With this review of Josephus, we have actually begun the historic case for the East Gate, which is already confirming the scriptural and prophetic case. We will now explore the historic case more fully.

THE HISTORIC CASE FOR THE EAST GATE AS A LANDMARK

We now know that there is a prophecy about this present-day gate being shut, and it is shut in apparent fulfillment of the prophecy, but is there any historic testimony that can also confirm that it is the correct gate and how long it has been shut? This was a question that I had to answer for myself. If you've read the initial portions of this book, you know that I have already disclosed my conviction in the truth of the Bible, and so as an engineer and scientist I also wanted to immediately go and start looking for the evidence. That's the way engineers and scientists make investigations. They start with an idea—a hypothesis, if you will—based on their current understanding of the world and the mechanisms in question, and then they attempt to design an experiment or search for data to confirm (or deny) their hypothesis. This is where I found myself after examining the scriptural and prophetic case for the East Gate.

Well, being that I was already working as an engineer and researcher on a university campus back in 2008, I decided to make a trip to the library. There, I found F. E. Peters's book on Jerusalem,[6] where he collected testimonies from pilgrims and visitors to the site that predated Suleiman's work on the walls and the East Gate, reporting its existence back into antiquity. Now, I was pretty sure that I had stumbled onto something important. The gate was much older than Suleiman. Combined with the prophetic implications of the gate being shut, it certainly merited more investigation. The implications were huge, because it could settle the debate about where the temple should be located! But I didn't immediately start thinking that I needed to get this information published. In fact, I just filed it in my pet theory category, but I kept working on the idea and collecting and reading original source material on the subject.

Now, back to the historic testimonies I found referenced in Peters's book on Jerusalem, taken together as a whole, these testimonies clearly demonstrate that the gate was in existence long before Suleiman began his work on the walls of Jerusalem. This firmly establishes its preexistence, and they affirm the gate's Solomonic origins. They also document that the gate was already nailed shut in Suleiman's time, and that the city's inhabitants believed it had been in this condition for centuries, if not longer. This confirms that this gate has been shut for at least a millennium. To begin with, Al-Muqaddasi (c. 985) mentions two arches to this gate (the Golden Gate), the southern one called Bab e-Rahma (Gate of Mercy) and the northern one Bab e-Tauba (Gate of Repentance), and says that both were closed.[7] The double gate is also mentioned by Nasir i-Khosrau (c. 1047),[8] but some of the most detailed and compelling accounts are reproduced here. Included for reference are the accounts from Niccolo da Poggibonsi a fourteenth-century Franciscan monk representing a Christian viewpoint, and a Muslim cleric named Mujir al-Din (c. 1496) that provides a critical corroborating viewpoint from a non-Christian perspective.

Niccolo da Poggibonsi

You reach beside the walls of Jerusalem a Muslim cemetery. Do not enter, but go straight ahead, for the Muslims do not wish that Christians enter their churches and either kill them or force them to renounce their faith. *And there you find the Golden Gate and the wall of the Temple of the Lord.* This gate is very large and consists of two gates, one beside the other . . . The gate faces east and is all covered with iron attached with stout nails, but now many nails have been removed for the Christians take them, when they can, because they have great power. The wood at the back of the gate is cypress. *This gate was never opened,* and this not because they [the Muslims] did not want to but because they could not since Christ left by it on Palm Sunday.[9]

Mujir al-Din

The first [of the gates of the Haram] is the double entry let into the eastern wall. It is of it that the Quran speaks [57:13] "And between them will be erected a wall that will have a gate. Inside will sit mercy;

outside and facing it, punishment." In fact, the valley that is behind this gate is that of Gehenna. These two gates are inside the wall and are next to a part of the Haram. One is called the Gate of Repentance, and the other the Gate of Mercy. *Presently they are impassable. Over these gates and inside the Haram is a vaulted construction built by Solomon*; it is the only building inside the Haram whose construction goes back to Solomon. This place is visited by pilgrims; it has an imposing appearance and commands respect. One of the older inhabitants of the city once told me that *the two entries [of the Golden Gate] were sealed by the Commander of Believers Umar ibn al-Khattab [in AD 635] and that they will not be reopened until the descent of the Lord Jesus, son of Mary, upon whom be blessings.* From all appearances, however, they were closed in the fear of an attack on the Haram and the city by the heretic enemy since the gates lead out into the countryside and there would be little use in leaving them open.[10]

Upon close inspection of these texts, we see that not only were the gates present and intact in the wall, but they were also made of cypress and were housed within a vaulted stone structure believed to have been made by Solomon. Both accounts are long before the walls of Jerusalem were restored by Suleiman the Magnificent (c. 1537–1541). These accounts also match very well with the East Gate structure visible today, with the exception of the stone walling up the doorways and increasing the overall height of the gate structure. We also are informed that the gates were perpetually closed, and that they were reportedly kept shut for defensive purposes, going back to at least AD 635. In fact, in the almost continuous periods of insecurity that followed the destruction of Jerusalem in AD 70 and the fact that they led out to nowhere but a very steep hillside, it's not difficult to understand why they would have constantly been kept shut.

These testimonies should satisfy us that the gates are more ancient than the Muslim conquest of Jerusalem, but the question remains whether or not this could be an original gate from before the time of

Titus's destruction of Jerusalem. To answer that question we can refer to Josephus's account of the destruction of Jerusalem, which gives several important clues. The first is the suggestion that the East Gate was not totally destroyed and was in fact kept intentionally for its testimony to posterity and as a meeting place.

> And now the Romans, judging that it was in vain to spare what was round about the holy house, burnt all those places, as also the remains of the cloisters, *and the gates, two excepted; the one on the east side and the one on the south*; both which, however, they burnt afterward. . . .
>
> And now the Romans, upon the flight of the seditious into the city, and upon the burning of the holy house itself, and of all the buildings round about it, brought their ensigns to the temple, and set them over against its eastern gate; and there did they offer sacrifices to them, and there did they make Titus imperator, with the greatest acclamations of joy.[11]
>
> Now, as soon as the army had no more people to slay or to plunder, because there remained none to be objects of their fury (for they would not have spared any, had there remained any other such work to be done) Caesar gave orders that they should now demolish the entire city and temple, but should leave as many of the towers standing as were of the greatest eminency; that is, Phasaelus, and Hippicus, and Mariamne, and so much of the wall as enclosed the city on the west side. This wall was spared, in order to afford a camp for such as were to lie in garrison; as were the towers also spared, in order to demonstrate to posterity what kind of city it was, and how well fortified, which the Roman valor had subdued. . . .
>
> But [Titus] permitted the tenth legion to stay, as a guard at Jerusalem.[12]

So, how do we know from these passages that the East Gate was preserved? First of all, Josephus wrote that the East Gate was specifically spared. Even though he said that it too was later burned, we can be sure that it was not destroyed completely because it was primarily of stone, not wood, so fire would only be partially destructive in any case. Next, the army chose to place their ensigns (flags) at the East Gate, offer sacrifices to them, and make Titus imperator there in the same spot. This confirms that it was kept as a nice area and maintained a regal character befitting their honor as soldiers. Finally, Josephus tells us that a west wall was preserved to provide a base camp for the garrison of the Tenth Legion in Jerusalem. (There are also archaeological findings that support that the Tenth Legion was indeed camped on the Temple Mount during this time, which we'll discuss later in this chapter.) Understanding that the army was camped there helps us recognize that Josephus was not talking about walls on the western edge of the city, but what today is called the Western Wall or Wailing Wall. This wall certainly communicates to posterity the grandeur that Jerusalem possessed in the days before its destruction. Therefore, Josephus's testimony also supports what should be obvious: that the Western Wall is part of the original Temple Mount wall.

The next account of the East Gate is the testimony of Prudentius (c. 394), who said that this gate (also called *Porta Speciosa* in Latin, or "Beautiful Gate," by Byzantine pilgrims) was a great work of Solomon and was near the Pinnacle of the Temple (*Pinna Templi*).[13] Certainly, it is odd that the Golden Gate is not mentioned by the Bordeaux pilgrim in AD 333, but that isn't proof it wasn't there, particularly, because he only mentioned two of the gates of Jerusalem in his entire account, and only gave an actual name to one of them. We do have a clear reference to the Golden Gate, though, by the Piacenza pilgrim (c. 570), who also called it the *Porta Speciosa*, and he affirmed that it was a gate of the temple. We know it was the Golden Gate because he called it out as he was coming up from Gethsemane to the gate of Jerusalem on the east, approximately where today's Lion's Gate is located.

> This valley of Gethsemane is also at this place called Jehoshaphat. We climbed by many steps up from Gethsemane to the gate of Jerusalem. There is an olive grove on the right of the gate; in it is the fig-tree from which Judas hanged himself. Its trunk still stands there, protected

by stones. This gate of the city is next to the Gate Beautiful which was part of the Temple, and its threshold and entablature are still in position there.[14]

We also have the account of Arculfus, bishop of Gaul (c. 670). In this account we see the general locations of most of the modern gates (the Jaffa Gate, Damascus Gate, Herod's Gate, the Golden Gate, and the Dung Gate). And while there is some interpretation required, there is no compelling reason to believe that in AD 670 Arculfus was not describing the stairs of the Golden Gate that lead, exactly as described, down into the Kidron Valley (valley of Jehoshaphat).

> As to the situation of Jerusalem, we shall now write a few of the details that the sainted Arculf dictated to me, Adamnan; but what is found in the books of others as to the position of that city, we shall pass over. In the great circuit of its walls, Arculf counted eighty-four towers and twice three gates, which are placed in the following order in the circuit of the city: the Gate of David, on the west of Mount Sion, is reckoned first; second, the Gate of the Place of the Fuller; third, the Gate of St. Stephen; fourth, the Gate of Benjamin; *fifth, a portlet, that is a little gate, by which is the descent by steps to the Valley of Jehoshaphat;* sixth, the Gate Thecuitis.[15]

By these accounts we can be sure that the Golden Gate of today is an original gate of the temple and that Suleiman did not relocate it from in front of the Dome of the Rock to its present-day location. On the contrary, it is exactly where it has always been. In fact, a careful search of the recorded history about Suleiman reveals that he intentionally walled it up, possibly for defensive reasons, but also to prevent the messianic prophecy regarding the East Gate (see Ezekiel 43) from coming to pass.[16]

BIBLICAL AND RABBINIC TESTIMONY ABOUT THE EAST GATE AND TEMPLE ALIGNMENT

Another question to answer in this section concerns how certain it is that the East Gate was in fact directly aligned with the temple. This point is of paramount importance to establish if we propose to use it as a landmark for the temple location. At first, I didn't think this really needed to be proven because Jewish scholarship on the subject seemed to be without disagreement on this issue, so it appeared to be settled fact. However, I did find that not all of the archaeological scholarship was in agreement, so I decided that this too would have to be explored in depth.

This question, however, can only be resolved by looking at biblical and rabbinic sources, since no secondary or secular sources appear to deal at all with this precise question. The first place to look would be the biblical references. Unfortunately, the Scriptures themselves do not say a lot about the orientation of the temple and its gates. Nevertheless, with some logical inference we can get a good idea. For example, in 1 Chronicles 9:24 the gatekeepers (and the associated gates) are described as lying in the cardinal directions from the temple:

> The gatekeepers were on the four sides, to the east, west, north and south.

If the East Gate was, for instance, actually located in the north-eastern corner of the Temple Mount, rather than directly east of the temple, this verse would be a poorer fit. Consequently, we can say that the most literal understanding of this verse is that the gates were in general alignment.

In Ezekiel 40 we read that in the prophet's vision, the east gate faced the temple, which affirms that, at least in a future vision of the temple, this is the case. The description is consistent with a central alignment of the outer eastern gate with the central east-west axis of the temple itself, because the text describes the eastern gate as facing the temple. Since gates are square and look straight ahead, an offset gate would not properly face the temple, because to "face" something, you need to be directly pointed at it.[17] Thus, if the Golden Gate was offset to the Temple, then this description would not be accurate.

> *Then he went to the east gate.* He climbed its steps and measured the threshold of the gate; it was one rod deep. The alcoves for the guards

were one rod long and one rod wide, and the projecting walls between the alcoves were five cubits thick. And the threshold of the gate next to the portico facing the temple was one rod deep. (Ezekiel 40:6–7)

Based on Hebrews 8, the vision of the East Gate directly facing the temple should also apply to the First and Second Temples. Why? Because the author of Hebrews affirmed that the earthly temple is to be a copy of God's temple in heaven. And if all of the earthly temples copy the same heavenly design, then we can be sure that the First and Second Temples had the same core temple design that Ezekiel described in his vision. This is a reasonable deduction for at least the temple edifice proper. There are clearly differences in the outer court in lieu of the Court of the Women and the larger surrounding sacred district of Ezekiel's temple, which are logically associated with needs and uses in that time.

> . . . for there are already priests who offer the gifts prescribed by the law. They serve at a sanctuary that is a copy and shadow of what is in heaven. This is why Moses was warned when he was about to build the tabernacle: "See to it that you make everything according to the pattern shown you on the mountain." (Hebrews 8:4–5)

Next, we turn to the writings of Jewish rabbis to look for explicit confirmation of what we infer from Scripture—that the Shushan/ Golden Gate was located along an east-west axis with all the eastern gates of the temple and the entrance to the Holy of Holies. And when we do, we find that the historical accounts given by the Mishnah and Talmud also confirm that the eastern gates were all aligned with the temple.

> One should not show disrespect to the Eastern Gate, because it is in a direct line with the Holy of Holies. (Berakhot 9:5)

> One may not deport himself light-headedly opposite the eastern gate (of the Temple) [outside the Temple Mount, in the lower wall at the foot of the Temple to the east], for it is aligned with the Holy of Holies. [All of the gates were aligned with one another: the eastern

gate, the gate of the ezrath nashim (Court of the Women), the gate of ezrath Yisrael (Court of Israel), the entrance of the Ullam (Entrance Hall), the sanctuary, and the holy of holies—in the days of the first Temple.] (Commentary on Mishnah Berakhot 9:5 by Obadiah Bartenura, c. 1445–1515, translated by Rabbi Shraga Silverstein)

There were five gates to the Temple Mount: The two Huldah gates on the south were used both for entrance and exit; The Kiponus gate on the west was used both for entrance and exit. The Taddi gate on the north was not used at all. The Eastern gate over which was a representation of the palace of Shushan and through which the high priest who burned the red heifer and all who assisted with it would go out to the Mount of Olives. (Middot 1:3)

All the walls that were there [in the temple] were high except the eastern wall, for the priest who burned the red heifer would stand on the top of the Mount of Olives and direct his gaze carefully to see the opening of the Sanctuary at the time of the sprinkling of the blood. (Middot 2:4)

The Mishna describes: When they reached *the gate through which one exits to the east, they turned from facing east to facing west toward the Holy of Holies,* and said: Our ancestors who were in this place during the First Temple period did not conduct themselves appropriately and stood "with their backs toward the Sanctuary of the Lord, and their faces toward the east; and they worshipped the sun toward the east" (Ezekiel 8:16), and we, our eyes are to God. The Sages taught: By inference, from the fact that it is stated: "And their faces toward the east," don't I know that "their backs were toward the Sanctuary of the Lord"? The Sanctuary was to the west. (Sukkah 53b, emphasis added)

From the Mishnah Berakhot it is clear that the gates were aligned all the way to the Eastern Gate, and Rabbi Obadiah Bartenura's commentary, made in the sixteenth century, is even clearer on this point. By Rabbi Shraga Silverstein, we have it reported explicitly that all of the gates, starting with the Eastern Gate, were in line. Thus, there was perfect alignment from the Holy of Holies out to the Eastern Gate, which is now called the Golden Gate. The other comments from the rabbis all support this understanding. In summary, having looked closely at the original sources for the claim that the Eastern Gate was aligned with the temple, this question should be settled by the works themselves. And even though the scriptural references are not entirely explicit, the rabbinic sources are. Granted, the rabbinic sources were recorded by men, so they are not inerrant. However, the traditions have been preserved in as faithful a way as men can produce.

A quick side note: The existence of the Mishnah and the Talmud are a testament to the fact that the rabbis clearly believed there was a difference between their own thoughts and musings and the Scriptures, which they believed to be divinely inspired.[18] Rather than alter anything in the scriptures they copied (besides occasional scribal notes in the margin), they exclusively recorded their own thoughts, opinions, procedures, and other information in these separate documents. Writings like the Talmud and the Mishnah contain the detailed writings of very serious and devout men over the centuries, but they have always been regarded as lesser than and separate from the Scriptures themselves. This is really important to understand. The Bible has been faithfully copied to preserve as accurately as possible exactly what was written by the original authors. Throughout its history, devout men have treated the Scriptures as holy and completely above revision. There is simply no credible evidence for continued revision over time. That hypothesis is completely refuted by the Dead Sea Scrolls (c. 250 BC–AD 68) and papyri fragments of New Testament documents that exist from the second century AD on.[19]

THE PRACTICAL ARGUMENT FOR THE EASTERN
GATE ALIGNMENT WITH THE TEMPLE

A very down-to-earth question can also be asked about the Golden Gate. Why is it even there if not because of something to do with the temple? If there was no design-based reason to have an eastern gate directly in front of the temple, it is difficult to imagine any other compelling reason to build an ornate gate in that part of the steep hillside. Why would anyone put a gate there if not for decorative purposes? It's too steep to be a practical entrance, as seen in Figure 18.

Figure 18: The Steep Ascent to the Golden Gate, view from the Kidron Valley below. *[Author's photo]*

At best you might put a small gate as an emergency exit or a sentry gate in that part of the Eastern Wall. But an incredibly large and elabo-rate gate? That's much harder to understand. Particularly when 680 feet (207 meters) to the north, you find the Lion's Gate, which probably was previously in the general location of the Sheep Gate. In this part of the city, the approach to the gate is on a relatively light slope, and you have a realistic location for a highly trafficked entrance into the city. A gate as elaborate as the Golden Gate wouldn't have been a sentry gate, and it doesn't make sense for an emergency exit either. The Jews had other, secret-tunnel exits from the city out into the Judean wilderness as escape routes to the east, as recorded in the account of the attempted escape of Zedekiah (2 Kings 25:1–7) and by both Cassius Dio and Josephus. There just isn't an easily explained reason to have a gate in this part of the wall pre– or post–AD 70, particularly given the history of Jerusalem after its destruction and the fact that the geography in this area has not significantly changed in the past four thousand–plus years. That side of the Temple Mount has always been on a steep hill. Therefore, there needs to be a good reason to build a gate there, and apart from alignment with the temple, there just doesn't seem to be one. To further support that point, Josephus recorded the following, talking about the side of Jerusalem protected by a valley and only a single wall, which can only be this eastern side of the temple:

> The city of Jerusalem was fortified with three walls, on such parts as were not encompassed with unpassable valleys; for in such places it had but one wall. But on the outsides, these hills are surrounded by deep valleys, and by reason of the precipices to them belonging on both sides, they are everywhere impassable. Now of these three walls, the old one was hard to be taken, both by reason of the valleys, and of that hill on which it was built, and which was above them. But besides that great advantage, as to the place where they were situated, it was also built very strong; because David and Solomon, and the following kings, were very zealous about this work.[20]

Israeli archaeologist Dan Bahat has also commented on the strange placement of this gate and reasoned that there is no good reason for an Umayyad or later construction of the gate in this area; however, he notes that it is also generally in line with the Church of the Holy Sepulchre and proposes that it could have been placed there in the time of Emperor Heraclius (c. AD 630) for his triumphal entry into Jerusalem.[21] While history does record that Heraclius entered the eastern gate in front of the Mount of Olives, it does not record that it was built for his arrival. In fact, in a very early account it is reported that he was even denied entry into Jerusalem until he dismounted from his horse and removed his royal attire to enter in humility.[22] Such an account would be inconsistent with building the gate solely for his arrival under pomp and circumstance. In fact, in a ninth-century source the gate is referred to as the eastern gate that Christ entered through, affirming that this gate indeed pre-dates Heraclius and was not built for his arrival:

> When the King of the heavens, the Lord of all the earth, entered through this gate on his way to fulfilling the mysteries of the passion, he did not appear in purple or shining diadem, nor did he ask for a strong horse to carry him, but sitting on the back of a humble donkey he left his servants a paradigm of humility.[23]

Thus, it is actually more reasonable to assume that (1) the gate was already in existence and (2) that Heraclius entered it because it possessed special significance. The logical conclusion from these accounts is that the Golden Gate of today is the same gate that Jesus entered on Palm Sunday, and therefore is also the Shushan Gate of Herod and even the Eastern Gate of Solomon, at least in the original portions of the gate that have survived. This doesn't mean that the gate was never repaired or further embellished, but simply that it is, for all intents and purposes, exactly where it has always been. And as Josephus pointed out, this portion of the wall was "built very strong, because David and Solomon, and the following kings, were very zealous about this work." This brings us to the archaeological case for the Eastern Gate, which for many will be the most convincing line of reasoning.

THE PIÈCE DE RÉSISTANCE: THE ARCHAEOLOGICAL CASE FOR THE ORIGIN OF THE EASTERN GATE

Perhaps I have made some progress in convincing you that the current Golden Gate could be an original temple construction that was repaired and modified, and historically has been in continual existence. However, you'd still like to know if there is any solid archaeological reason to believe this is the case. There actually is.

Some important observations were made about the Golden Gate (*Porte Dorée*) by Melchior de Vogüé back in 1864. He reported that there are two monolithic gateposts visible in the interior of the gatehouse of the Eastern Gate and made a detailed sketch of the largest monolith, as shown in Figure 19. The gateposts are of a size and construction that is consistent with the oldest and lowest portions of the Temple Mount walls. And in the post-Herodian era, it is difficult to support a construction hypothesis of the primary walls and arches, including monoliths of the size reported, during a later period.[24] Thus, of necessity, its design and construction in its oldest elements must be from at least the Second Temple period.

Figure 19: (Left) Photo of the interior of the Golden Gate showing the monolithic gateposts in situ. (Right) A close-up sketch of the southern gatepost. [from M. de Vogüé, 1864][25]

Picking up on de Vogüé's findings, Dr. Leen Ritmeyer, a leading archaeological voice and expert on the archaeology of the Temple Mount, also asserts that the Golden Gate is not a new gate in the Eastern Wall. He is one of the few archaeologists who has actually had the opportunity to conduct any serious studies of the interior of the Golden Gate.[26] Speaking of the monolithic gatepost stones within the Golden Gate documented by Melchior de Vogüé, Dr. Ritmeyer wrote:

> Inside the gateway, two large monolithic gateposts have survived. The northern one is 15 feet (4.5 m) high while the height of the southern one is 11 feet (3.4 m). The top of the southernmost post is level with the top of an ancient stone course that can still be seen in the Eastern Wall to the immediate south of the Golden Gate. The second post is one stone course higher. As the monoliths line up with the adjoining masonry in the eastern wall, they appear to have been constructed contemporaneously, although they may have been inserted at a later date, i.e. Hasmonean or Herodian. *We shall see later that this masonry dates from the First Temple period* . . . As Herod left the line of the original East Wall untouched, this gate would have been in use during his time, as no other Herodian eastern gate has been found. . . .
>
> These monolithic gateposts may have been part of the earliest wall section of the Temple Mount walls. Even if they were inserted at a later date, it follows that as no remains of any other pre-Herodian eastern gateway are known, the site of the Golden Gate is the only possible location for the earlier Shushan Gate. The location of this early gate in the Eastern Wall does not line up with the axis of the Temple. However, as we will see later, this does not disqualify it as an original gate of the Temple Mount.[27]

Dr. Ritmeyer's finding, that the Golden Gate is from the First Temple period (definitely before Herod) and is the ancient Shushan Gate of the temple, is incredibly important. He noted that the monoliths are aligned with the ancient stone courses of the adjoining masonry of the Eastern Wall, which supports the conclusion that they "may have been a part of the earliest wall section of the Temple Mount walls." He also conceded that they could have been inserted at a later date; however, I would say no. First of all, the largest monolith is arguably around 9 m³ in volume and weighs around 23,000 kilograms (25 tons). That is an incredibly large stone to move in after the wall is already constructed. Second, the stones are both in line with the wall and leveled with each course, which is an alignment and setting that would be difficult to achieve. Finally, if that was the case, there would be evidence that the wall was posthumously cut and reset to accommodate the monoliths. Therefore, if they weren't already there, then the entire portion of the wall would have to have been reset to hide the fact that they were added later. Therefore, one can logically conclude that they had to be, as Dr. Ritmeyer affirms, a part of the original wall. This means that the gate and the oldest part of the east wall are (1) contemporaneous and (2) arguably datable to the First Temple period.

There are dissenters from this view who ascribe the Golden Gate to the Umayyad period (seventh century).[28] However, the argument is style and design based, rather than based on logical deductions from the physical structure of the gate, such as the monoliths, which are difficult to interpret as later artifacts, as Dr. Ritmeyer has pointed out. To support stylistic arguments for Umayyad construction, accounts regarding the Eastern Gate from centuries earlier also have to be disregarded. Instead, the arguments must rely solely on subjective assessments of style. The remains of a stone arch, reported by James Fleming when he fell into a tomb in front of the Golden Gate,[29] are also cited as proof that the monoliths are not monoliths at all. It is claimed that they must be smaller stones because they "stand upon the smaller stones of the lower gate." However, this is not the case. First of all, the arches seen are both in front of and between the monoliths reported by de Vogüé—they cannot be underneath them; it is physically impossible. The monoliths are in line with the east wall of the Temple Mount and are spaced wider than the double gate itself. The point of Fleming's entry into the tombs is in front of the Golden Gate spaced well out from the wall and in the area now marked by a black wrought-iron fence, as shown in Figure 20. The monoliths were also reported by J. L. Porter, the president of Queen's College in Belfast, in 1886, making a third eyewitness account of the stature of these stones.[30] Therefore, the attempt to reduce the size of the monoliths from 3.4 meters and 4.5 meters to 0.8 meters based on a photograph of an area not related to the monoliths is a clear example of how such an important landmark has been hidden in plain sight through misidentification.

Figure 20: Area in front of the Golden Gate where archaeologist James Fleming fell into a tomb and photographed a stone archway about eight feet below the present opening of the gate. A wrought iron fence now keeps visitors away from the area (white arrow). Approximate monolith locations are shown with white dashed arrows back at the main east wall but are only visible inside the Golden Gate. *[Author's photo]*

Not only that, but in reality, the arches are probably not a gate at all, but the remnants of the supporting structure for the walkway that would have undoubtedly been needed to approach the Golden Gate in the days of the temple.[31] Since it is on a steep incline, without some type of ramp or stairway the gate would be almost inaccessible. Nevertheless, the arch seen below the Golden Gate is further proof that the Golden Gate does indeed mark the location of the original Eastern Gate of the temple, as Dr. Ritmeyer affirms. Why? Because the arch is directly below the present gate and part of the older wall. So, it still confirms that this was the location for the eastern temple entrance going back to its earliest times and confirms this location as a point of alignment for the temple.

Recognizing the Golden Gate as an original gate of the temple is an incredibly important finding for which Dr. Ritmeyer deserves significant recognition. Nonetheless, he also recognizes the problem that identifying the Golden Gate as the original Shushan Gate poses for a Dome of the Rock temple location. Most Jewish scholars agree that the Shushan Gate was aligned with the temple, and based on the review of the rabbinic sources earlier, I think it should be clear that it indeed was. However, Dr. Ritmeyer also supports the view that the Dome of the Rock's *al-Sakhra* is the true foundation stone that marks the former location of the Holy of Holies. Since the Dome of the Rock is not in line with the Golden Gate, he attempts to resolve the conflict by concluding that the tradition regarding the Eastern Gate being in alignment with the Temple is in error. He posits that the Shushan Gate was never aligned with the temple; only the other two inner gates of the temple were in alignment.[32] However, we have already discussed that the rabbinic records clearly state that all of the eastern gates were in alignment all the way through the Shushan Gate. This fact is arguably implied in the biblical texts, as well. One can also logically conclude that the Eastern Gate was aligned with the temple because the location is otherwise totally unsuitable for such an elaborate gate.

Therefore, if one accepts that the gate is the original Eastern Gate and that it was formerly aligned with the temple, then al-Sakhra cannot mark the temple location because it is not aligned with the Golden Gate. Hence, while there are some reasons to think that the foundation stone of the Holy of Holies could be al-Sakhra, in fact it is not. The main reasons to disqualify al-Sakhra have already been discussed in chapter 2, and I will attempt to address any remaining objections in chapter 4. Hopefully, however, the case for the Golden Gate marking the true location of the holy temple is becoming clearer and clearer.

The archaeological tradition for the Golden Gate being a post–AD 70 construction can be traced back to around the time of Charles Warren, who supported this idea and stated that the Golden Gate was not mentioned by writers until the 1100s and was therefore not an original gate. We now know that this is not correct, either. Josephus mentioned the gate in his *Wars of the Jews* (book 6, chapter 6), which was reviewed earlier in this chapter. Here's what Warren reported:

> None of the early writers speak of the Golden Gate before Justinian. Antony Piacenza and Saewulf in 1102 are the first to describe this monument, and the latter does not carry its oral history back further than the time of Heraclius (the beginning of the seventh century), and from the Arabic writers, Mejr ed Din and Jelal ed Din (fifteenth century), that Omar found no building over or near the Sakhrah rock.[33]

First of all, Warren failed to recognize the reference to the Golden Gate that he quoted in his own survey report from Arculfus, the holy bishop of Gaul, who visited Jerusalem around AD 670. He missed it because it was not called out by name but was instead described. Despite that, Arculfus's description makes it clear that he was talking about the Golden Gate when he said that it was "a portlet, that is a little gate leading by a flight of steps to the valley of Jehoshaphat (Cedron)."[34] Now, while "little" may be a fairly subjective term, the term "portlet" and the flight of steps and reference to the Kidron Valley (Valley of Jehoshaphat) are dead giveaways. Not to mention the earlier accounts of Josephus (c. AD 100), Prudentius (c. 394), and the Piacenza pilgrim (c. 570) that we discussed earlier in this chapter. Consequently, it is difficult to understand how Warren could have so erroneously concluded that the history of the Eastern Gate could not be older than Heraclius (c. 610–641). But sadly, that tradition caught on, so the gate is generally believed to be post-Herodian by most people today.

Another important archaeological observation that supports the assessment of the age of the ornate stonework of the Golden Gate is the weathering observed in the Eastern Gate stones compared to that of similar stone carving work in the area that is of a known or accepted age. In Figure 21, we see some close-up pictures of the north side of the Eastern Gate stone structure within the Temple Mount complex.

Figure 21: North side of the Eastern Gate, showing large, well-worn stones and a decorated pilaster with a pattern of concentric rectangles found on the northern side of the Golden Gate from inside the Temple Mount (left), and a close-up image of the top of the pilaster to observe the degree of weathering (right). *[Author's photos]*

There is a significant amount of weathering in the obviously older stone of the side structures. The stone in this portion of the gate is significantly larger and more weathered than the smaller stones of the upper and walled-in portions of the gate. The smaller stones found on the top of the gate and filling its doorways would be associated with Suleiman the Magnificent's restoration and sealing up of the gate. The other stonework is clearly from an earlier time. But how much earlier?

A good example of weathering in a similar limestone material—a sepulcher in the Kidron Valley that has been dated to the Second Temple period—is found just to the east of the Temple Mount. It can help answer the question of how much earlier the main Golden Gate structure was constructed compared to when it was walled up. This sepulcher is a wonderful example of carved bedrock stone left out in the elements, as shown in Figure 22.

Architectural historian James Fergusson recognized the sepulcher as a Second Temple structure in 1878,[35] but this has also been affirmed more recently by the Israeli Antiquities Authority and foreign archaeologists.[36]

The structure is often called Absalom's Tomb, although that attribution is not generally believed by scholars or archaeologists and has changed more than once over the centuries. Nevertheless, by comparing the degree of weathering, we see that they could be of the same age. This may be harder to tell from a cursory inspection of a photograph; it is much more obvious in person. Hence, it presents a good qualitative comparison to substantiate a possible Second Temple date or earlier for the ornate carvings of the sides, columns, and arches of the Eastern Gate. My point here is that what we see on the outside of the gate is not incongruous with other known and aged carved stone monuments in the area. Obviously a more careful study of the entirety of the Golden Gate masonry is needed in this regard, in order to separate original structures from later repairs, but a detailed study of the masonry was also called for by Auld and Hillenbrand:

> A close examination of the masonry of the Golden Gate, which to my knowledge has never been made and is beyond the scope of this chapter, will be needed if the construction history of this gate is to be elucidated.[37]

Figure 22: Absalom's Tomb in the Kidron Valley, to the left of the Temple Mount in Jerusalem (top),[38] and a close-up view for a comparison of weathering with the nearby Eastern Gate (bottom). *[Author's photos]*

While arguably a comparison of this type is rudimentary, I think it helps confirm that the Golden Gate is not a post–AD 70 construction. Taken together with the reports of Melchior de Vogüé and the candid assessments of Dr. Ritmeyer, I would say that the archaeological case confirms the historic case that, while there may have been repairs made by the Byzantines, Umayyads, and even Suleiman I, the Golden Gate seen today preserves the essence of the original Shushan Gate.

Interestingly, pilgrims have continuously professed belief that this was the gate of Solomon's temple from antiquity all the way up to the 1800s. And it is still the popular opinion of laypeople who look at the gate (unless they've already been convinced otherwise by some publication they have read). The Golden Gate has remained through all of its recorded accounts as the messianic gate, the gate that would one day mark the end of the age. What is important, as far as establishing the Eastern Gate as a landmark, though, is simply establishing that it dates to the time of at least Herod and the Second Temple period. If the gate is from Herod's time or before, then we establish it as an important landmark of the First and Second Temple periods. Obviously, if it is a *post*–AD 70 construction, then it is not.

The weight of evidence, though, heavily supports that the core of the gate is from the time of Solomon, as believed and reported by pilgrims down through the ages. And even those who say that the gate is more recent, still often report that the present gate sits on top of an older gate in the same location.[39] But again, this simply demonstrates that the history of the Golden Gate is not widely understood (even by scholars) and that the dissemination of wrong information has led to wrong conclusions about where the temple was located. Ironically, it is still popularly believed today by Jews and Christians that the Messiah will enter Jerusalem through this gate,[40] and even Muslims believe this gate will play a role in the final judgment.[41]

Finally, another argument for the Eastern Gate being in its proper location is that no other Herodian-era gate locations exist in the wall. It would be, for all practical purposes, impossible, even after damaging or destroying such a large gate, to lose its location. The stones that make up the gate are quite large and would not have been scattered far from the site. For example, in all of the archaeological digs found in Israel of ancient fortified cities (Ai, Tel Arad, Hazor, Tel Meggido, etc.), archaeologists have always found the city gates, no matter how badly destroyed the city was. This is, of course, not just true in Israel, but probably without exception around the world. There is always evidence left behind. Gates can certainly be deliberately moved, which would be much more difficult to detect than simply destroying them, but you can't easily erase the evidence that it was ever there. That is one of the primary tenets of both archaeology and police detective work. There are always things left behind. When there is no evidence found in a certain place, it is generally assumed that it did not exist. Now, there are problems with that, because some things can be moved, and some things can be destroyed, but not everything, and generally not heavy stone and deep foundations. We might look in the wrong place, but things don't simply vanish. Dr. Ritmeyer was right about there being no other pre-Herodian gate because people have looked, and there is nothing there. As he said, "The site of the Golden Gate is the only possible location for the earlier Shushan Gate." Therefore, while the Golden Gate of today was repaired and sealed off by the Ottomans, it is the Eastern Gate of the Temple, known as the Shushan Gate of the Second Temple period, and almost certainly is actually the East Gate of Solomon, as popularly reported for almost two millennia.

THE ALIGNMENT OF THE EASTERN GATE AND THE DOME OF THE SPIRITS

Next, to ascertain exactly where the temple actually stood, we need to look at the stone under the Dome of the Spirits and determine if it is in the right place on the Temple Mount in general (in terms of its east-west positioning) and if it is aligned with the Eastern Gate (relating to its north-south positioning). As already discussed, the Eastern Gate is undoubtedly the original Shushan or Golden Gate of the former Second

Temple and reasonably of the First Temple as well. So, is the Eastern Gate aligned with the threshing floor–like rock under the Dome of the Spirits? Yes! A line parallel with the northern wall (6 degrees south of west) and passing underneath the middle of the Dome of the Spirits will also pass through the middle of the Golden Gate. That's incredible! Dr. Asher Kaufman noted this alignment in his book *The Temple Mount: Where Is the Holy of Holies*.[42]

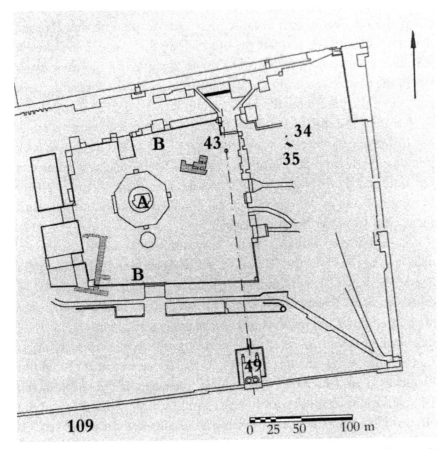

Figure 23: Simplified map of the central-northern part of the temple area. Number 43 designates the Dome of the Spirits (Tablets), and number 49 marks the Golden Gate. The arrow points west.

Figure 23 clearly shows that the Dome of the Spirits is in a straight line with the Eastern Gate. Surprisingly, Kaufmann noted that this alignment is from the First Temple, which he said was aligned precisely 6.2 degrees south of west. But inexplicably, he then devised another alignment for the Second Temple (9 degrees south of west) coordinated with a rock mass and wall remains uncovered on the site and a location on the Mount of Olives where the high priest could have performed the red heifer ritual. The reasoning for this was not altogether clear to me, but perhaps it was in part because of reports at the time that claimed that the Golden Gate was not the original Shushan Gate. Nevertheless, it stands as an excellent contribution to uncovering the mystery of where the temple was really located by discovering the threshing floor and hence the datum for the Holy of Holies.

So, does the shift in alignment from 9 degrees to 6 degrees make any difference to whether or not the high priest would be able to look into the temple from the Mount of Olives, another important point that Dr. Kaufmann brings up? No. With either alignment there are plenty of suitable areas where the high priest could have stood and seen into the temple from the Mount of Olives.

Next, I started thinking about how unlikely it was for these two objects to be in alignment. In fact, the odds of that stone being along the line of the East Gate by accident is clearly very small, but I decided to calculate exactly how small. So by my measurement, using a Google satellite image, shown in Figure 24, the alignment is within approximately ±1 meter, which is close to the accuracy of the measurement at this resolution. To be conservative, though, I doubled the accuracy estimate to within ±2 meters. I also estimated that at most, one-sixth of the width of the Temple Mount complex (east to west) would still allow space east of the Holy of Holies for the rest of the temple building and the temple courts. Therefore, the probability of this occurring by accident can be calculated by simply multiplying the ratio of a 2 meter-wide area in line with the gate, divided by the average length of the Temple Mount itself, which is 475.5 meters, and one-sixth of the length of the line in the east-west direction, which in formula form is: 2/475.5×1/6. Therefore, the probability that a large piece of flattened bedrock would just happen to be in the correct location is only 1 out of 1,426. In other words, there is only a 0.07 percent chance that the stone in the floor under the Dome of the Spirits and the East Gate are aligned by accident. But, the more eye-opening way to say this is that there is a 99.93 percent chance that the gate and the threshing floor are aligned on purpose! Now, I don't know how you think about probabilities, but a 99.93 percent chance of it being on purpose puts me in the category of beyond a reasonable doubt!

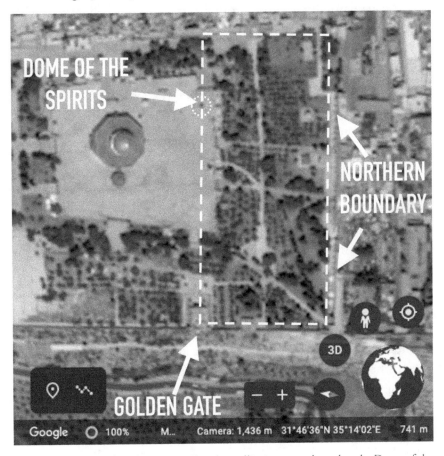

Figure 24: A rectangle is drawn on a Google satellite image to show that the Dome of the Spirits is aligned with the Golden Gate, and the line that bisects both is also parallel with the north boundary of the Temple Mount.

But, it's actually even more significant to have made this calculation if you think back to the last chapter, where we learned that the platform was leveled to the bedrock under the Dome of the Spirits. I discussed the forensic evidence that the polished and pockmarked surface was produced by threshing, and not by the builder of the platform chiseling and leveling the bedrock in that area as his reference point for the platform. Here's one more reason that the chiseling-and-leveling hypothesis at the Dome of the Spirits is unlikely: if that were the case, then there is only *a 0.07 percent chance* that this elevated area of bedrock would have naturally occurred in this perfect point of alignment with the Golden Gate!

In keeping with this location and alignment, one can also see that a 500-cubit square (~860 feet) fits almost perfectly within this area, depending, of course, on the exact dimension of a cubit that one chooses to use. In this case, I've drawn the square using an estimate for the long cubit measurement, which is believed to have been used for the temple and was probably around 20.67 inches.[43] The Golden Gate is approximately 456 feet from the northeast corner of the Temple Mount. Using that conversion, there would be room for a 500-cubit square centered on the Golden Gate, with about 50 feet to spare on the northern boundary of the temple mount platform, as illustrated in Figure 25. If the actual cubit was slightly shorter, then it would fit even easier; however, using 20.67 inches per cubit appears to be a good match and provides more circumstantial evidence to support that this is indeed where the Jewish temple once stood.

As for whether or not this northern boundary is the original boundary of the Temple Mount, antiquarian George Williams supported the view that it is, as did landscape artist W. H. Bartlett, both of whom visited the site in the mid-nineteenth century.[44] Furthermore, there are large ashlar stones like those of the Western Wall at the northeast corner of the Temple Mount on both the outside of the wall and inside it at the current Gate of the Tribes. This provides further evidence that this was the true northern boundary of the Temple Mount.

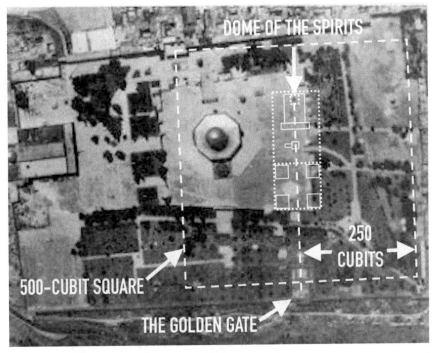

Figure 25: Author's diagram showing a notional overlay of temple structures on an aerial photograph of the Temple Mount.

SUMMARY

When one takes a fresh look at the Eastern Gate and reviews the historic testimony that we have about it, along with recent archaeological evidence, it is easy to see that what we have, right in front of us, is an ancient landmark, silently pointing the way to the temple and whispering to all who have ears to hear that the temple site has not been lost. This point is so crucial. *If we know that we have located the ancient Shushan Gate, which we also now know as the East(ern) Gate or the Golden Gate, and we know that the temple was aligned with that gate, then there really can be no doubt about its alignment along that axis. It simply cannot be anywhere else.* Once it is accepted that the Golden Gate reliably marks the site of the original temple Eastern Gate, then we should no longer be talking about a temple location anywhere but in front of it. It's as simple as that.

When we combine this with the discovery of the threshing floor and understand that there is a 99.93 percent chance that the two are aligned on purpose, or in other words there is no better than a 1 in 1,426 chance that it's an accident, then we have all we need to establish the former location of the Jewish temple. *Remember, all it takes to establish a fixed location is a datum and a point of alignment. We now reliably have both.*

It's just math! Okay, it's not math; it's some forensics, logic, and a little engineering. But my point is that this discussion has now become very deterministic and objective because we have established reliable landmarks. It should now be very easy for the average person to understand how we know where the temple was. Going forward, there really can no longer be any doubt about where the Jewish temple was located. Obviously, this first section has not exhaustively dealt with every known aspect of the Temple Mount structures and archaeology beyond the temple location. I will address many of them in the next section, though, in the context of addressing objections based on other possible locations. But I have largely left other secondary features of the Temple Mount alone because they are subordinate questions once we have established these two landmarks.

It is critical to grasp in this first part that what has been revealed by recognizing the Shushan Gate and the threshing floor, which have literally been hiding in plain sight, can now serve as the reference points for interpreting all of the other features found on the Temple Mount. The ability to fix these two points with certainty makes the interpretation of everything else that much easier. It's like getting the border of a puzzle completed and then being able to begin to fill in the interior. I'd like to close this section with a view of the Temple Mount from the east, looking at the area that once housed the Jewish temple (Figure 26) so that you can imagine what the implications of this discovery really are.

Figure 26: View of the Temple Mount from the east, showing the approximate 500-cubit area and the alignment of the Golden Gate and the Dome of the Spirits (white dashed lines).[45]

PART II

ADDRESSING THE OBJECTIONS

The first to plead his case seems right, until another comes and examines him.

(PROVERBS 18:17 NASB)

The Dome of the Rock viewed from the northwest. *[Author's photo]*

4

WHY THE TEMPLE WASN'T AT THE DOME OF THE ROCK

NO BOOK on such a controversial and well-studied subject can stand without properly addressing as many of the potential objections as possible. Part 1 was mainly focused on presenting the evidence for a northern placement, aligned with the Eastern Gate. In this section, I will attempt to reasonably address the potential objections of opposing views and their legitimate arguments for alternate locations. If this section is successful, it will begin to change the way people think about the Temple Mount and the idea of rebuilding a Jewish temple. Giving up a long-held belief is very difficult indeed. It creates cognitive dissonance in the brain, which, by itself, often encourages us to stop listening to a new idea before it is fully heard. There can also be a fear of the consequences of an idea that drives people to deny even obvious realities. Nevertheless, I believe that the truth must win out in the end. It is my great hope that if the first part is even remotely convincing, then after hearing an analysis of the opposing arguments, you will be able to reach a confident conclusion.

In this fourth chapter, we will address the view that is held by the vast majority of scholars and laypeople alike: that the Dome of the Rock now sits where the Jewish temple used to stand. This view has the weight of historic support going back to the ninth century. It is also the most widely held and is supported by a large number of scholars, including J. Lightfoot (1664), H. Menke (1868), K. Furrer (1876), C. R. Conder (1884), J. Porter (1886), C. Schick (1896), C. M. Watson (1896), C. Mommert (1903), J. L. Leeper (1903), G. Dalman (1909), F. Hollis (1934), L. Vincent (1954), L. Ritmeyer (1985), D. Jacobson (1990), D. Bahat (1990), A. Yisrael (1993), and C. Richman (1997). These authors hold essentially the same fundamental view about the location of the former temple, albeit with various subtle differences in the overall arrangement of the courts and so on. In my opinion, however, the best case for defending this position has been presented in recent times by Dr. Leen Ritmeyer.[1] Consequently, this is the presentation of the position that will be given the principal attention. His book also contains a treasure trove of information on the Temple Mount, which has been very helpful to unraveling this great mystery. Nevertheless, the quality of his work notwithstanding, there are multiple objections to his stated view that the Dome of the Rock covers the former location of the temple. To avoid getting bogged down in a multitude of minor points, I will try to keep the discussion focused on the key points. The areas addressed in this section are:

1. Historic testimony about the location of the temple: *Does the weight of historic testimony about the location of the temple support the Dome of the Rock location?*

2. The morphology of the al-Sakhra rock: *Does it match what we expect for a threshing floor?*

3. Argument from silence for the Dome of the Rock location: *Where is the corresponding landmark-based evidence for the East Gate and a flat threshing floor at the Dome of the Rock location?*

4. The reported fosse in the northern part of the Temple Mount: *Is the northern portion of the Temple Mount really disqualified from being a potential temple location because of a possible ancient fosse running through this area?*

5. All other landmarks being nonexclusive to the Dome of the Rock: *Are there any cited landmarks that exclusively support a Dome of the Rock location? Or are all of the in situ evidences cited actually inherently nonexclusive because they could be used to support any number of other theoretical positions?*

In an attempt to really address current objections to the views presented in this book, I also tried to contact a dozen leading archaeologists for peer review and comment on my core arguments and evidences. Many were simply too busy to be able to conduct a detailed review, but others were clearly unwilling to entertain any discussions related to reviving Dr. Asher Kaufman's views, even if it was based on new arguments and evidences. However, I was able to have some productive dialogue with some for which I am very grateful. The main objections to the northern placement view are related to the theory that the Golden Gate was a construction of the Byzantines for Heraclius and the theory that there was a northern defensive fosse within the current Temple Mount area. The first objection is answered by the evidences presented in chapter 3, and the northern fosse objection will be dealt with in this chapter.

HISTORIC TESTIMONY ABOUT THE LOCATION OF THE TEMPLE

When we consider the case for the placement of the First and Second Temples over the location currently occupied by the Dome of the Rock, the strongest argument in favor of locating the temple at the Dome of the Rock is the historic belief that the dome was built around the stone known as al-Sakhra, which marked the Holy of Holies of the temple and was the "foundation stone" of Jewish writings. But when did this belief begin? Clearly, the Dome of the Rock was built to venerate or protect and display the stone placed at its center (see Figure 27). The design implies that the rock was believed to have some special significance at the time of the construction of the dome, but what is really recorded about these early origins and beliefs?

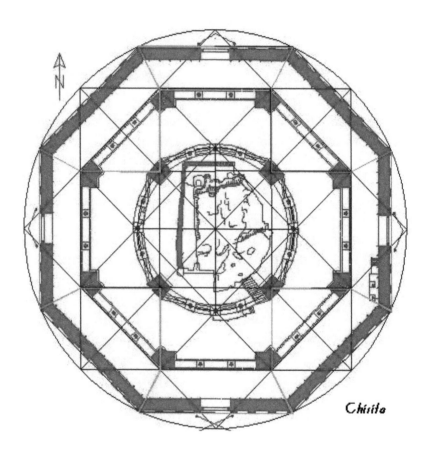

Figure 27: Geometric design of the Dome of the Rock.

When we want to understand the history of the Temple Mount since its destruction, we have to begin with Titus. The best account of the destruction of the temple comes from Flavius Josephus (c. 37–100). He recorded that Titus so utterly destroyed the temple complex in AD

70 that it wouldn't have been easy to tell anything about where it used to be located because of all the rubble from the fallen temple and its surrounding structures. In fact, wrote Josephus, Jerusalem and its walls were "so thoroughly razed to the ground by those that demolished it to its foundations, that nothing was left that could ever persuade visitors that it had once been a place of habitation."[3] In light of that, we know that most of the identifiable landmarks were obliterated within the Temple Mount itself (but not all of the walls, as we discussed in part 1).

Next on the scene of Jerusalem was Emperor Hadrian. Cassius Dio, a Roman historian (c. 155–235), recorded that Hadrian set out to build up and rename Jerusalem as Aelia Capitolina (beginning around AD 129–130) in honor of the Roman god Jupiter, and that he also set up a temple on the site of the former Jewish temple, all of which soon led to a bitter revolt.

> At Jerusalem he (Hadrian) founded a city in place of the one which had been razed to the ground, naming Aelia Capitolina, and on the site of the temple of the god he raised a new temple to Jupiter. This brought on a war of no slight importance nor of brief duration, for the Jews deemed it intolerable that foreign races should be settled in their city and foreign religious rites planted there.[4]

Based on this testimony, we can conclude that it was actually Hadrian who first tried to determine where the former temple had been located because he wanted to set up another temple where he thought the Jewish temple had been. But could he have gotten it wrong? First, had Emperor Hadrian ever seen the former Jewish temple? The answer is no. Publius Aelius Hadrianus was born January 24, AD 76, almost six years after the destruction of the temple. Could there have been people alive who still remembered seeing the temple and its location sixty years earlier? Perhaps, but they would have been very old by that time, and only children when they saw it before it was destroyed. Furthermore, only Jews would have had a great knowledge of the temple and its design, since the site was mostly off-limits for non-Jews. The Jews also likely wouldn't have wanted to tell Hadrian much of anything about the temple. It was Rome that had destroyed it. It was Hadrian's policies and constructions on the Temple Mount that led to the start of the Bar Kokhba Revolt (AD 132–136). Therefore, it is highly unlikely that he would have had the support of the Jewish community to identify the former site of the Holy of Holies and the temple. Left to his own devices, he would have been dependent on his own reasoning and biases and whatever was left of the evidence at hand, which would have been scarce.

Thus, what landmarks would Hadrian have had to identify the temple location? For one, we know that the rock in the center of the Dome of the Rock, *al-Sakhra*, would have been the highest natural landmark in the complex. It is also located approximately in the middle of the whole rectangular temple mount, so it could have been easy to assume that this was the temple's former location. Hadrian had also made it clear through his policies that he had no intention of rebuilding the temple but rather was intent on removing the Jewish presence from Jerusalem and creating a completely Roman colony.[5] Since Hadrian's intentions were clear, he could easily have been encouraged to believe that this central rock marked the former location rather than told the true location, particularly, if he had tried to persuade or compel by force any Jews at that time to show him where it would have been.

There is a historical mystery associated with Hadrian, and specifically what he did build in Jerusalem as he built Aelia Capitolina on the ruins of Jerusalem. The mystery comes from some vague and esoteric references recorded in the *Chronicon Paschale*, a well-respected seventh-century anonymous chronicle of world history from Creation to AD 629.[6] It records some of the things that Hadrian built when he was in Jerusalem, including two baths (*duo Balnea publica*), a theater (*Theatrum*), the *Tricameratum* (possibly the temple to the Capitoline Triad), the *Tetranymphum*, the *Dodecapylum*, and the *Codrum*. This last one, the *Codrum*, or possibly *Quadra* (both of which are possible Latin renderings from the Greek), has been theorized to be the current Dome of the Rock platform on the Temple Mount.[7] However, combined with the testimony of the Bordeaux pilgrim in AD 333 regarding the statues of Hadrian present at that time, it is certainly possible that Hadrian built the trapezoidal platform that is present on the Temple Mount today as a base for the display of the statues and his temple to Jupiter. Before this time that whole site would have been in disarray due to the temple's destruction. Therefore, as the first major builder to return to this area, Hadrian would have needed a foundation or platform for the building and statues. Otherwise, he would have had only rubble to build on. While this conclusion is inferential, it is also just common sense and is well supported by the historical accounts of Hadrian, not just in Jerusalem, but everywhere he went.

> Finally, after his (Hadrian's) return to Rome from Africa, he immediately set out for the East, journeying by way of Athens. Here he dedicated the public works which he had begun in the city of the Athenians, such as the temple to Olympian Jupiter and an altar to himself; and in the same way, while travelling through Asia, he consecrated the temples called by his name [Note: They were, in fact, temples dedicated to the cult of the emperors, including Hadrian himself, who was worshipped in the cities of Asia Minor as well as in the Olympieion at Athens]. *Historia Augusta*[8]

> For Hadrian ordered a temple without an image to be built in every city, and because these temples, built by him with this intention, so they say, are dedicated to no particular deity, they are called today merely Hadrian's temples. *Historia Augusta*[9]

> And in the building (in aede) itself, where stood the temple which Solomon built ... There are two statues of Hadrian, *and not far from the statues there is a perforated stone*, to which the Jews come every year and anoint it, bewail themselves with groans, rend their garments, and so depart. *Bordeaux Pilgrim*[10]

There is also some modern archaeological support for the account of the Bordeaux pilgrim from a dig at Tel Shalem in Israel in 1973. A portion of a bronze statue of Hadrian was recovered there, as seen in Figure 28. This confirms that Hadrian also set up a statue of himself in Israel.[11]

Figure 28: Bronze statue of Emperor Hadrian found in Israel at Tel Shalem. *[Author's photo taken at the Israel National Museum]*

It is also not unreasonable to think that the statue found at Tel Shalem was similar to or even originally located on the Temple Mount. First, there is no report of other full-sized bronze statues of Hadrian being placed in Tel Shalem, so the statue could only have been found in secondary use.

No one really knows what happened to the statues of Hadrian mentioned by the Bordeaux pilgrim after AD 333, but if use of the Tel Shalem fort continued into the fourth century, the statue could have later been moved there. Furthermore, in addition to the testimony of the Bordeaux pilgrim of a statue of Hadrian on the Temple Mount, another archaeological find also supports the legitimacy of the statue. A stone with an inscription was found upside down and in secondary use as a repair in the southern wall of the Temple Mount near the blocked entrance of the former Double Gate.[12] The stone bears an inscription that is consistent with a plaque that could have been at the base of one of the two statues, identifying Hadrian's successor Titus Hadrianus Antoninus Augustus Pius (c. AD 138) as the subject (Figure 29). The stone reads:

TITO AEL HADRIANO

ANTONINO AUG PIO

P P PONTIF AUGUR

D D

Translation of the Latin:

TITUS AEL[ius] HADRIANUS

ANTONINUS AUG[ustus] PIUS

the F[ather] of the F[atherland], PONTIF[ex], AUGUR

D[ecreed] by the D[ecurions]

Now, whether or not this stone is actually from one of the two Hadrian statues reported by the Bordeaux Pilgrim, it still shows how legitimate material from Hadrian's time was redistributed elsewhere after its original location was destroyed. If whatever originally held this stone was destroyed and its material reused, then it should not be surprising that a statue of Hadrian could have been partially damaged but reused elsewhere, even outside of Jerusalem.

Figure 29: Inscription stone from the time of Emperor Hadrian (c. 135) in secondary use in the wall on the southern end of the Temple Mount. *[Author's photos]*

Why is all of this important? Because it settles the debate about whether or not Hadrian really built anything substantial on the Temple Mount. This is important to resolve as we attempt to understand the changes on the Temple Mount, because it influences our presuppositions in the search for the location of the Jewish Temple. Based on these testimonies and the few archaeological findings that have been made, it is no longer reasonable to doubt that Hadrian indeed built some kind of structure on the Temple Mount. Charles Warren came to the same conclusion.

> There is reason to suppose that this was done in the reign of the Emperor Hadrian, and that at the same time a temple to Jupiter was erected on the sister site of holiness, the rock on which the Temple of Solomon had stood.[13]

We know that in 333 there were two statues of Hadrian still standing in the Temple Mount area. We can also be sure that the statues would have to have been on a rebuilt platform of some type, or else they would have been standing among the temple ruins. Hadrian would have needed a platform for both his temple and the statues that were reported to be there. It is likely that Hadrian's platform would not have been destroyed, even though his temple was torn down. This would explain why the Dome of the Rock is built on a platform on which it is not centered. Particularly, because the Dome of the Rock is centered around al-Sakhra (as shown in Figure 27). We can therefore assume that the platform was already in existence because there is no obvious alignment of the platform to the Dome of the Rock, which sits off-center both to the west and south of the platform center, as shown in Figure 30. Consequently, when we look at the design of the Dome of the Rock, which is centered so perfectly and geometrically around the al-Sakhra stone, and then look at the offset and nonsymmetrical layout of the platform to the same stone, we know that they were not built contemporaneously. If the platform had been constructed at the same time, surely it would have reflected a similar symmetry in its construction, as well. That is not to say that the platform itself has not been enhanced and repaired by the Umayyads and others since the construction of the Dome of the Rock, but it cannot be a part of the original design in its overall dimensions and layout. Therefore, the most likely explanation is that the platform itself was a part of an earlier construction, for example, by Hadrian, which might have occupied the area indicated by the dashed line in Figure 30.

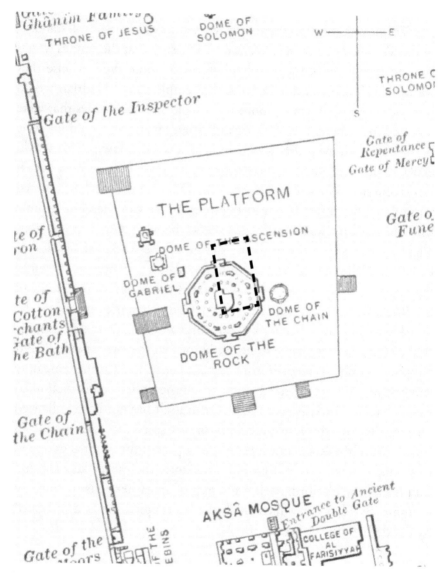

Figure 30: Plan view of the Temple Mount platform and Dome of the Rock from 1899 with author addition indicating a possible earlier building marked by a dashed line.[14]

The next emperor on the scene who could have had a hand in modifying the Temple Mount was Emperor Constantine the Great (AD 272–337) and his mother, Empress Helena (AD 248–330). Eusebius recorded that Helena discovered the place of Golgotha buried beneath a temple to Aphrodite (Venus) in Jerusalem.[15] The temple was destroyed, the site purified, and Emperor Constantine ordered the construction of a church on the spot where today we see the Church of the Holy Sepulchre. It is also recorded that Constantine ordered the destruction of pagan temples throughout his empire and that he finished his church, which was named *Anastasis,* or Resurrection, in 335.[16] What's not clear is what he may have done or not done on the Temple Mount. With the account of the Bordeaux pilgrim from AD 333, we can at least be sure that the statues of Hadrian were still standing at that time. Whether or not he tore down a temple to Jupiter on the Temple Mount as well as a temple to Venus (Aphrodite) is unclear, but some think it likely.[17] It does not appear that Constantine tore down the statues of Emperor Hadrian, though, because they are also reported by Saint Jerome (c. 394).[18] Thus, it may be that either this site was left alone, or only the temple structure was taken down. What we do know is that there are no solid reports of anything substantial being built on the Temple Mount under Emperor Constantine. And while there has been some confusion by some trying to attribute Emperor Constantine's work at the church of the Anastasis to the Temple Mount,[19] it is far too speculative and circumstantial to undermine the current site of the Holy Sepulchre.

Thus, Hadrian is still the most likely builder of the current Temple Mount platform, as opposed to an earlier Herodian origin or later Umayyad construction. What happened after Hadrian built his platform and temple and set up his statues on the Temple Mount, however, is not fully known. We only know from the historic records that after the statues of Hadrian were seen in 333, an attempt to rebuild the temple was supported by Emperor Julian around AD 361–363.[20] Julian (c. 355–363) allowed the Jews to tear down the former buildings and clear the area for setting new foundations, but the work was interrupted and never completed. After that time and before the surrender of Jerusalem in 637, the area went into disrepair and disregard.

The Christian lawyer Sozomen recorded the attempt to rebuild the

Jewish temple in Emperor Julian's day. His account is valuable in that it gives us a glimpse into the state of the Temple Mount almost thirty years after the Bordeaux pilgrim. At this point it is said that the Jews cleared the ground where they hoped to rebuild their temple. They "removed the ruins of the former building," which presumably means they cleared away the remains of Hadrian's temple.

> . . . for he [Emperor Julian] sent for some of the chiefs of the race and exhorted them to return to the observance of the laws of Moses and the customs of their fathers. On their replying that because the temple in Jerusalem was overturned, it was neither lawful nor ancestral to do this in another place than the metropolis out of which they had been cast, he gave them public money, commanded them to rebuild the temple, and to practice the cult similar to that of their ancestors, by sacrificing after the ancient way. The Jews entered upon the undertaking, without reflecting that, according to the prediction of the holy prophets, it could not be accomplished. They sought for the most skillful artisans, collected materials, cleared the ground, and entered so earnestly upon the task, that even the women carried heaps of earth, and brought their necklaces and other female ornaments towards defraying the expense. The emperor, the other pagans, and all the Jews, regarded every other undertaking as secondary in importance to this. Although the pagans were not well-disposed towards the Jews, yet they assisted them in this enterprise, because they reckoned upon its ultimate success, and hoped by this means to falsify the prophecies of Christ. Besides this motive, the Jews themselves were impelled by the consideration that the time had arrived for rebuilding their temple. When they had removed the ruins of the former building, *they dug up the ground and cleared away its foundation*; it is said that on the following day when they were about to lay the first foundation, a great earthquake occurred, and by the violent agitation of the earth, stones were thrown up from the depths, by which those of the Jews who were engaged in the work were wounded, as likewise those

who were merely looking on. The houses and public porticos, near the site of the temple, in which they had diverted themselves, were suddenly thrown down; many were caught thereby, some perished immediately, others were found half dead and mutilated of hands or legs, others were injured in other parts of the body. When God caused the earthquake to cease, the workmen who survived again returned to their task, partly because such was the edict of the emperor, and partly because they were themselves interested in the undertaking. . . . But all parties relate, that they had scarcely returned to the undertaking, when fire burst suddenly from the foundations of the temple and consumed several of the workmen. This fact is fearlessly stated and believed by all; the only discrepancy in the narrative is that some maintain that flame burst from the interior of the temple, as the workmen were striving to force an entrance, while others say that the fire proceeded directly from the earth. In whichever way the phenomenon might have occurred, it is equally wonderful. . . . If any one does not feel disposed to believe my narrative, let him go and be convinced by those who heard the facts I have related from the eyewitnesses of them, for they are still alive. Let him inquire also of the Jews and pagans who left the work in an incomplete state, or who, to speak more accurately, were not able to commence it.[21]

It was also reported by Mujir al-Din, a Muslim historian writing in 1496, that when Umar ibn al-Khattab conquered Jerusalem in 637, the Temple Mount had become a trash heap and the area of the Noble Rock was transformed into a stable. The reference to a stable around the Noble Rock is especially interesting, because the large flat platform built by Hadrian could have served very well as a place to have stables. By Mujir al-Din's reckoning, it was Helena, the mother of Emperor Constantine, who first ordered the abandonment and desecration of the Temple Mount and helped found al-Qumama, the Islamic name for the Church of the Anastasis, or Holy Sepulcher. But what is clear is that by 637 it would have been difficult to recognize anything that was found on the Temple Mount, particularly, after the basic constructions of the Tenth Legion living there in the time of Titus, a temple to Jupiter in the days of Hadrian, a failed attempt by Julian to rebuild the Jewish temple, and finally, centuries of neglect and deliberate disregard.

> Destroyed by Titus, the city of the Holy House was, after the persecution of the Jews, rebuilt little by little. It remained prosperous until the departure of Helena, mother of Constantine the Victorious, for this city of Jerusalem. Her son was first king at Rome, then he transferred his capital to Constantinople, had its wall constructed and became a Christian. The name of this city was Byzantium but he gave it that of Constantinople. Helena, the mother of Constantine, thus left for Jerusalem in search of the cross of Christ, the cross on which the Christians pretend that Jesus was crucified. Once she was in Jerusalem, she had the wood of the cross discovered and to this end instituted the Feast of the Cross and had built the church of al-Qumama [Anastasis] over the tomb in which, according to the Christians' pretensions, Jesus had been buried. She also had built the place opposite the Qumama known to this day as the Dargah [probably the patriarchal residence]; the church at Bethlehem; the one on the Mount of Gethsemane where the tomb of Mary is located. She had the Temple of Jerusalem leveled down to the ground—it was that which was in the sanctuary—and she ordered that the filth and scourings of the city be thrown on its place. The place of the Noble Rock was transformed into a stable. That state of affairs remained until the arrival of Umar Ibn al-Khattab, who took the noble city of Jerusalem.[22]

Thus, after all of this, we have the beginning of the Islamic traditions regarding the Temple Mount, and the beginning of the accounts of al-Sakhra. Three hundred years later, at the time of the conquering of Jerusalem in 637 by Umar, son of Al-Khattab, we find the first mention of "the Rock" (presumably al-Sakhra). It is generally assumed that the rock in question was the Jewish foundation stone of creation and marked the site of the Jewish temple, but in reality, the earliest Islamic histories, testimonies, and records suggest that is not the case. When we examine the earliest Muslim records related to the rock on the Temple Mount, we find that they are not focused on the temple of the Jews, but on the actions of Muhammad.

According to the history of al-Tabari (c. AD 915), the Temple Mount site was cleansed from being a dung heap, and "the Rock" was identified and discussed, but the first mosque location, that is, the "place of prayer," was deliberately chosen to the south, or in front of, the rock, to avoid venerating anything Jewish. This was decided after consultation with a Yemenite Jew named Ka'b al-Ahbar, who previously had converted to Islam. This explains why al-Aqṣā Mosque is on the southern end of the enclosure.

> According to Abu Maryam, the client of Salamah, who said: I witnessed the conquest of Jerusalem with 'Umar: he set out from al-Jabiyah, leaving it behind until he came to Jerusalem. He then went on and entered the mosque (Temple Mount). Then he went on toward the *mihrab* of David, while we were with him, he entered it, recited the prostration of David, and prostrated himself, and we prostrated ourselves with him.

> According to Raja b. Haywah—persons who were present at the event: When Umar came from al-Jabiyah to Jerusalem and drew near the gate of the mosque, he said "Watch out for Ka'b on my behalf!" When the gate was opened for him, he said: "O God, I am ready to serve you in what you love most." Then he turned to the mihrab, the mihrab of David, peace be upon him. It was at night and he prayed there. It was not long before dawn broke, and then Umar ordered the mu'adhdhin to sound the call for prayer. Then he moved forward, led the prayer, and recited Surat Sad with the people . . .

> . . . Then he (Umar) prayed another rak'ah and went away. He said: "Bring Ka'b to me." Ka'b was brought to him. Umar said: "Where do you think we should establish the place of prayer?" Ka'b said: "Toward the Rock." Umar said: "O Ka'b, you are imitating the Jewish religion!

I have seen you taking off your shoes." Ka'b said: "I wanted to touch the ground with my feet." Umar said: "I have seen you. Nay, we shall place the *qiblah* in the front of it, the messenger of God likewise made the front part of our mosques the *qiblah*. Take care of your own affairs, we were not commanded to venerate the Rock, but we were commanded to venerate the Ka'bah."

Umar made the front part of the mosque its *qiblah*. Then he stood up from his place of prayer and went to the rubbish in which the Romans buried the temple (*bayt al-maqdis*) at the time of the sons of Israel. (When he came to the Byzantines, they had uncovered a part but left the rest [under the rubbish].) . . .

. . . By the time it was evening nothing remained of the rubbish.[23]

Here we see the mention of a prominent rock, which presumably is what was later identified as al-Sakhra and where today the Dome of the Rock is located. However, in this account, there is no mention of the rock being the place associated with Sura 17:1 in the Quran, where Muhammad makes a night journey to the "farther Mosque" that became al-Aqsa in Jerusalem. This could of course be because the story about Muhammad's night journey was not widely known yet (c. 637). What we see here is that the Muslim conquerors associated the rock with something that is possibly Jewish, because Umar suspected that Ka'b was trying to return to his Jewish roots. But nothing is explicitly stated about why the rock was significant in this account. What we do know is that at this time, a close association of the mosque with al-Sakhra was being avoided intentionally.

The lack of early details to support a Jewish temple association with the Dome of the Rock was also reported by James Fergusson in 1878:

As before I mentioned, I am not aware of the existence of any quotation from any Mahomedan author, who wrote before the Crusades, which asserts that either Abd-el-Malek or anyone else erected any circular or octagonal building at Jerusalem, though there are ample details regarding the square one that khalif did erect. Nor do I know of any passage which would convey the idea that the Moslems understood the Sakhra to be a rock . . .

. . . Even to the present day the Mahomedans have only the haziest ideas possible as to what the great Sakhra really is intended to represent. I do not gather from any author that they really believe it to be the Altar, or the foundation of the Altar, of the Jewish Temple. *They know, as we do, that there is nothing in the Bible, or the Talmud, or in any ancient author, to countenance the idea, that the Altar was a rock or founded on a rock; what we do know is that it was in Solomon's time of brass, in Herod's of loose stones, but there is no mention of the rock anywhere.* It seems only something that somebody has asserted and everyone repeats, without any one enquiring whence the tradition arose.

The principal Mahomedan tradition regarding it is, that it was from this rock that Mahomet (Muhammad) ascended to heaven, on his celebrated night journey to that place.[24]

They were not trying to establish the location of the Temple when they chose the location of the first mosque built on the Temple Mount. In fact, there was a deliberate effort to not venerate the rock. The *qiblah*, or direction of prayer, was placed toward Mecca, and it was placed deliberately well to the south of the Rock referenced by Ka'b. Now, what we don't know for sure is why Ka'b, a converted Jew, chose the rock as the place and direction for a house of prayer. We can guess, as Umar did, that Ka'b was secretly still trying to align to the former temple, but he didn't say that. In fact, the most reasonable understanding of this interaction is found in the context of the change in *qiblah* that Muhammad had decreed (c. AD 623) to move the direction of prayer to Mecca. Before that, Muslims had prayed toward Jerusalem and the Holy Land. The best interpretation of these events is that Umar wanted to make certain that the *qiblah* was not changed back to anything Jewish. In reality, he could have just been affirming the change in the direction of prayer from Jerusalem to Mecca and didn't want any confusion by having the rock in the way. In either case, Umar was emphatic about not venerating the rock, but rather the Ka'ba, and distanced himself from Ka'b's recommendation by placing the mosque at the southernmost end of the Temple Mount complex.

There is also a later account of this event reported in the fourteenth century by Muthir al-Ghiram that suggests that the temple location was actually believed in those days to be north of al-Sakhra, which supports the northern location proposed in this work. Here, al-Ghiram wrote that Ka'b actually wanted to put the place of prayer north of the rock and near the Gate of the Tribes, which is located at the far northeast corner of the Temple Mount complex. While this still does not really tell us much about where the temple was located, it severely undermines the idea that the Dome of the Rock was intentionally built on top of the al-Sakhra rock to cover over and venerate the location of the Jewish temple. If this was truly the case, then this conversation between Ka'b and Umar should have been significantly different from what is reported here:

> Then the caliph himself went there (Temple Mount), and Ka'b (al-Ahbar) with him. Umar said to Ka'b: "O Abu Ishaq, do you know the position of the Rock?" Ka'b answered: "Measure from the well which is in the Valley of Gehenna so and so many ells; there dig and you will discover it," adding, "at this present day it is a dungheap." So they dug there and the rock was laid bare. Then Umar said to Ka'b, "Where do you say we should place the sanctuary, or rather, the qibla?" Ka'b replied: "Lay out a place for it behind [that is, to the north of] the Rock and so you will make two qibla's that, namely, of Moses and that of Muhammad." And Umar answered him: "You still lean toward the Jews, O Abu Ishaq. The sanctuary will be in front [that is, to the south of] the Rock." Thus, was the Mosque [of al-Aqsa] erected in the front part of the Haram area.

> Al-Walid relates further, as coming from Kulthum ibn Ziyad, that Umar asked of Ka'b; "Where do you think we should put the place

of prayer for Muslims in this Holy Sanctuary?" Ka'b answered: "In the further (northern) part of it, near the Gate of the Tribes." But Umar said: "No, since the fore part of the Sanctuary belongs to us."[25]

The next mystery concerns the history of the construction of the Dome of the Rock. Its unique octagonal structure is similar to a couple of early churches from the time of Constantine and the Byzantines, namely, the Church of the Kathisima and the Church of St. Peter in Capernaum.[26] This has led some to doubt its Umayyad origin. The modern belief is that the Dome of the Rock was built by Abd el Malik and completed in 691. If that is the case, then it was he who first determined the location of the Dome of the Rock to be placed around al-Sakhra about fifty years after Umar secured control of Jerusalem. However, there is at least some controversy for sole attribution to Abd-el-Malek. First of all, in the inscriptions within the Dome of the Rock there is a contradiction, because they are also ascribed to Abd-Allah-al-Mamun (c. 786–833), the successor of Harun-Al-Rashid, admittedly as a modification to an original attribution to Abd-el-Malek (c. 646–705).[27] A simple explanation for this would be later damage to and rebuilding of the structure. However, Fergusson has pointed out that two observers in the time of the Crusades did not record the presence of any Islamic inscriptions; therefore, they may be posthumous epigraphs. John of Wurzburg and Theodoricus, both of which recorded detailed descriptions of the interior and exterior of the Dome of the Rock, then called the Templum Domini, mentioned none of the Islamic inscriptions that are so prominent today. Most likely, then, the inscriptions are more modern (post-Crusades and after the supposed date of its original construction and inscription) and therefore are not at all useful for determining the building's true origins. Either way, the most significant thing about the inscriptions is what they don't say. To quote Fergusson's objections on this point:

> The truest test, however, of the age of this inscription, is its contents. If we assume that it was written either by Abd-el-Malek, or

by Al-Mamun, or by anyone else, in a building which they believed to have been erected on the site of Solomon's temple, it is not only inapplicable but unintelligible. If they believed the great Sakhra to be either the site of the Holy of Holies or of the Altar of the Jewish Temple, it seems quite impossible that no reference should be made to the fact, and that the names of David or Solomon do not occur in any part of it, and that no allusion to their greatness or their works should occur in it, not even a prayer for the rest of their souls. . . . It begins, of course, with the usual paragraphs in honour and praise of the founder of their religion, and of the unity of God. Then follows a very emphatic denial of the trinity, "He neither begettteth nor is begotten," which, however, is so common an expression as not to be important here. Then follows what is certainly most unusual, "Verily, Jesus, the Son of Mary, is the Apostle of God, and his word which he cast over Mary, and spirit from him. O God, pray for thy Apostle Jesus, the Son of Mary. Peace be upon me the day that I am born, and the day I die, and the day I am raised to life again"; and so on to the end. The whole of the latter half of the inscription is, in fact in honour of Jesus and his mother, and the idea of any Mahomedan inscribing that on a building supposed to be a rebuilding of the Temple of Solomon, and having no reference to Christ, seems too absurd to be entertained for one moment.[28]

From this passage, we see that there are good reasons to conclude that the area of the Dome of the Rock was not chosen because of a belief that there was a connection with the Jewish temple. I think Fergusson is right. If there was truly an original belief that this was the location of the temple, then there would most likely be words inscribed to that effect. Nevertheless, the structure was built post-Hadrian, and I favor early Umayyad construction followed by rebuilding and revision, notwithstanding the strange similarity to other early Christian churches. There is more evidence for an Umayyad source, and the Dome of the Rock presents a unique design that is clearly suitable for circumambulation (walking around in a circle), like that which had already begun around the Ka'ba stone in Mecca by that time. It is debated whether or not this was done by Abd el Malik intentionally to compete as a pilgrimage destination,[29] but the design is not inconsistent with the encouragement of circumambulation. They also reported that there was no direct mention in the inscriptions of the Dome of the Rock as to why the rock is included as the centerpiece of the structure. However, they confirmed that it became the firm belief that this was the site Muhammad visited in his nocturnal journey and where he ascended into heaven leaving behind the imprint of one foot. One of the earliest accounts connecting Jerusalem with the night journey of Muhammad is from Ibn Ishaq in the eighth century.[30] The association of al-Sakhra with the temple of the Jews, however, is not an association in early Islamic historical accounts. For example, there is another mention of the rock by Muslim historian Ya'qubi, writing around AD 874.

> "So this is now appointed to you (as a place of worship) in place of the Holy Shrine of Mecca. And this Rock, of which it is reported that the Apostle of God set his foot when he ascended into heaven, shall be to you in the place of the Ka'ba." Then Abd al-Malik built above the rock a dome and hung it around with curtains of brocade, and he instituted doorkeepers for the same, and the people took up the custom of circumambulating the rock, even as they had paced around the Ka'ba, and the usage continued thus all the remaining days of the dynasty of the Umayyads.[31]

What these Islamic accounts tell us, then, is that the association of the al-Sakhra rock as the precise location of the Jewish temple is not recorded as an early tradition and was not reported until the fourteenth century. So where did the belief come from? The answer to that question may be found from Christian sources writing around AD 876. It seems that the Christian historian Eutychius, the patriarch of Alexandria, was the first to assert that the rock seen by Umar was the same as the Jews' foundation stone and the place of the Holy of Holies.

The patriarch said to him: "I will give to the Commander of the Faithful a place to build a sanctuary where the kings of Rum were unable to build. It is the rock where God spoke to Jacob and which Jacob called the Gate of Heaven and the Israelites the Holy of Holies. It is in the center of the world and was a Temple for the Israelites, who held it in great veneration and wherever they were they turned their faces toward it during prayer."[32]

But in the ninth century, Christians had already been without access to the Temple Mount for more than two centuries, because the inhabitants of Jerusalem surrendered in 637 to the Muslim forces led by Umar, son of Al-Khattab. After al-Aqsa Mosque was firmly established on the Temple Mount, all non-Muslims were prohibited from entering the Haram el-Sharif. After that, apparently thanks to Christian sources, the tradition became firmly established that al-Sakhra marked the site of the former Holy of Holies. Evidence that Christians no longer had access to the site, and therefore could not claim to have any deep insight beyond hearsay into Temple Mount features, can be inferred from a fragment by Photius (a contemporary of Eutychius), answering question 316 to Amphilochius (c. 867). This is the earliest clear Christian testimony about an Islamic (Saracen) mosque on the Temple Mount, and the account confirms that Christians believed that where the Saracens (Muslims) had their mosque was near the Holy of Holies and was located within the "court of Solomon."

> The court of Solomon, itself the ancient Holy of Holies, but now occupied by the godless Saracens and providing them with a site for a mosque, has not been familiar to any one of the Christians in Jerusalem, for Christians cannot enter the places kept holy by Saracens.[33]

Now, whether Photius was referring to the Dome of the Rock or al-Aqsa is unclear in this passage. Therefore, it seems that Eutychius maybe the first—of the surviving accounts, at least—to make the assumption that the Holy of Holies was under or near an Islamic mosque within the Temple Mount. But once this idea took root, it became persistent.

We even see that this idea was becoming a Jewish belief by the twelfth century, as recorded by Benjamin of Tudela, who visited Jerusalem around 1180.[34] His accounts are a little unclear because on one hand he says the Gate of Gushpat (Gate of Jehoshaphat) faces the ancient temple, now called *Templum Domini*, which aren't actually aligned (unless there was another structure standing there that has since been destroyed). But on the other hand he references the "sanctuary of Omar ben al Khataab," who "erected an edifice with a very large and magnificent cupola, that was built upon the site of the sanctuary." And he also says that "in front of this place is the western wall, which is one of the walls of the Holy of Holies," which would seem to indicate al-Aqsa. This makes the account sound a little contradictory, because one could infer three different locations from his descriptions. He was clear in identifying the location of the Temple Mount as the former location of Solomon's Temple, palace, and stables. Now, it could be that he was generally remarking that these buildings were all in the area of the temple and not really affirming that they were covering the exact location of the Holy of Holies.

> The other building is called the Temple of Solomon; it is the palace built by Solomon the king of Israel . . .

> Jerusalem has four gates—the gate of Abraham, the gate of David, the gate of Zion, and the gate of Gushpat, which is the gate of Jehoshaphat, facing our ancient Temple, now called Templum Domini. Upon the site of the sanctuary Omar ben al Khataab erected an edifice with a very large and magnificent cupola, into which the Gentiles do not bring any image or effigy, but they merely come there to pray. In front of this place is the western wall, which is one of the walls of the Holy of Holies. This is called the Gate of Mercy, and thither come all the Jews to pray before the wall of the court of the Temple. In Jerusalem, attached to the palace which belonged

to Solomon, are the stables built by him, forming a very substantial structure, composed of large stones, and the like of it is not to be seen anywhere in the world. There is also visible up to this day the pool used by the priests before offering their sacrifices, and the Jews coming thither write their names upon the wall. The gate of Jehoshaphat leads to the valley of Jehoshaphat, which is the gathering-place of nations. Here is the pillar, called Absalom's Hand, and the sepulcher of King Uzziah.[35]

While it is debatable which former temple location Benjamin was actually affirming, Isaac ben Joseph clearly affirmed this idea after he visited Jerusalem in 1334. He stated that an Ishmaelite building was occupying the former site of the Jewish temple. He also affirmed earlier reports that Jews in the time of the Islamic control of Jerusalem used to pray at the Gate of Mercy, which is one of the Islamic names for the Golden Gate, on the east side of the city.[36] This is not insignificant, since this would have placed the Jews of that time praying at the Golden Gate, directly toward the Dome of the Spirits, not the Templum Domini (Dome of the Rock), providing that the Muslim name for the Golden Gate is really what was being referred to here (as noted by F. E. Peters).[37] There are also Jewish accounts (c. 1334) from Isaac ben Joseph, a visitor to Jerusalem who also recorded what was said in those days about the Temple Mount.

> It was on Mount Moriah that in the olden days the Temple of Solomon (to whom be salvation) was reared; and from that august Temple it received its name of the Mountain of the Temple. Alas, by reason of our sins, where the sacred building once stood, its place is taken today by a profane temple, built by the king of the Ishmaelites when he conquered Palestine and Jerusalem from the uncircumcised. The history of the event was in the wise.
>
> The king, who made a vow to build up again the ruins of the sacred edifice, if God put the Holy City into his power, demanded of the Jews that they should make known the ruins to him. For the

uncircumcised (that is, the Christians) in their hate against the people of God, had heaped rubbish and filth over the spot, so that no one knew exactly where the ruins stood. Now there was an old man then living who said: "If the king will take an oath to do what he demanded." When he had shown him the ruins of the Temple under a mound of defilements, the king had the ruins cleared and cleansed, taking part in the cleansing himself, until they were all fair and clean. After that he had them all set up again, with the exception of the wall, and made them a very beautiful temple, which he consecrated to his God.

It is this wall which stands before the temple of Umar ibn al-Khattab, and which is called the Gate of Mercy. The Jews resort thither to say their prayers, as Rabbi Benjamin (of Tudela) has already related.[38]

This testimony also seems to confirm the Golden Gate location as a focus of prayer toward the temple from another early Jewish source.[39] And while it is unclear which gate Benjamin of Tudela was referring to, Isaac ben Joseph was clearly associating the Gate of Mercy with the gate of the same name referred to by Muslims. Therefore, it could certainly be understood that Jews were actually praying at this gate on the outside of the city. This would also make sense if they were denied access to the city. Furthermore, the proliferation of Muslim graves in front of the gate would easily explain why Jews stopped praying there.

What can we glean from all of this history? There really are no historical associations of the Dome of the Rock and the site of the Jewish temple until the ninth to fourteenth centuries. The idea likely began in Christian traditions, followed by Jewish and Islamic sources, and eventually became popular lore. However, there is no definitive reason to believe this based on a review of the earliest Islamic and Christian sources, and even the early Jewish sources are unclear on this point. Therefore, the historic argument, which is the best argument for the Dome of the Rock location of the temple, wilts under close scrutiny.

MORPHOLOGY OF THE AL-SAKHRA ROCK

Another point, which was touched on earlier, is that one of the best evidences presented for the al-Sakhra rock being the foundation stone is that it has cutouts and features that demonstrate it is a revered rock. But we aren't looking for a sacred rock per se. We are looking for a threshing floor. One of the more potentially convincing arguments revolves around cutouts in the surface of the rock. It is reported that there is an area cut into the top of al-Sakhra that measures 1.31 by 1.0 meters, which is about the same length as the ark of the covenant, but 20 centimeters wider.[40] Dr. Ritmeyer proposes that this cutout in the rock was made by Solomon, and that it was 20 centimeter wider to accommodate a scroll of the Law of Moses, which he believes was carried on the outside of the ark; however, while there is an extensive case built for it, it still lacks conclusive evidence and therefore stands ultimately on conjectures that cannot be proven. There is also no scriptural or rabbinic record of a depression being cut into the threshing floor to hold the ark of the covenant. The ark was made to be carried and set down in multiple locations as it was carried from site to site with the tabernacle for approximately five hundred years before the temple was built. It would have been more than stable set on a flat threshing floor, and consequently would not have needed a special provision cut into the rock. Furthermore, the irregularities and natural formations all over the rocks' surface speak to simply a large piece of natural bedrock, as seen in Figure 31. Therefore, there are plenty of reasonable explanations for the features observed on the al-Sakhra stone, but no good explanations for why an originally flat surface would need a depression cut into it for the ark.

There is also a cave located below and within the al-Sakhra rock, which is completely incongruous with all scriptural and rabbinic sources. Nowhere is a cave ever mentioned with respect to the temple and the Holy of Holies. Granted, there is no mention of one even within the Temple Mount complex, but as a part of the larger complex, this is much more believable than within the Holy of Holies. It is possible that the cave was only discovered after the destruction of the Temple Mount, which would account for its absence in scriptural and rabbinic sources. The collapse of the temple structures or a later earthquake could certainly be a mechanism for opening up an undiscovered cavern in the bedrock, post–AD 70. We just don't know everything that happened after the destruction of the temple, but we do know there is no mention anywhere of a cave being in the Holy of Holies.

To justify why al-Sakhra isn't flat today, it has been speculated that it is no longer flat because of the large quantity of stone that Crusaders quarried off to sell as relics and because "they cut away most of the northern part of the Rock so that [their] shrines could be built at ground level."[41] However, during the time of the Crusades, they actually built a level platform over the al-Sakhra rock because it wasn't flat. Therefore, it makes little sense that the rock was grossly mutilated from a flat stone and then a platform was built over it to make it flat again. All in all, there is just no resemblance to a threshing floor exhibited anywhere on its top surface. Additionally, the cutout that resembles an area for the ark of the covenant is just as likely to be a location where square pieces of stone were quarried out of bedrock for relics (as obviously occurred in numerous other locations, in square or rectangular patterns). Finally, as discussed previously, Hadrian was likely the builder of the current platform on which the Dome of the Rock sits. Thus, the large cutouts in this rock could have originally been used as the cornerstone to support a wall of Hadrian's temple, rather than something associated with the Jewish temple. The fact that the large trapezoidal platform is built around the rock but isn't centered to it overall is strongly suggestive of it being a building support, not a building centerpiece. If you look at the lower right-hand corner of the picture in Figure 31, you can see that there are two large cutouts at different elevations, but at right angles to each other (also reported by Ritmeyer[42]). These could have supported a corner of a building quite nicely. However, since the area inside that corner was obviously not a surface for threshing, it wasn't the Jewish temple. Having eliminated that possibility, a more logical deduction would be that it's a surviving piece of evidence from the temple that Hadrian built.

Figure 31: The al-Sakhra rock at the center of the Dome of the Rock (top view). The white arrow marks the proposed location for the ark of the covenant.[43]

There is one more major feature on the al-Sakhra stone, though, that is believed to confirm a connection with the Jewish temple. The idea comes from one of the earliest accounts about any rock on the Temple Mount, which was recorded by the Bordeaux pilgrim. This was discussed in chapter 2, regarding his description of a "pierced rock" or "a perforated stone" that is "not far from the statues." He said that the "Jews come every year and anoint it, bewail themselves with groans, rend their garments, and so depart." So, if we believe that the Jews of

AD 333 did know exactly where the temple was supposed to be located, then we are looking for a stone that is not far from where Hadrian's statues would have been set up.

There are two viable candidates for the "pierced stone" that the pilgrim saw: (1) the stone in the Dome of the Rock and (2) the stone under the Dome of the Spirits. Both are bedrock stones and are about 265 feet (80 meters) apart. There is one stone that is pockmarked and level with the platform (under the Dome of the Spirits) at an elevation of 742.9 meters (2,437 feet),[44] and another elevated only 0.9 meters (3 feet) above it (under the Dome of the Rock).[45] The "pierced stone" description could be met by the pockmarked stone underneath the Dome of the Spirits or arguably by the hole made in the rock that leads to the cave under the Dome of the Rock. However, the hole in al-Sakhra is a man-made hole 2 feet 7 inches (80 centimeters) in diameter through more than five feet of bedrock. The hole was first mentioned in 1173 by Ali of Herat, and based on examinations of the cave that it bores into, is it believed to have been made by the crusaders to create a chimney for the lamps and candles that were kept inside the cave that had been turned into a shrine.[46] Thus, this rock would be very difficult to describe as "pierced" in AD 333 when the pilgrim was visiting the Temple Mount. This leaves us only one candidate that we can verify today as the pierced stone, and that is under the Dome of the Spirits. Its entire surface is highly pitted or pockmarked in texture and could certainly be described as "pierced," which is a common consequence of threshing upon such a surface.

One final comment: Remember that the threshing floor was chosen not because it was the highest point in the surrounding area but because it was a good flat surface for threshing grain. When men are looking for monuments, they choose the highest spot, but Araunah wasn't looking for a place to build a temple when he chose his threshing floor. Therefore, it's easy to see how with two rocks to choose from, men chose the more prominent rock, which was near the center of the platform, rather than the humbler and more hidden rock that was level with the paving stones of the platform. If you've seen the movie *Indiana Jones and the Last Crusade*, I think you can imagine the scene where the wrong cup was chosen when searching for the Holy Grail . . . "He chose poorly."[47] But armed with this information, we can choose wisely.

ARGUMENT FROM SILENCE FOR THE DOME OF THE ROCK LOCATION

Consequently, when we consider the case for a placement of the First and Second Temples over the location currently occupied by the Dome of the Rock, there is an argument from silence for the Dome of the Rock location, because it lacks the specific evidence for identifiable landmarks presented in part 1 of this book. There is no satisfying threshing floor candidate at this location, and there is no gate in the eastern wall in front of this area, either. There is only circumstantial evidence and conjecture to support the Dome of the Rock location. The presumed existence of these items, which have not been found or verified, cannot be cited as evidence or set up as alternatives to the threshing floor and Golden Gate landmarks discussed in part 1. Therefore, the only counter to the evidence produced in part 1 is to simply argue against the validity of the evidence presented for the Dome of the Spirits and the Golden Gate, since no other convincing competing candidates have been found.

A good example of this point can be illustrated by an attorney who is simply trying to prove that the accused is innocent of the crime, but without being able to identify the true culprit ("I don't know who did it . . . but it wasn't him"). The argument for the Dome of the Rock location is silent on these points in the positive, and is forced to presume that (1) the threshing floor cannot currently be identified, because it is somewhere yet to be discovered (or it used to be flat, but now isn't), and (2) that either (a) the final outer Shushan Gate (East Gate) was not actually aligned with the temple, or (b) the current Golden Gate is not the original Shushan Gate of the Second Temple period. And so, the original Eastern Gate is also yet to be discovered.

However, on the first point, that a suitable threshing floor has never been found, the flat stone underneath the Dome of the Spirits cannot be so easily dismissed. The argument for the Dome of the Spirits cannot be undone by simply presuming that a better threshing floor must exist elsewhere. And one certainly cannot then use that presumption to weaken the argument that a suitable threshing floor is observed underneath the Dome of the Spirits.

Furthermore, while it may not be immediately obvious, the positioning of the Dome of the Spirits is in a much better position for locating the Temple in terms of its east-west placement than is the Dome of the Rock.[48] This is because the rest of the temple, the Court of Israel, and the Court of the Women all lie to the east of the Holy of Holies. If the threshing floor is not sufficiently westward (like the bedrock under the Dome of the Spirits), then it is difficult to interpret the dimensions of those items in a way that the whole temple complex comfortably fits within the Temple Mount area. Or one is forced to presume that the al-Sakhra stone was where the altar was located and not the Holy of Holies, but that presumption places the temple in a position that would appear to be too far west.

Consequently, the fact that on the Temple Mount there is a large, flat stone that (1) would be suitable for a threshing floor, (2) is best explained as being a part of the mountain bedrock itself, (3) is found where we expect the threshing floor of Araunah to be, and (4) is precisely aligned with the Golden Gate, goes unanswered, because there is no counterpoint found in the area of the Dome of the Rock. This is positive evidence that has no peer among the other temple placement views. The threshing floor was how the temple was originally located, so its importance cannot be overstated, and its identification should be paramount in our search for the temple location.

On the second point, a claim that the temple was not aligned with the Eastern Gate (Shushan Gate) has been shown to be false, based on the testimony of rabbinic writings and logical inference from the Scriptures. Rabbinic testimonies about the East Gate explicitly state that the East Gate was in alignment with the temple, so there can be no doubt about the East Gate having been in a basic east-west alignment with the temple. Furthermore, a claim that the current Golden Gate is not the original gate has also been shown to be untenable based on both historic and archaeological grounds, as discussed in chapter 3. Because of the presence of ancient monolithic gateposts found within the gate itself, strong historic testimony going back to the time of Josephus, and the lack of any other such Herodian era gates in the eastern wall (as evidenced by the exploratory digs of Charles Warren and visible inspection today), there can be no doubt that the Golden Gate was the location of the gate in the Second Temple period. Accordingly, there is a strong argument against the Dome of the Rock location, based solely on the fact that the two primary means of locating the temple have excellent support for a northern location, but no corresponding evidence for the Dome of the Rock location.

THE REPORTED FOSSE IN THE NORTHERN PART OF THE TEMPLE MOUNT

There is another point that is suggested as a reason that the temple could not have been in the northern portion of the Temple Mount in the time of Herod and earlier. It has been proposed that the five-hundred-cubit-square pre-Herodian temple area could not have been farther north than the fosse reported by Warren in his explorations of the Temple Mount, which was about 52 feet north of the northwest corner of the current temple platform.[49] If this was true, then it would make it more difficult to have had the temple aligned with the Golden Gate and situated near this deep trench. The problem with this view, however, is first of all that the hypothesis is highly speculative. It imagines that the small depression in the bedrock, found by Sir Charles Warren when he was making measurements of the depth of the bedrock within the Temple Mount, is the remnant of either: 1) the large fosse described by Strabo, the Greek historian and geographer, that was 250 feet long and 60 feet deep, or 2) the defensive trench that protected the temple area and delayed the attack of Pompey in 63 BC as described

WHY THE TEMPLE WASN'T AT THE DOME OF THE ROCK

by Josephus. Ritmeyer postulates that Warren's measured depression is evidence that the artificially cut defensive fosse was made within the Temple Mount complex, and that it was later filled in as part of the attack against Jerusalem and subsequent destruction of the temple (c. AD 68-70). However, this is not in agreement with the account recorded by Josephus, who described the Jews digging a defensive valley fosse north of the Fortress Antonia, not south of it. Its purpose was to separate the Bezetha hill north of the Temple Mount from the fortress Antonia. He was not describing a defensive valley between the Temple Mount and Tower Antonia, as shown here.

> It was Agrippa who encompassed the parts added to the old city with this wall, which had been all naked before; for as the city grew more populous, it gradually crept beyond its old limits, *and those parts of it that stood northward of the temple*, and joined that hill to the city, made it considerably larger, and occasioned that hill, which is in number the fourth, and is called "Bezetha," to be inhabited also. It lies over against the tower Antonia, but is divided from it by a deep valley, which was dug on purpose, and that in order to hinder the foundations of the tower of Antonia from joining to this hill, and thereby affording an opportunity for getting to it with ease, and hindering the security that arose from its superior elevation; for which reason also that depth of the ditch made the elevation of the towers more remarkable. This new-built part of the city was called "Bezetha," in our language, which, if interpreted in the Grecian language, may be called "the New City."[50]

The renowned scholars Edward Robinson, Eli Smith, and George Williams all affirmed that the fosse was north of the current Temple Mount.[51] In fact, Williams, a fellow of King's College in Cambridge, wrote: "The great trench on the North of the Haram, known as *Birket Israil* (Pool of Israel—*shown in Figure 33, page 146*), does so entirely answer to the description of the fosse on the North of the Temple, as given both by Strabo and Josephus, that I cannot question their identity."

However, it is also possible that the trenches mentioned by Strabo and Josephus (regarding Pompey's attack on the temple in 63 B.C.) are not one and the same, but in fact were separate defensive features.

To that point, there are two additional candidates for fosse-type features north of the Temple Mount. For example, there is a possible connection with the pools of Bethsaida, mentioned by the Bordeaux pilgrim, as a derivation from Bethzatha or Bezetha.[52] The use of the large fosse described by Strabo to later create pools for storing water seems more plausible for such a geographical feature, rather than assuming that the natural variations in the bedrock of the Temple Mount area were once a large man-made defensive fosse. Furthermore, there is no evidence of an ancient defensive wall to the south of where some suppose the fosse was located within the Temple Mount. Wherever the fosse was located there must also have been a large defensive wall to the south of it because the purpose of the fosse was to make it more difficult to breach the defensive wall. The northern wall of the Temple Mount meets this criterion, but nowhere inside the current thirty-six-acre Temple Mount could.

There is also another area that could possibly satisfy Strabo and Josephus' descriptions. Till this day, there are still the visible remains of a hill that was cut away to create a gap between the northern Old City wall and the hill that is now occupied by the Rockefeller Archaeological Museum, as shown in Figure 32. I propose that this feature is also a plausible explanation for Strabo's fosse; however, it would mean that Josephus' description of the "new city" as opposed to the "old city" is still basically the same today as it was then. This could challenge the current accepted understanding of the development of Jerusalem and its extent in the first century. However, either way, there is more evidence for a defensive fosse location outside of the Temple Mount than inside of it.

Figure 32: Picture of the cut in the hillside north of the Old City wall in Jerusalem in front of the Rockefeller Archaeological Museum which would fit the size description by Strabo. This area was certainly cut for defensive reasons to eliminate an approach to that portion of the northern wall from high ground. *[Author's photo]*

The purpose of presenting these alternate points of conjecture is not to prove in this book that one or the other is the solution to the question of the northern fosse, but simply to show that they are hardly less speculative than the idea that there was a deep trench or moat-like feature within the northern area of the Temple Mount. Therefore, the objection raised about the possible fosse has insufficient evidence to deny the possibility of the Temple being located in the northernmost portion of the complex.

Finally, there is evidence that the original 500-cubit square of the Temple extended all the way to the north boundary of today's Temple Mount, because, as already shown, the north end of the complex extends approximately 250 cubits north of the Golden Gate. Dr. Ritmeyer confirms that the Golden Gate is the original pre-Herodian Shushan or true East Gate of the temple complex but does not address this surprising coincidence. We know that the original eastern gate stood in the middle of a 500-cubit square, and the Golden Gate is right about 250 cubits from the northern boundary. Surely, this is no mere happenstance!

THE OTHER CITED LANDMARKS ARE NONEXCLUSIVE
TO A DOME OF THE ROCK PLACEMENT

There are a few tantalizing clues to the locations of former buildings on the Temple Mount that lie partially exposed in some locations or have been temporarily revealed during various construction activities over the years. Some of these have already been discussed, such as the features cut into the al-Sakhra stone. Others are just too esoteric to deal with in depth because they just aren't definitive enough to reveal anything conclusive about the temple. One example would be Asher Kaufman's justification for moving the alignment of the Temple from six degrees south of west to a true east-west alignment, based on angles he measured on the remains of hewn rock, wall remains, and a large flagstone.[53] The problem with his conclusions is that they are based on many assumptions that can't be properly validated and could be explained by any number of alternative theories, like later constructions under Hadrian, the Byzantines, or the Umayyads to name a few. Evidence of this type is commonly cited in many of the theories published to date regarding where the Jewish temple was formerly located. And more such clues continue to emerge as people seek to better understand the history of the Temple Mount, where no formal archaeological investigations have been allowed.[54] I love these findings, and collectively they support the obvious fact of an ancient Jewish presence on the Temple Mount and build the evidence base for our understanding of the development and progression of the site. They do not make a contribution, however, to the attempt to ascertain exactly where the temple was located because they have not been fully excavated, explored, and placed in the context of the substructure of the rest of the Temple Mount. They are triggers for the imagination, but they cannot tell a complete story. Therefore, they can be used to support any number of different ideas, while lacking the ability to say something truly definitive. For this reason, I have completely avoided any of the highly nuanced and subtle interpretations of those remnants. In the end, they can be used to paint a variety of different pictures, but none of them exclusively verify a single placement location and consequently don't merit discussion as viable landmarks.

SUMMARY

The best reason to believe that the Dome of the Rock rests over the site of the former Jewish temple, is because for a thousand years or so, this has been the popular belief. Certainly, since the late ninth century it may have been believed in Christian circles that the Dome of the Rock was built over the Holy of Holies. But as we examine the reports of Islamic historians, early pilgrims, and Roman historians, a different picture emerges from the earliest accounts. We can see how the precise location of the temple could have been lost and then influenced by the early structures that were first rebuilt there.

Despite logical conjecture and similarities with certain aspects of current Temple Mount structures, the Dome of the Rock cannot be the correct temple location for the following reasons:

1. Early Islamic sources identify al-Sakhra as the place Muhammad ascended into heaven, not as the former location of the Jewish temple.

2. The features of the al-Sakhra rock are inconsistent with scriptural and rabbinic sources.

3. The morphology of the al-Sakhra rock does not match a threshing floor.

4. There is no other evidence of a threshing floor in front of or behind the Dome of the Rock.

5. There is no eastern gate in the wall opposite the Dome of the Rock.

6. There is no conclusive evidence of a deep fosse to prevent the use of the northern portion of the Temple Mount in the time of Herod or earlier.

7. There are no other verifiable and exclusive landmarks that support a Dome of the Rock location.

Therefore, the weight of evidence falls in favor of the Dome of the Spirits, not the Dome of the Rock, with its strongest witness being the Golden Gate in the eastern wall. However, the weight of tradition can often overwhelm the weight of evidence, and the Dome of the Rock wins by the current tradition metric. Nevertheless, my hope is that by putting these evidences side by side, the true location will finally be revealed.

View of the southern end of the Temple Mount.[1]

5

WHY THE TEMPLE WASN'T
TO THE SOUTH

AS WE CONSIDER THE POSSIBILITY that the temple was located on the Temple Mount enclosure, but somewhere south of the Dome of the Rock, we see a variety of views, ranging from just a few feet south from people such as Charles Warren,[2] to actually hanging off the edge of today's Temple Mount enclosure, as proposed by Norma Robertson.[3] The great challenge for any proposal in the south, however, is a lack of archaeological confirmation. All of the proposals in this portion of the Temple Mount rely on highly speculative arguments that simply cannot be substantiated and rest on the thinnest of reasoning bolstered by very imaginative drawings of former walls and buildings that simply haven't been found to exist.

Nevertheless, one of the earliest proposals for a southern location was presented by James Fergusson in 1878.[4] A diagram of Fergusson's plan for the temple is shown in Figure 33. One of the first problems with his plan is that his temple area is nowhere near 500 cubits, he doesn't even reach 400 cubits, and he doesn't allow room for the temple courts, altar of sacrifice, and so on. In other words, his layout is disqualified from the beginning based on rudimentary knowledge of the temple layout and practices.

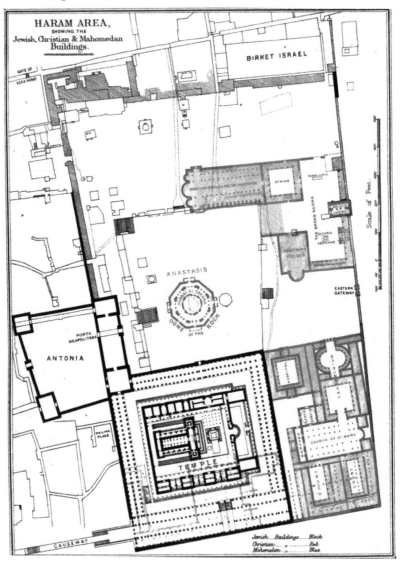

Figure 33: Proposed Temple location: James Fergusson (c. 1878)[5]

Fergusson partially based his theory on a belief that there was a relationship between the Second Temple period tombs at the southern end of the Temple Mount enclosure on the east side, down in the Kidron Valley. I think he correctly observed that they are contemporary with the temple but tried to significantly increase their connection. He suggested that they were spaced apart at a distance that was associated with the width of the original temple structure and noted that they were also square to the temple, indicating an intentional alignment.

This southern location is also the closest spot between the Mount of Olives and the Temple Mount, so if there was anywhere a bridge between the two, it would be more likely to have been on the south rather than farther north, where the distance is much greater. At this point in the wall, there is also the evidence of past openings or other structures connecting to the wall near the top, as shown in Figure 34.[6] However, since this area is also near an obviously repaired portion of the upper wall, it would be difficult to say with certainty that this was a former entrance and not something else, or just stones in secondary use.

Figure 34: Possible former eastern entrance or structure at the southeast corner of the Temple Mount (white arrows). *[Author's photo]*

To that point, in 1880 Charles Warren issued a refutation of Fergusson only two years after Fergusson's work on the subject was published.⁷ As his primary support, he referenced his contour plan of the Temple Mount to refute Fergusson. I have included Warren's map here with a few additions to help clarify the viable areas for the temple, as shown in Figure 35. And while Warren proposed his own southern location a few feet to the south of the al-Sakhra stone, he was hardly convinced of his own proposal. Additionally, his southern proposal was so near to the rock as to hardly count as a "southern" viewpoint.

> The sides of this mount are very steep on the south-west side. Where Mr. Fergusson would place his hypothetical temple, the slope is so steep that it would be impracticable to attempt to climb up without using hands as well as feet, the rise in one place being 60 feet in 100 feet horizontal; and again, 110 feet in 250 feet horizontal.
>
> It is to be observed that the south-west angle of the Noble Sanctuary reaches right across the Tyropoeon Valley, and ascends 30 feet of the hill on the opposite side; it is self-evident that this could not have been the original position of the Temple, but is an extension. . . .
>
> This is very much in favour of the Sacred Rock itself being the Holy of Holies, and I am not positive that the position I assign it (a few feet south of the rock) is the absolute position; I only assert that in the position where I place it, it fulfils the conditions required most thoroughly, and that Mr. Fergusson is altogether in error in his disposition.⁸

The area marked with a black dotted line on the plan of Mount Moriah in Figure 35 represents areas that are both of sufficient elevation and appropriately spaced from the west and east walls to allow for the building of the temple and its courts. What we see here is also what Warren asserted, which is that it is essentially impossible for the former temple to have been anywhere except within the area that is today occupied by the Temple Mount platform and just a little south of it. The reason for this, as stated earlier, is that you first need open, flat, and exposed bedrock for the threshing floor of Arunauh present before any part of the Temple Mount enclosure was constructed. And it needs to be in an area that is near today's western side so that all of the temple and its courts can open up to the east, and still be within the overall enclosure of today. The only area of original mountain that satisfies those criteria are shown in Warren's contour map, which he made by physically taking coring measurements down to the bedrock all over the Temple Mount.

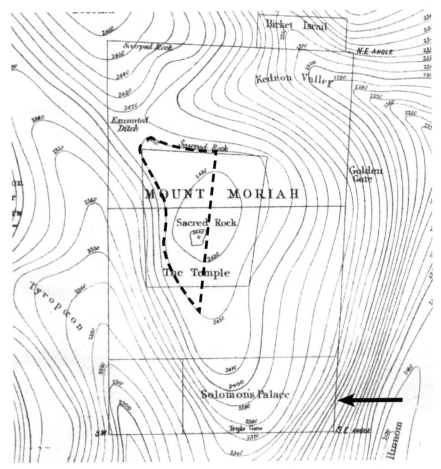

Figure 35: Charles Warren's contour map of Mount Moriah and the Temple Mount area marking the original mountain slopes. Indicated are: (1) a possible area for a threshing floor that allows room for building the temple (black dotted line); (2) Dome of the Spirits (black circle); and (3) remains of an opening or structure in the outer southeast wall (black arrow) marks.[9]

Despite the compelling visible landmark of an ancient opening or structure in the upper southeast wall area, which is now filled in, it could not have been the East Gate of the Second Temple period. This can be stated with absolute certainty because there was no mountain in this area to have threshed upon. If there wasn't a threshing floor there, then there was no temple there, and if the temple was not there, then whatever the repaired wall section represents, it was not the Shushan Gate.

A BRIDGE CROSSING ACROSS THE KIDRON VALLEY

Proponents of southern placement views will also contend that this southern location is the only place that could have logically supported a bridge across the Kidron Valley as described in the Mishnah in association with the sacrifice of the red heifer:

> They made a causeway from the Temple Mount to the Mount of Olives, an arched way built over an arched way, with an arch directly above each pier (of the arch below), for fear of any grave in the depth below. (Parah 3.6)

But to that point, Dr. Leen Ritmeyer addresses the issue well by pointing out that the Hebrew word used is *kevesh*, which is generally translated as a ramp, not a bridge.[10] He also astutely points out that a bridge would have to be around 180 feet tall at the middle in order to span the distance across the valley using a level bridge at the current elevation of the Temple Mount. So even if one built a bridge at the narrowest spot (located at the southern end of the Temple Mount), it would have been an amazing feat of engineering skill. If such a structure did exist in the past, then at least some evidence of its remains should have been found. Since no such archaeological evidence exists, then there is no tenable argument that a bridge of this type ever existed in the first place. Furthermore, there is no clear corroborating testimony from Josephus, either. Surely, if such an amazing bridge existed in his time, then he would have mentioned it in great detail. Consequently, the best view on this point is what Dr. Ritmeyer suggests, which is an elevated ramp following the contour of the valley, and not a bridge at all. In which case, there is no reason to have a ramp structure anywhere but where you also have a gate exiting the eastern wall. As discussed previously, in the chapter on the East Gate, the only archaeologically confirmed gate in the east wall is the Golden Gate.

We simply don't know what else may have been connected to the southern portion of the upper wall. For example, 1 Kings 9:24, Jeremiah 31:40, and 1 Chronicles 11:7–8 all speak about terraces that were made in the area of Solomon's palace and the City of David. It is written that there were some that extended out east into the Kidron Valley. The remains in the southeast corner of the wall could actually be evidence that other structures were originally built off that portion of the wall, namely, the terraces mentioned in the Bible. Or as mentioned earlier, they could just be hurried repairs with stones in secondary use. Personally, I think the terrace option and the breaks in the stonework in the southeast portion of the wall deserve more attention, but that is outside the scope of the present discussion of the temple.

> After Pharaoh's daughter had come up from the City of David to the palace Solomon had built for her, he constructed the terraces. (1 Kings 9:24)

> The whole valley where dead bodies and ashes are thrown, and all the terraces out to the Kidron Valley on the east as far as the corner of the Horse Gate, will be holy to the LORD. The city will never again be uprooted or demolished. (Jeremiah 31:40)

> David then took up residence in the fortress, and so it was called the City of David. He built up the city around it, from the terraces to the surrounding wall, while Joab restored the rest of the city. (1 Chronicles 11:7–8)

THE GOLDEN GATE WAS NOT THE SHEEP GATE

To really develop a southern view theory, in light of all the other historic and rabbinic testimony already given, plus the archaeological evidence presented regarding the Golden Gate, then the Golden Gate would have to be identified with another gate. It could be suggested, for example, that the Golden Gate was the Sheep Gate mentioned in John 5:2 and Nehemiah 3:1. This suggestion is only tenable, however, if one believes that the area north of the Temple Mount walls was outside of Jerusalem in the days of the First and Second Temples. This suggestion, however is, clearly not possible, since John 5:1 clearly locates the Pool of Bethesda within the city walls of Jerusalem and also near the Sheep Gate.

> Now there is in Jerusalem near the Sheep Gate a pool, which in Aramaic is called Bethesda and which is surrounded by five covered colonnades. (John 5:2)

And even back in Nehemiah's time, there was a Sheep Gate in the walls of Jerusalem, which, since it was repaired by Nehemiah, as we read in Nehemiah 3:1, was also in existence during the time of Solomon's temple. The account of Nehemiah's repairs of the walls of Jerusalem begins at the Sheep Gate in verse 1, and then continues in a counterclockwise direction to either the north or the west, but based on John 5:2, I would argue strongly that it was to the north and that the Sheep Gate of Nehemiah in Jesus' time was in the vicinity of today's Lion's Gate. That being said, we pick up the account again in verse 28 above the Horse Gate. This was possibly the Single Gate at the southeast corner of the Temple Mount and led into what has been known far into antiquity as Solomon's Stables. Therefore, the next repairs being described are to the eastern wall of the Temple Mount leading up to the Inspection Gate (Miphkad Gate). Now, opinions do vary on which other names this gate was known as, if any. But I would argue that this is the same as the Shushan Gate. Why? Because the altar of the red heifer on the Mount of Olives was called the Miphkad altar. Consequently, the idea that this was the eastern outer gate of the Temple Mount that led out to the Mount of Olives and then up the Miphkad altar would be perfectly congruent with that name. Then later, when the gate was presumably adorned with an image of Shushan in Babylon, it became more commonly known as the Shushan Gate.

Eliashib the high priest and his fellow priests went to work and rebuilt the Sheep Gate. They dedicated it and set its doors in place, building as far as the Tower of the Hundred, which they dedicated, and as far as the Tower of Hananel. . . .

Above the Horse Gate, the priests made repairs, each in front of his own house. Next to them, Zadok son of Immer made repairs opposite his house. Next to him, Shemaiah son of Shekaniah, the guard at the East Gate, made repairs. Next to him, Hananiah son of Shelemiah, and Hanun, the sixth son of Zalaph, repaired another section. Next to them, Meshullam son of Berekiah made repairs opposite his living quarters. Next to him, Malkijah, one of the goldsmiths, made repairs as far as the house of the temple servants and the merchants, opposite the Inspection [Miphkad] Gate, and as far as the room above the corner; and between the room above the corner and the Sheep Gate the goldsmiths and merchants made repairs. (Nehemiah 3:1, 28–32)

As we read the passage in Nehemiah, we see that repairs to the walls were needed from the Miphkad Gate to "the room above the corner" (most likely a reference to the northeast corner of the Temple Mount, which shows evidence of a tower there in antiquity[11]), and then repairs were completed from there back to the Sheep Gate, making a full circuit of the walls. If you have visited Jerusalem and walked its walls, it is much easier to understand these descriptions, but they clearly start and stop at the same point and make a counterclockwise progression from place to place, allowing us to understand their order in the wall.

Admittedly, we need to make some inferences here, but they do not require large leaps of logic. Furthermore, if the argument could be made that the Golden Gate was the Sheep Gate, then the repaired area of the wall shown in Figure 34 (possibly a former double entryway into the Temple Mount area) would need to be the ancient remains of the East Gate and the Miphkad Gate of Nehemiah. However, as already discussed, the eastern gates of the temple were all in line with the threshing floor and the Holy of Holies. If this southeast gate was the Shushan/Miphkad Gate,

153

then the threshing floor should be in line with this gate, which is only about 25 meters (47 cubits) from the southern end of the Temple Mount enclosure wall. So, unfortunately for this view, it simply is not possible. From a review of Warren's contour map in Figure 35, we can see that the mountain bedrock is not flat and prominent in the south of the enclosure. This area is on an incline and at least 60 meters below the present level of the platform. There would also need to be another 203 cubits of Temple Mount to the south to support a 500-cubit-square around the threshing floor, which there isn't. This means that at best, it was a former entrance on the east that was similar to the entrance on the western end at Robinson's Arch, as suggested by Ritmeyer.[12] However, even on that point, the case is questionable, since Warren attempted to investigate this very point by digging east of this location for 50 feet, and then digging further north and south branches and more east-west branches, but never encountered any piers on which a bridge could have been set in this area.[13] Consequently, it is more likely that this is simply a repaired area of the wall with stones in secondary use, as already mentioned.

We can also look to the Madaba Map for some inspiration. The map (c. 542–570) was found as a mosaic tile floor in the early Byzantine Church of Saint George in Madaba, Jordan. While it admittedly is not to scale and requires some imagination and a good understanding of Jerusalem's principal elements, I think it shows the main gates of the city, including the Golden Gate of the Temple Mount, as shown in Figure 36. The top of the map is east. This makes the gate on the left the Damascus Gate (a), the gate on the bottom center right is more or less the Jaffa Gate (b), the top gate is the precursor of the Lion's Gate (or Sheep Gate) (c), and just right of that gate is another smaller and square gate that would be the Golden Gate (d). This interpretation would also be consistent with the testimony of the Piacenza Pilgrim (c. 570), who was a contemporary of the Madaba Map, quoted in chapter 3. He reported that there was still a gate of the temple in the eastern wall next to the gate of the city that led in from Gethsemane and the Valley of Jehoshaphat (Kidron Valley).

Figure 36: Madaba Map, indicating the gates of the city. Their modern names or approximate equivalents would be: (a) Damascus Gate, (b) Jaffa Gate, (c) Lion's Gate, and (d) Golden Gate.[14]

Finally, if we recognize that the Miphkad Gate is another name for the Golden Gate, then we also know an important fact about its history, namely, that it was not demolished when Jerusalem was razed by the Babylonians, because it is not listed as being rebuilt in Nehemiah 3. But even if the Miphkad Gate was part of a second outer eastern wall, which was repaired by Nehemiah, rather than the Temple Mount enclosure walls (as concluded by Ritmeyer[15]), we still have no record of the eastern gate in the Temple Mount enclosure wall being repaired. And so, the point still stands that the Golden Gate was not destroyed and had to be in line with the temple. Accordingly, this means that except for possible embellishment after the time of Nehemiah and the repairs made by Suleiman the Magnificent, this really is substantially the same gate going back to the time of Solomon.

THE NEED FOR WATER ON THE TEMPLE FROM AN AQUEDUCT
Another southern placement view, proposed by Tuvia Sagiv, supposes

the altar was located at the al-Kas fountain, which is to the south of the Dome of the Rock and its platform but is north of al-Aqsa Mosque.[16] The theory is based on the rock levels at the Temple Mount and known aqueduct elevations in the area that are below the elevation of the present platform. In this view, the central and northern locations for the temple are excluded because of the need for priests to have accessible water on the Temple Mount without working (raising water from the cisterns) on the Sabbath. However, this is not a tenable argument. The priests were exempt from the prohibitions against work related to their temple services; therefore, the assertion is unfounded.

> Or haven't you read in the Law that the priests on Sabbath duty in the temple desecrate the Sabbath and yet are innocent? (Matthew 12:5)

Additionally, the argument assumes both that the water had to reach the elevation of the temple platform and that there was no siphon effect (only elevation differences) to deliver the water to the required height. As a result, it must therefore be assumed that the Temple Mount retaining walls were built by Hadrian after the destruction of the temple, and that the original temple elevation was 16 meters below present levels in order to achieve the required elevations. However, this line of reasoning is completely unsupported by any known archaeological evidence regarding the temple walls and platform. Furthermore, the history of the Temple Mount has already been well documented in this book and shows that this is simply impossible. Josephus described the main part of the Temple Mount being left in place, and later sources provide nothing to substantiate such a monumental project by Hadrian, who has no other buildings to his credit of the style or magnitude of the Temple Mount. Furthermore, the levels of the cisterns are well below the temple platform, and so would have had no trouble being filled by the ancient aqueduct on whose remains he has based his conclusions.

THE LOCATION OF THE TEMPLE BASED ON
THE ANGLE OF SIGHT OF AGRIPPA II

Another argument proposed by Tuvia Sagiv is that the original temple elevation also had to be both lower in elevation than the present and located in the southern portion of today's Temple Mount, based on his assumptions regarding the former location of the Hasmonean palace.[17] The problem with this idea is again a lack of archaeological evidence to support the exact location of the palace or its precise design. Without specific and detailed information about the exact location and structure of the building, no useful argument can be constructed to definitively argue either for or against a specific temple location.

SUMMARY

A southern placement is mostly an antiquated and minority viewpoint. The best support for it is its proximity to the Mount of Olives at the narrowest point of the Kidron Valley and the possible indications of a corresponding structure and opening in this part of the wall. While, I too, find this portion of the wall of great interest for further study, it is not a part of the discussion about where the temple once stood, because the original mountain is far too low in this area. Therefore, Araunah's threshing floor could never have been in this southern location. The temple could not have been any farther south than where the upper bedrock ends on the Temple Mount. The rest of the southern areas are actually heavy fill areas for the massive retaining walls that surround the Temple Mount.

View of the southern end of the Temple Mount enclosure and the northern end of the City of David.[1]

6

WHY THE TEMPLE WASN'T AT THE CITY OF DAVID

PERHAPS THE NEWEST and most divergent view regarding the temple location was first proposed by meteorologist and minister Dr. Ernest L. Martin.[2] This view has also been further developed and supported by Marilyn Sams and Bob Cornuke.[3] The view asserts that the temple was actually located in the northern portion of the City of David, just to the south of the Ophel area and the Temple Mount. The view proposes that what is called the "Temple Mount" today was actually the Fortress of Antonia. In other words, the view is that the temple was never on what we today call the Temple Mount but was to the south of it, on structures that were so utterly destroyed in AD 70 that we cannot find any surviving evidence of them. Since the publication of these views, the idea has also been popularized on the internet in relatively informal presentations on various websites, YouTube, and the like.

This is another convenient in absentia argument, because the proposed evidence is the lack of evidence. In other words, that there is no archaeological evidence of even one foundation stone of the temple in the City of David/southern Ophel area is proof that the Temple was there. It's believed to be proof because "not one stone was left on another," just as Jesus predicted (see Matthew 24:2). The great problem for this view is that in this area there has been a great deal of archaeological excavation, and there is simply no evidence to support the assertion. Nevertheless, to credibly refute this view, I will present and discuss the cores of the arguments.

The primary arguments for this view claim that

1. not one stone was left on another, so the Temple Mount we see today cannot be the true one

2. the Antonia Fortress was actually what is called the "Temple Mount" today

3. early Christian and Muslim sources (before the tenth century) affirm the southern location view

4. the Temple was located in the immediate vicinity of the Gihon Spring because of ancient testimonies and the need for water at the temple

5. Scripture affirms that the Temple was located on Mount Zion, which is in the City of David

In the following pages, we'll evaluate these claims in the light of Scripture, historic testimony, archaeological observation, and logical inference. Many of the evidences already presented should be enough to dispel most of these points, but they will be reviewed to clearly point out the deficiencies of this view. In addition, this view is unable to produce a credible threshing floor location or temple landmark of any sort. In short, there are significant flaws in the reasoning for this view that I will expand on more fully in this chapter.

"NOT ONE STONE HERE WILL BE LEFT ON ANOTHER"

Probably the best argument to support a location other than the traditional site of the Temple Mount platform comes from Jesus' comment in Matthew 24 that "not one stone will be left on another." The argument asserts that surely Jesus meant the platform of the temple as well as the entire temple and its outbuildings when he prophesied their destruction. This argument can have some appeal as we gaze at the awesome walls still standing, deprived of all that stood on the platform before AD 70. Nevertheless, this conjecture is flawed for a number of reasons. Let's review the passage before we examine the argument.

> Jesus left the temple and was walking away when his disciples came up to him to call his attention to its buildings. "Do you see all these things?" he asked. "Truly I tell you, not one stone here will be left on another; every one will be thrown down."
>
> As Jesus was sitting on the Mount of Olives, the disciples came to him privately. "Tell us," they said, "when will this happen, and what will be the sign of your coming and of the end of the age?" (Matthew 24:1–3)

The first thing that is important to notice is that Jesus asked his disciples, "Do you see all *these* things?" That means that they were looking at the buildings while they were standing among them. If they had been far away, the text would say, "Do you see all *those* things."[4] Next, the disciples asked their question of Jesus as he "was walking away" from the temple. So again, the context and language clearly imply that Jesus was still in the immediate vicinity of the temple when he made his comment about not one stone being left on another. Finally, they must have also still been surrounded by crowds when Jesus made his comment because later, after they reached the Mount of Olives, his disciples asked him about it "privately." Once they left the Temple Mount, they would have left the crowds behind. We can also be sure that Jesus wasn't outside the Temple Mount lower down in the Kidron Valley. From

down in the Kidron Valley, one would not have been able to even see
the temple itself or its buildings due to the steep angle looking up at
the walls. From down in the valley, Jesus could not have said, "Do you
see all these things?" while referring to buildings that were not within
view. Finally, Luke 21 also makes it clear that Jesus made his comment
while they were still in the temple courts and that they were actually
looking at the temple itself and its buildings when he answered them.

> Some of his disciples were remarking about how the temple was
> adorned with beautiful stones and with gifts dedicated to God. But
> Jesus said, "As for what you see here, the time will come when not
> one stone will be left on another; every one of them will be thrown
> down." (Luke 21:5–6)

Therefore, Jesus was definitely still standing on the Temple Mount
itself when he made this comment, perhaps in the Court of the Women
or the Court of the Gentiles, but definitely still on the Temple Mount. In
this case, the Temple Mount structure was below his feet, and it would
not be described as a building. He would clearly have been referring to the
temple and its ornate buildings within the five-hundred-cubit-square wall
that surrounded the entire temple and designated the area where only Jews
could enter. All of this would have been in front of Jesus and his disciples
or all around them. It is unreasonable to insist that he was also referring
to areas outside of the five-hundred-cubit temple square and even to the
very ground beneath their feet. Simply asserting that the temple and all
these buildings would be thrown down is sufficient to fulfill the prophecy.
There is no contradiction with Scripture to allow the Temple Mount
platform to remain intact. Particularly when we remember that only the
five-hundred-cubit-square area that sat on top of and within the Temple
Mount was the area of the holy temple and was off-limits to non-Jews.
The other outer areas of the Temple Mount were accessible by non-Jews,
including people like Herod, who was not allowed into the temple area
itself, but they could enter the surrounding areas and the Royal Stoa.

The whole point boils down to this: Could Jesus' words about "not one stone" being left on another still be true if the walls of the Temple Mount, including the Western Wall, were not also destroyed along with the temple and all of its supporting structures? I think the clear answer is yes. The destruction of only the temple itself, its buildings, and everything within the five-hundred-cubit-square area of the temple, which stood within the larger area of the outer walls of the Temple Mount enclosure, completely fulfills Jesus' statement. It is faulty logic to assert that Jesus' statement intrinsically includes the outer Temple Mount enclosure walls, which were never a part of the holy area designated as the temple.

Furthermore, even if Jesus was referring to the Temple Mount enclosure walls, then a supernatural event, like the parting of the Red Sea, would be required to completely demolish and uproot the foundation footings and walls of such a monumental structure. Just for a basic understanding of the labor and manpower required to build (or tear down) the Temple Mount platform, we should think about how big the Temple Mount structure really is. In its total fill volume around Mount Moriah, the Temple Mount platform is larger than the Great Pyramid at Giza.[5] Let that sink in a minute. Not only that, but the largest stone in the Temple Mount walls is the Western Stone, a megalithic stone measuring 13.6 by 3 by 3.3 meters and weighs about 570 tons! Is it practical to think that the Temple Mount walls could have ever been so thoroughly razed by the attacking Roman forces? Would they really expend the effort to move such massive stones? They would not even have had the manpower or engineering knowledge available to them to transport stones of this size. It makes even more sense when you consider that Josephus called the walls that enclosed the area of the Temple Mount "the most prodigious work ever heard of by man" and said that the robustness of the construction "preserved the joints immovable for all future time."[6] This is a good description for the Temple Mount ashlar stones we see today! The bottom line is that the walls were just too massive . . . not for God to level supernaturally, but certainly for a Roman legion who could barely penetrate the defenses in the first place.

Now, on this point Dr. Martin might have disagreed, because he proposed that a wall of similar magnitude was around the temple in a southern location at the City of David; but he claimed that it was so totally eradicated that no trace of it remains.[7] But to suggest that there was another retaining wall structure of similar magnitude to the south of the present Temple Mount is preposterous and without evidence of any kind. If there ever was another Temple Mount–like retaining wall enclosure to the south (and there couldn't have been a temple there without one), then there is just no way that all of the archaeological evidence for it could have been so completely and utterly erased and hidden from modern discovery. Furthermore, the retaining walls are so large that it is completely impractical and unrealistic to assume that a similarly sized structure could have ever been completely destroyed by the Roman Tenth Legion. The temple buildings, yes, but 570-ton megalithic stone blocks, no way. The reason for the difficulty locating evidence on the Temple Mount is clear. No proper archaeological excavation is currently allowed there. But to the south there has been a lot of archaeological exploration, and nothing to substantiate Dr. Martin's theory has ever been identified. Therefore, the best conclusion is not that the Romans did the impossible by completely erasing all traces of the temple in the City of David, or that God, in his anger, supernaturally demolished them, but rather that the temple just wasn't there.

Finally, excavations at the Pool of Siloam (which was one of the main mikvah pools for ritual purification of people going to the temple) have also uncovered the path that led from there to the temple. The ancient paving stones that led from its purifying waters up to the Temple Mount have been fully excavated, as shown in Figure 37. This path goes straight from the Pool of Siloam up to the southwest corner of the Temple Mount at Robinson's Arch and has been dated to the time of Jesus and the Second Temple.[8] Since the path leads directly to the Temple Mount, and not somewhere to the south of it, how could the temple have been anywhere else?

Figure 37: Portion of the Excavated Walkway from the Pool of Siloam to the Temple Mount accessed from the City of David. *[Author's photo]*

THE FORTRESS ANTONIA

Another key argument in favor of this view is that the Fortress Antonia could not have been as small as indicated by modern scholars when they draw the fortress as only a small fraction of the size of the Temple Mount enclosure. It is argued that the fortress in the time of Herod and Jesus would have housed at least five thousand and as many as ten thousand people, so an area at least the size of the thirty-six-acre Temple Mount is what we should be looking for. Since no other remains of this magnitude have been found north of the Temple Mount, then it must be the Antonia Fortress, and the temple was then south of the Temple Mount and the Ophel area in the northern part of the City of David. However, this argument is highly speculative and self-defeating.

To start with, we don't know for sure how many men were stationed at Fortress Antonia before the Temple's destruction. So, assertions up to this point about the necessary size of Fortress Antonia are just unsubstantiated speculation. We do know that later, when the Tenth Legion was stationed at Jerusalem, it would have accommodated between five thousand and ten thousand people, but that was after the destruction of the temple. In this time period, the Roman army actually set up camp on the Temple Mount. Josephus recounted that Titus left the Tenth Legion in place in Jerusalem, and then established their camp on what can logically be concluded was the Temple Mount complex.[9] He reported that the complex was not completely destroyed, but rather it was used as an encampment and as a monument to the power of Rome for having conquered such massive fortifications. While his descriptions still require some imagination and common sense (since the descriptions left by Josephus are not as fully detailed as one might like), they are sufficient to make this point clear, particularly when one considers the modern archaeological evidence from excavations by Benjamin Mazar and the Temple Mount Sifting Project. Excavations at the foot of the walls at the southern end of the enclosure, directed by Benjamin Mazar from 1968 to 1978 and later compiled and published by Eilat Mazar, confirm that the Roman legion was present in this part of Jerusalem.[10] Additional evidence to support their conclusions were found by the Temple Mount Sifting Project, whose team discovered clay roof tiles with impressions designating the Tenth Roman Legion in some of the debris excavated directly from the Temple Mount.[11] Therefore, arguments about the necessary size of the fortress based on the size of a full Roman legion after the destruction of Jerusalem are untenable.

Next, the argument that "since the Romans needed a space the size of the thirty-six-acre Temple Mount, it must be their garrison" is self-defeating because the exact same reasoning could be used to claim the area as the Temple Mount. We know that the temple enclosure held a five-hundred-cubit square, which, as shown previously, nicely fits within the Temple Mount enclosure. Therefore, you could just as easily claim the thirty-six-acre area based on the size of the temple as on the size of a Roman legion. So, the argument is useless for any attempt to prove purpose based on size alone. Finally, while it seems of great historic and archaeological interest—to answer questions regarding Fortress Antonia's dimensions, location, and conditions throughout Jerusalem's many destructions, as well as its rebuilding into Aelia Capitolina and subsequent rule by Byzantine, Ummayad, Crusader, and Ottoman empires—it is not a cornerstone of the question regarding the temple's location.

EARLY SOURCES AFFIRM A CITY OF DAVID LOCATION?

Another claim of this view is that all of the sources before the tenth century affirm a City of David southern location, not a Temple Mount location. This is just patently mistaken and false. What purveyors of this view have presented as historic proof is nothing but revisionist misinterpretations of the events. The readings of the ancient testimonies are so far out that it is almost comical to spend time refuting them. However, so that I can avoid the appearance of an ad hominem attack or a straw man refutation, I will relate a few of the key pieces of evidence presented by Dr. Martin from the historic record and show how they have been misused or misinterpreted. I will refrain from dealing with most of them, however, because it would be like reading the grading results of a poorly written term paper.

The first one I'll deal with concerns the al-Sakhra stone under the Dome of the Rock. Dr. Martin began by mixing up historic accounts and their locations to suit his theory. For example, he claimed that Josephus noted that the Fortress Antonia was built on a large rock seventy-five feet tall and acknowledged that the term generally refers to a mountain, not a small stone. But he then jumped to the conclusion that the al-Sakhra stone is the tip of the giant rock that Josephus was referring to. He wrote explicitly, "When one looks at the geographical evidence for this area of Jerusalem, Josephus could only be describing the rock now under the Dome of the Rock in the Haram."[12] This assertion is preposterous. This part of Jerusalem is made of almost nothing but solid rock. There are all kinds of large rock hills and outcroppings that could have been a fortification in the ancient past. The al-Sakhra stone is simply a visible outcropping of the bedrock beneath the Temple Mount and is dwarfed by the overall dimensions of the enclosure.

It's not all bad, though. Dr. Martin did rightly observe that the Dome of the Rock stone could never have been a threshing floor and that there is no mention in the Bible or any other source of a natural outcropping of rock associated with the temple.[13] On this we agree, and it is why that rock could never have been the threshing floor of Araunah. However, he then mixed up more ancient testimonies to support his views. He made this the site of the basilica of Saint Sophia, which was reported by the Piacenza pilgrim (c. 570) to have held an oblong stone on which Pilate had the accused stand during trials. This stone was alleged to have borne the impression of Jesus' footprints.[14] This is convenient because it supports Martin's theory that the impression was of Muhammad's foot (singular), but it is an entirely fanciful idea. And besides the two footprints becoming one, there are major problems with his statement. First, the description of an oblong stone is much more likened to a carved podium stone than a natural outcropping of rock because it was used for prisoners to stand on during a trial so that they could be seen by all. Second, by all accounts the Temple Mount area was a refuse dump at that time, so there would not have been an active church there.[15]

This misidentification leads to another obvious mistake, however, by insisting that Umar (Omar) built the al-Aqsa mosque at the south end of the Temple Mount enclosure because he wanted to be away from the Jesus stone (al-Sakhra) and point his back toward it.[16] Martin made another error by affirming that "he (Omar) had not the slightest compunction in praying toward Mecca through the former site of the actual Temple of Solomon and that of Herod (over and near the Gihon Spring) with its ruins directly south of the al-Aqsa Mosque."[17] But Dr. Martin seemed unaware that originally Muslims prayed toward Jerusalem, not Mecca, and that it wasn't until later on that Muhammad changed their direction of prayer (*quibla*) toward Mecca and the Ka'bah stone. At that point, it became anathema for Muslims to pray anywhere else, and it is recorded that Omar took clear steps to move the mosque to the south of where they thought the temple had once been located because of its Jewish connection, not because of a Christian connection with Jesus. The earliest Islamic account, recorded by al-Tabari, should make this point clear.[18] In short, Omar (the conquering Islamic general) accused his advisor, Ka'ab, who was a convert to Islam, of trying to imitate his Jewish religion, not Christianity. The qibla had recently been changed, and Omar was very clear that he did not want to be facing the former temple in prayer, so he placed the mosque (al-Aqsa) at the farthest southern location. It is literally the opposite situation from what Dr. Martin suggested.

In conclusion, many of the early witnesses have already been thoroughly cited in this book and should be enough to refute the claim that they support a City of David location. I'm sorry to say it, but in the 476 pages of *The Temples That Jerusalem Forgot*, very few of the ancient testimonies are used or interpreted correctly. Furthermore, the interpretations don't just deviate from almost any accepted scholarly view; they are in conflict with even the plain meaning of words in their proper context.

MOUNT MORIAH OR ZION?

Another argument in favor of this view relies on connecting the name "Zion" exclusively to the City of David, and thereby understanding every temple reference as referring to the City of David and not the main part of Jerusalem or Mount Moriah to the north.[19] In this view the Temple Mount of today is excluded, and the temple was actually located in the City of David, to the south. This view asserts that the City of David is called Zion, and Scripture also refers to Zion as God's "holy mountain," "his dwelling place," "the mountain of the LORD," "the temple of the God of Jacob" and other names that suggest that the temple was in Zion (see, e.g., Psalm 2:6, 76:2; Isaiah 2:3). I'm simplifying a little here, but these references are taken to mean that the temple was in the City of David.

However, while the name Zion did refer to the City of David, it is also used very broadly in Scripture to refer to the temple and the whole region of Jerusalem, as you will see in the numerous verses I will quote later in this section. So, if "Zion" is a broadly used term, one cannot logically argue that any reference to the temple as Zion means that the temple was actually in the City of David, because the term does not exclusively apply to the City of David. Scripture is so explicit on this point. For example, Zion is clearly equated with the City of David in 2 Samuel, but in Isaiah, the prophet calls out Mount Zion separately from Jerusalem.

> Nevertheless, David captured the fortress of Zion—which is the City of David. (2 Samuel 5:7)

> The moon will be dismayed, the sun ashamed; for the LORD Almighty will reign on Mount Zion and in Jerusalem, and before its elders— with great glory. (Isaiah 24:23)

Reading these verses, it should be clear that the name Zion is being equated with the City of David and connected with Jerusalem. And yet, Scripture also refers to Zion as God's "holy mountain" in Psalm 2:6 and as "the city of the Great King" in Psalm 48:2. The best way to reconcile the usage of Zion, therefore, is to understand that "Zion" can be used as a general reference to Jerusalem and the Temple Mount, as well as a specific reference to the City of David and even Mount Moriah. This is further supported by Isaiah 2:3, which equates Zion and Jerusalem.

> I have installed my king on Zion, my holy mountain. (Psalm 2:6)

> Beautiful in its loftiness, the joy of the whole earth, like the heights of Zaphon is Mount Zion, the city of the Great King. (Psalm 48:2)

> Many peoples will come and say, "Come, let us go up to the mountain of the LORD, to the temple of the God of Jacob. He will teach us his ways, so that we may walk in his paths." The law will go out from Zion, the word of the LORD from Jerusalem. (Isaiah 2:3)

Remember the nation you purchased long ago, the people of your inheritance, whom you redeemed— Mount Zion, where you dwelt. (Psalm 74:2)

Most important, we are told that the temple was located on Mount Moriah, not Mount Zion, even though Zion is a name for Jerusalem and the Temple Mount in general. We see this clearly in 2 Chronicles, where we learn that the temple was built on Mount Moriah. Contrary to the usage of the name Zion, "Mount Moriah" is only used to refer to a specific mountain, where the threshing floor was found. In fact, we see that Mount Moriah is very clearly a specific part of Jerusalem:

Then Solomon began to build the temple of the LORD in Jerusalem [general location] on Mount Moriah [specific location], where the LORD had appeared to his father David. It was on the threshing floor of Araunah the Jebusite, the place provided by David. (2 Chronicles 3:1)

Scripture also says that the temple was located outside of the City of David in Jerusalem, as described in 1 Kings 3:1:

Solomon made an alliance with Pharaoh king of Egypt and married his daughter. He brought her to the City of David *until he finished building his palace and the temple of the LORD, and the wall around Jerusalem.* [emphasis added]

As you can see, this passage conveys that the temple and the City of David were separate locations, which also agrees with 2 Chronicles 3:1. The temple had to be outside the City of David based on the descriptions in these verses. We can be sure of this because according to 1 Kings 3:1, Solomon kept his Egyptian wife in the City of David, which was outside of Jerusalem and the Temple Mount, while he was building them. If they were in the same place, then this passage would not make sense.

The next important objection to the view that the temple was in the City of David is that Scripture says that before the building of the temple, the ark of the covenant was kept in the City of David. After the completion of the temple, the ark was brought up from the City of David and placed in the newly consecrated temple:

> Then Solomon summoned to Jerusalem the elders of Israel, all the heads of the tribes and the chiefs of the Israelite families, to bring up the ark of the Lord's covenant from Zion, the City of David. (2 Chronicles 5:2)

> Then King Solomon summoned into his presence at Jerusalem the elders of Israel, all the heads of the tribes and the chiefs of the Israelite families, to bring up the ark of the Lord's covenant from Zion, the City of David. All the Israelites came together to King Solomon at the time of the festival in the month of Ethanim, the seventh month.

> When all the elders of Israel had arrived, the priests took up the ark, and they brought up the ark of the Lord and the tent of meeting and all the sacred furnishings in it. The priests and Levites carried them up, and King Solomon and the entire assembly of Israel that had gathered about him were before the ark, sacrificing so many sheep and cattle that they could not be recorded or counted.

> The priests then brought the ark of the Lord's covenant to its place in the inner sanctuary of the temple, the Most Holy Place, and put it beneath the wings of the cherubim. (1 Kings 8:1–6)

Again, as we see in these verses, the ark was first stored in the City of David, then brought up and transferred into the temple. Based on a simple visit to the City of David and the Temple Mount, anyone can see that the Temple Mount is immediately north and at a higher elevation than the City of David. However, it is still not the highest point of Mount Moriah. In fact, the elevation increases ninety feet or so above the Temple Mount platform as you ascend even farther north toward the summit of Mount Moriah and into the Muslim Quarter of the Old City, which, as mentioned earlier, makes that site an ideal threshing floor location, because you want to be *near* the top of a hill, but not *at* the top of the hill.

In a video interview, Cornuke argues that this passage in 1 Kings 8 could also have meant that Solomon and the assembly went up and made sacrifices, then brought the ark back down to the City of David.[20] He believes that the Ark was brought up from the City of David, not to be placed in the Temple, but to be used, along with the old Tent of Meeting— the Tabernacle built by Moses—in a one-time, final closing ceremony with the Ark of the Covenant using the old Tent of Meeting apart from the newly constructed Temple. But this is pure conjecture, and it redefines the plain meaning of the text, presenting a narrative that adds details that are not present in Scripture in order to support his view. He argues in another video that an ancient source, Hecataeus of Abdera (c. fourth century BC), located the temple in the midst of the city,[21] which Cornuke infers must have meant the City of David. The oversight of that assertion is that Jerusalem was a large city in the fourth century BC (over 120,000 people according to Hecataeus), which encompassed and greatly expanded the ancient citadel that David conquered to the north and west. The current Temple Mount would then be much better described as being in the center of Jerusalem at that time than a City of David location.[22]

The point here is to separate what we know explicitly from Scripture from what we can deduce. It is not sound logic or consistent interpretation of Scripture to deny that these passages simply mean that the ark was kept in the City of David but was brought up to Mount Moriah when the temple was finished. And again, based on a simple visit to the site, it is not hard to visualize the reality described in these passages. In fact, standing on the southern end of the Temple Mount platform, one can easily look down and see the City of David and the general area where the ark and the tabernacle would have been located, 150–200 feet lower in elevation.

A final note: the threshing floor used to define the location of the temple could not have been within the City of David, which already belonged to David when he conquered it. If it had been inside the City of David, then he wouldn't have needed to purchase it. The threshing floor would have been part of a farm, and not found in a city. Requiring the threshing floor to have been inside the City of David makes this view untenable.

A NEED FOR RUNNING WATER AT THE TEMPLE?

The argument has also been made that there was a need for water at the temple, which is true. But it is then claimed that the temple would have had to be near water to support the large number of daily sacrifices,[23] or that ancient accounts report a spring within the temple.[24] Since Gihon Spring is the only spring in the area, then the temple must have been in the immediate vicinity of the Gihon Spring, namely, in the City of David. There are several problems with these arguments also.

First, let's address the account of Tacitus, who said that the Jewish temple contained an "inexhaustible spring." Dr. Martin cites this report as proof that the temple was located at Gihon Spring, since it is the only known spring within five miles of Jerusalem.[25] Tacitus is believed to have been born around AD 55 and to have lived in northern Italy,[26] so he would have been only a teenager when the temple was destroyed and it is very unlikely he would have had the opportunity to see the temple himself. In that case, Tacitus was probably reporting what he had heard about the temple, not what he'd actually observed. Furthermore, Tacitus's full quotation better supports the traditional Temple Mount view than refutes it.

> The temple resembled a citadel, and had its own walls, which were more laboriously constructed than the others. Even the colonnades with which it was surrounded formed an admirable outwork. It contained an inexhaustible spring; there were subterranean excavations in the hill, and tanks and cisterns for holding rainwater.[27]

Here's why this account supports the traditional view. Tacitus connected the "inexhaustible spring" description to subterranean cisterns, which can easily be understood to refer to the ready availability of water produced by the multitude of cisterns known to exist within the Temple Mount. Plus, he described citadel-like walls that were "laboriously constructed," which is also consistent with the massive ashlar stones of the Temple Mount walls. Martin also said that Eusebius, reporting Aristeas's account, also noted that there was a spring within the temple."[28] But this is another example of Martin reading a report the way he wanted to see it, and ignoring the fact that the comment is not definitive.

> There is an inexhaustible reservoir of water, as would be expected from an abundant spring gushing up naturally from within [the temple]; there being moreover wonderful and indescribable cisterns underground, of five furlongs [three thousand feet away], according to their showing, all around the foundation of the Temple, and countless pipes from them, so that the streams on every side met together [at the temple site].

As seen in this quotation, when Eusebius wrote "as would be expected from an abundant spring," he introduced the very real possibility that he was making an analogy to describe the abundance of water. He even called it a "reservoir." Now, just based on the grammar, I would say it could conceivably be either way. What you really can't say is that it definitively proves there was a spring within the temple precinct, particularly, considering that Eusebius was writing nearly three hundred years after the destruction of the temple and was quoting material written five hundred years or so before his time. This is not exactly the kind of testimony that constitutes irrefutable proof for a precise location, but it does affirm that there was a lot of water available at the site and an abundance of cisterns. It just falls way short of proving that the temple was located at Gihon Spring.

Next, the site was chosen by God, not men looking for an ideal temple site. God chose this site to be his footstool for his own reasons, but Araunah chose it as his threshing floor presumably because it was a good place for threshing. Araunah would not have needed water near the immediate area of his threshing floor; in fact the opposite. Chaff could have constantly made its way into the spring, had the spring been too close. In fact, threshing floors would almost never be found within settlements.[29] On the contrary, he would have wanted it to be in a lonely, windy place to carry away the chaff, which at that time was definitely not within the confines of the City of David.

Second, the Temple Mount had the Bronze Sea and numerous other baths made of bronze on the Temple Mount specifically for washing. We don't know how the water was emptied into these containers, but they were made of bronze with a likely 90 percent or so copper content, which would have made the baths antibacterial, lessening the need for changing the water.

Finally, from the survey and excavations performed by Charles Warren and published in 1884 and from subsequent archaeological confirmation, we learn that there are all kinds of cisterns beneath the Temple Mount that held vast amounts of water. So, there was a lot of water available at the Temple Mount. In fact, since there is a dense concentration of cisterns at the temple site, and relatively few by comparison in the rest of the Old City, it is certainly not inconsistent with the view that water was stored there for reasons other than just drought and siege protection. Not only that, but the remains of aqueduct pipes carrying water to the Temple Mount can still be seen in the Jewish Quarter of the Old City. The aqueduct used to cross on a walkway into the temple area, bringing water from Solomon's Pools near Bethlehem (which were fed by springs).[30]

Consequently, while it is certainly true that water was needed at the temple, the temple location was not determined by the location of a spring, but by the location of a threshing floor. Also, the bronze water vessels would have been naturally antibacterial, so we may be overestimating the frequency of water changes that would have been necessary. Lastly, the spring in its present location is easily within walking distance, and there are ample cisterns directly under the temple platform that were fed by aqueduct. So, water was plentiful and accessible. Therefore, there is nothing disqualifying about the traditional Temple Mount location from a water usage perspective. On the contrary, the traditional site has so many cisterns concentrated within its interior that it would be hard to explain them fully without a temple complex being located there.

THE TRUMPETING STONE

Another piece of evidence that denies the conjecture of an Ophel/City of David location is the trumpeting stone (also known as the Trumpeting Place inscription) found at the southwest corner of the Temple Mount during excavation work there. The find was not exactly in situ—at least it was not found where it originally sat at the top of the southwest corner of the enclosure. As reported by Dr. Leen Ritmeyer, it was found buried along with other rubble at the base of the corner, about 138 feet directly below where it is presumed to have once sat.[31] Thus, finding it broken and lying in situ, with other wall debris, presents convincing evidence that the stone was found where it rested after falling from the height above. While it may not be beyond the imagination of some to suppose that this stone arrived in its location after being transported from somewhere else far off, it does not seem reasonable to presume that, based on the condition of the excavation site. The stone is now located in the Israel Museum in Jerusalem, where it is on display for all to see, as shown in Figure 38.

The inscription reads (from right to left) *"l'bet hatqia l'hakh . . ."* While the last word is incomplete, most scholars believe the full inscription translated, "to the place of trumpeting to announce . . ." This would have been the place for sounding the shofar on the Sabbath and during temple festivals.[32] And one more piece of evidence can be observed on this stone. The chisel marks found there match the unique style of chisel marks that are principally observed on the drafted margins of the Western Wall–type ashlar stones of the temple enclosure (see Figure 14 and Figure 39).[33] This strongly suggests that this stone is contemporaneous with the great megalithic stones of the Temple Mount retaining walls. This would provide more evidence that the ashlar stones of the

Temple Mount belong to the time of the temple service and were certainly not post–AD 70. And if we can accept that the stone was truly originally located at the top of this southwest corner, it also tells you that no temple structure could have ever extended farther south than the current Temple Mount walls we see today.

Figure 38: Temple Trumpeting Stone on display in the Israel National Museum. It was found lying at the base of the southwest corner of the Temple Mount. *[Author's photo]*

FINAL COMMENTS

The amount of biblical, historical, and archaeological evidence in support of the traditional location for the Temple Mount is overwhelming. Attempts by Dr. Ernest Martin and others to resolve the historical, religious, and political conflict of the Temple Mount by reevaluating historical testimonies to reveal a new option is well-intentioned but ultimately, very flawed. There may be some useful insights and discussions of the historical sources and archaeological sites in Jerusalem worth considering for further study; however, there is simply no tenable argument for a temple location outside of the traditional Temple Mount.

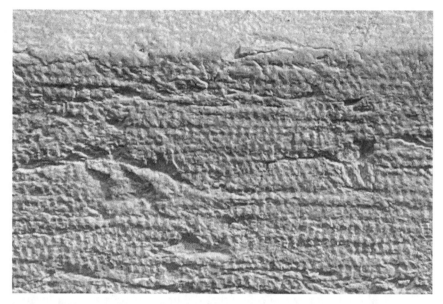

Figure 39: Close-up of the chisel marks on the Trumpeting Stone. *[Author's photo]*

The main points to refute a location south of the Temple Mount and including the City of David are these:

1. Scripture clearly records that the tabernacle and the ark were in the City of David before Solomon built the temple. Once the temple was complete, the ark was "brought up" and placed inside the temple that was built on Mount Moriah, which was not in the City of David.

2. Historical sources also confirm, when read carefully, that the existing Temple Mount structure was preserved and utilized.

3. Extensive cisterns have been found within the Temple Mount complex, which would have provided ample water storage for sacrificial activities. Furthermore, the temple location was based on the presence of the threshing floor that God designated to David, rather than on human election determined by a proximity to water.

4. Jesus' prophecy that not one stone would remain upon another was specifically spoken of the temple and its surrounding buildings. There is no contradiction with Scripture with the understanding that Jesus was standing on the Temple Mount platform when he made his comments, and therefore, he was not referring to everything under his feet, but to the buildings standing in front of him and his disciples.

5. This narrative is well supported by modern archaeological discoveries, which confirm not only the antiquity of the Temple Mount but also the presence of the Tenth Legion within their walls, and the path from the Pool of Siloam up to the Temple Mount has also been discovered, showing the way to the temple in the time of Jesus.

6. The Trumpeting Stone found at the base of the southwest corner also refutes any conjecture that the Jewish temple was ever located anywhere besides fully within the bounds of the current Temple Mount enclosure.

The evidence has been assembled, and all has been heard. The First and Second Temples of the Jewish people could not have been anywhere but on the Temple Mount platform we see today. And specifically, the temple really could not logically have been anywhere but centered over the Dome of the Spirits, in line with the Golden Gate, both of which are standing today. We really can now confidently assert, beyond a reasonable doubt, that this is the true former location of the Jewish temple.

So, what will we do with the answer to this great mystery?

PART III

WHAT NOW?

"Then the nations will know that I the LORD *make Israel holy, when my sanctuary is among them forever."*

Second Temple model in the Israel Museum, Jerusalem. *[Author's photo]*

7

TIME TO REBUILD THE TEMPLE

SO, WHAT NOW? For the past seven decades, a large part of the world has been relieved that the Jews haven't been able to rebuild their temple, and an increasing number don't believe there ever was a temple—or at least, not there. But this isn't really a problem for the world. It's an issue for Israel and the Jewish people. With the true location confirmed, specifically, on the north side of the Dome of the Rock, in an area that has been miraculously left clear for building and has ample area to lay its foundations on the current platform, there is at least a green light logistically. There are of course some very serious political implications. But it is still primarily a question for the people of Israel. Back in 2010, Arutz Sheva (Israel National News) conducted a survey of the Israeli public about rebuilding the Holy Temple.[1] Of those who responded, 49 percent want the holy temple rebuilt. But by the end of 2017, polls in Israel revealed that 68 percent of Israeli Jews want prayer on the Temple Mount,[2] and 72 percent of Jewish Israelis think Israel should maintain sovereignty over the Temple Mount.

Today, most Israelis believe that the Dome of the Rock would have to be torn down in order to rebuild the holy temple. If it becomes widely understood and accepted that this is not true, for the reasons stated in this book, then I think we could potentially see a big upswing in public opinion for rebuilding the temple. It also appears that general support for open and safe access, including prayer at holy sites, is also high, so going forward, there may be even more support for rebuilding the Jewish temple than in past years, particularly, when one considers the annexation of the Golan Heights and parts of Judea and Samaria based on the support of Donald Trump and the White House.[3] Continuing to support Israeli annexation may boost the confidence of Israelis to affirm their sovereignty over the land in other ways, as well.

But after so long, is it right to rebuild the temple when it would clearly be so controversial? Is it moral to risk violence for a building that has already been destroyed for so long? Well, personally, if there is no threat to Islamic buildings, and the rebuilding efforts are conducted lawfully and peacefully, then there is no need for violence. If violence resulted, it would be because of angry mobs trying to oppose the rule of law by force and tyranny. So, I think the moral question is easily answered, because otherwise you are blaming the victim for the evil acts of another. Furthermore, if it was the will of the people (even a minority) to reestablish the temple, it seems that denying a request to rebuild the temple would be a violation of their religious rights and liberties. Wouldn't it be wrong to deny a request to rebuild the temple just because another group didn't want them to and had threatened to become violent if they did? I agree it's a different question if it really did involve demolishing the Dome of the Rock to replace it with a Jewish temple, but as we have seen, that is not the case at all. In fact, it really is an entirely different question now. It's much more akin to the question, Should Jews be allowed to pray on the Temple Mount?—which is really the wrong question. The question should be, How can they allow anyone to be stopped from praying on the Temple Mount? Even with the excuse of preserving the greater good, prayer should be an inalienable right. But the political questions should be secondary to the spiritual ones.

IS IT TIME?

This is the million-dollar question. The general rabbinical opinion in Israel almost universally affirms that the holy temple should be rebuilt at some point; however, there is a wide range of opinions over exactly how this should be accomplished. Nevertheless, this has been an unbroken heart cry of the Jewish people for the past two thousand years as they continually pray for its return. But what does God say? What has been prophetically revealed to help guide us in answering that question? In this chapter, I will discuss the scriptural case for why the temple should be rebuilt and the preparations that have been made in modern times.

> Remember, O Lord, on David's behalf, all his affliction; How he swore to the Lord and vowed to the Mighty One of Jacob, "Surely, I will not enter my house, nor lie on my bed; I will not give sleep to my eyes or slumber to my eyelids, until I find a place for the Lord, a dwelling place for the Mighty One of Jacob."

> Behold, we heard of it in Ephrathah, we found it in the field of Jaar. Let us go into His dwelling place; Let us worship at His footstool. Arise, O Lord, to Your resting place, you and the ark of Your strength. Let Your priests be clothed with righteousness, and let Your godly ones sing for joy.

> For the sake of David Your servant, do not turn away the face of Your anointed. The Lord has sworn to David a truth from which He will not turn back: "Of the fruit of your body I will set upon your throne. If your sons will keep My covenant and My testimony which I will teach them, their sons also shall sit upon your throne forever."

> For the Lord has chosen Zion; He has desired it for His habitation. "This is My resting place forever; Here I will dwell, for I have desired

it. I will abundantly bless her provision; I will satisfy her needy with bread. Her priests also I will clothe with salvation, and her godly ones will sing aloud for joy. There I will cause the horn of David to spring forth; I have prepared a lamp for Mine anointed. His enemies I will clothe with shame, but upon himself his crown shall shine." (Psalm 132 NASB)

SHOULD CHRISTIANS SUPPORT
REBUILDING THE THIRD TEMPLE?

While this book clearly presumes that the temple will be rebuilt, many people wonder whether or not Christians should support the rebuilding of the temple at all. After all, didn't God ordain that his temple would be utterly destroyed? Some Christians would assert that God is done with his temple, and that it would be wrong to rebuild it, for sacrifices are no longer required to atone for the sins of humanity, because Jesus, the Lamb of God, has paid it all. I agree that sin sacrifices are no longer required because Jesus has paid the price of sin for all who believe, through his death on the cross. I do not agree, however, that the temple is no longer needed. I would say that Scripture is very clear about not only the presence of a temple in the last days, but also its presence throughout the millennial kingdom. Therefore, the holy temple is about more than just atoning for sin; it is also a physical representation of God desiring to be among his people. It is a beacon calling people to connect with God and a representation of his faithfulness and promises to his people. It is also about our thankfulness to God for his provision and our accountability before him. Finally, the temple is to be "a house of prayer for all nations":

For my house will be called a house of prayer for all nations. (Isaiah 56:7)

I know that for Christians this is a controversial subject, and it is hard to understand. So, I need to tread carefully here, but I want to remind Christian readers that Jesus' Jewish disciples continued to visit the temple after Jesus was resurrected and ascended into heaven. Paul the apostle did also. They went to pray, to offer sacrifices (not for atonement), and to preach Jesus as the Messiah. We have the accounts in the book of Acts. In these accounts we see Paul, Peter, John, and many of the early Jewish believers in Jesus continuing to visit the temple daily to pray and offer at least certain types of sacrifices while also preaching the gospel. And since there is no specific mention to the contrary, it is reasonable to assume that this practice continued up until the destruction of the temple, almost forty years after Christ's ascension.

> Every day they continued to meet together in the temple courts. They broke bread in their homes and ate together with glad and sincere hearts, praising God and enjoying the favor of all the people. And the Lord added to their number daily those who were being saved. (Acts 2:46–47)

> One day Peter and John were going up to the temple at the time of prayer—at three in the afternoon. Now a man who was lame from birth was being carried to the temple gate called Beautiful, where he was put every day to beg from those going into the temple courts. (Acts 3:1–2)

> The apostles left the Sanhedrin, rejoicing because they had been counted worthy of suffering disgrace for the Name. Day after day, in the temple courts and from house to house, they never stopped teaching and proclaiming the good news that Jesus is the Messiah. (Acts 5:41–42)

> When we arrived at Jerusalem, the brothers and sisters received us warmly. The next day Paul and the rest of us went to see James, and all the elders were present. Paul greeted them and reported in detail what God had done among the Gentiles through his ministry.

> When they heard this, they praised God. Then they said to Paul: "You see, brother, how many thousands of Jews have believed, and all of them are zealous for the law. They have been informed that you

teach all the Jews who live among the Gentiles to turn away from Moses, telling them not to circumcise their children or live according to our customs. What shall we do? They will certainly hear that you have come, so do what we tell you. There are four men with us who have made a vow. Take these men, join in their purification rites and pay their expenses, so that they can have their heads shaved. Then everyone will know there is no truth in these reports about you, but that you yourself are living in obedience to the law. As for the Gentile believers, we have written to them our decision that they should abstain from food sacrificed to idols, from blood, from the meat of strangled animals and from sexual immorality."

The next day Paul took the men and purified himself along with them. Then he went to the temple to give notice of the date when the days of purification would end and the offering would be made for each of them.

When the seven days were nearly over, some Jews from the province of Asia saw Paul at the temple. They stirred up the whole crowd and seized him, shouting, "Fellow Israelites, help us! This is the man who teaches everyone everywhere against our people and our law and this place. And besides, he has brought Greeks into the temple and defiled this holy place." (They had previously seen Trophimus the Ephesian in the city with Paul and assumed that Paul had brought him into the temple.)

The whole city was aroused, and the people came running from all directions. Seizing Paul, they dragged him from the temple, and immediately the gates were shut. While they were trying to kill him, news reached the commander of the Roman troops that the whole city of Jerusalem was in an uproar. He at once took some officers and soldiers and ran down to the crowd. When the rioters saw the commander and his soldiers, they stopped beating Paul. (Acts 21:17–32)

TIME TO REBUILD THE TEMPLE

"When I [Paul] returned to Jerusalem and was praying at the temple, I fell into a trance and saw the Lord speaking to me. 'Quick!' he said. 'Leave Jerusalem immediately, because the people here will not accept your testimony about me.'" (Acts 22:17–18)

Since all this is true, we should not say that it is wrong for there to be a temple or for Christians to visit it and pray there. Paul, who himself continued with many Torah and temple practices, did not argue against Jews continuing in some of them, but he vigorously defended his conviction that the Gentiles did not need to do those things (like circumcision for example). Therefore, it's important to understand that Jewish Christians had different standards of behavior, as evidenced in Acts 5 and 15. The apostles were not teaching Jews to become Gentiles, or Gentiles to become Jews. They were teaching Jesus as the Messiah, and that the forgiveness of sins was through Him.

> Certain people came down from Judea to Antioch and were teaching the believers: "Unless you are circumcised, according to the custom taught by Moses, you cannot be saved." This brought Paul and Barnabas into sharp dispute and debate with them. So Paul and Barnabas were appointed, along with some other believers, to go up to Jerusalem to see the apostles and elders about this question. The church sent them on their way, and as they traveled through Phoenicia and Samaria, they told how the Gentiles had been converted. This news made all the believers very glad. When they came to Jerusalem, they were welcomed by the church and the apostles and elders, to whom they reported everything God had done through them.

> Then some of the believers who belonged to the party of the Pharisees stood up and said, "The Gentiles must be circumcised and required to keep the law of Moses."

> The apostles and elders met to consider this question. After much discussion, Peter got up and addressed them: "Brothers, you know that some time ago God made a choice among you that the Gentiles might

hear from my lips the message of the gospel and believe. God, who knows the heart, showed that he accepted them by giving the Holy Spirit to them, just as he did to us. He did not discriminate between us and them, for he purified their hearts by faith. Now then, why do you try to test God by putting on the necks of Gentiles a yoke that neither we nor our ancestors have been able to bear? No! We believe it is through the grace of our Lord Jesus that we are saved, just as they are."

The whole assembly became silent as they listened to Barnabas and Paul telling about the signs and wonders God had done among the Gentiles through them. When they finished, James spoke up. "Brothers," he said, "listen to me. Simon has described to us how God first intervened to choose a people for his name from the Gentiles. The words of the prophets are in agreement with this, as it is written:

> *"After this I will return and rebuild David's fallen tent.*
>
> *Its ruins I will rebuild, and I will restore it,*
>
> *that the rest of mankind may seek the Lord,*
>
> *even all the Gentiles who bear my name,*
>
> *says the Lord, who does these things"*—
>
> *things known from long ago.*

It is my judgment, therefore, that we should not make it difficult for the Gentiles who are turning to God. Instead we should write to them, telling them to abstain from food polluted by idols, from sexual immorality, from the meat of strangled animals and from blood. For the law of Moses has been preached in every city from the earliest times and is read in the synagogues on every Sabbath. (Acts 15:1–21, emphasis added)

Based on verses 16–18 above (which are quoted from Amos 9 from the Greek Septuagint), I would say that physically rebuilding the temple, or at least a tabernacle tent, with Gentile support is encouraged. Now,

I know that this can be a really difficult subject, and I don't want to sound as though I'm advocating that Christians follow Judaism. I'm trying to remind us all of the close connection between Christians and Jews, because Jesus the Jewish Messiah is Jesus the Savior of the Gentile world. Christians are to love the Jewish people "on account of the patriarchs" (Romans 11:28). At the same time, we also need to remember a couple of additional passages where Paul taught that there is a spiritual temple, which the physical temple represents, that is made up of his children by the indwelling of the Holy Spirit, through faith in Jesus Christ. We are also "fellow citizens" with Israel, so I think we should give them our support, because citizenship comes with both benefits and obligations. Hear Paul:

> Don't you know that you yourselves are God's temple and that God's Spirit dwells in your midst? If anyone destroys God's temple, God will destroy that person; for God's temple is sacred, and you together are that temple. (1 Corinthians 3:16–17)

> Consequently, you are no longer foreigners and strangers, but fellow citizens with God's people and also members of his household, built on the foundation of the apostles and prophets, with Christ Jesus himself as the chief cornerstone. In him the whole building is joined together and rises to become a holy temple in the Lord. And in him you too are being built together to become a dwelling in which God lives by his Spirit. (Ephesians 2:19–22)

I know every Christian may not agree with these statements. I'm also quite sure that most Muslim nations will not immediately support the rebuilding of the Jewish temple either, even though we now know it would not threaten the existence of the Dome of the Rock or Al-Aqsa Mosque. Finally, many Jews who fear the loss of peace in the region will continue to oppose rebuilding the temple because they fear it would initiate all-out war. Still, the rebuilding of the temple is a question for the people of Israel to decide, but hopefully with the support of the

Christian community in the U.S. and around the world. But ultimately, the temple is a house for God, the place that he has called his treasured possession and where he has said he will rest the soles of his feet. So, the call to rebuild the temple must come from him.

A Call to Build the House of the LORD

In the second year of King Darius, on the first day of the sixth month, the word of the LORD came through the prophet Haggai to Zerubbabel son of Shealtiel, governor of Judah, and to Joshua son of Jozadak, the high priest:

This is what the LORD Almighty says: "These people say, 'The time has not yet come to rebuild the LORD's house.'"

Then the word of the LORD came through the prophet Haggai: "Is it a time for you yourselves to be living in your paneled houses, while this house remains a ruin?"

Now this is what the LORD Almighty says: "Give careful thought to your ways. You have planted much, but harvested little. You eat, but never have enough. You drink, but never have your fill. You put on clothes, but are not warm. You earn wages, only to put them in a purse with holes in it."

This is what the LORD Almighty says: "Give careful thought to your ways. Go up into the mountains and bring down timber and build my house, so that I may take pleasure in it and be honored," says the LORD. "You expected much, but see, it turned out to be little. What you brought home, I blew away. Why?" declares the LORD Almighty. "Because of my house, which remains a ruin, while each of you is busy with your own house. Therefore, because of you the heavens have withheld their dew and the earth its crops. I called for a drought on the fields and the mountains, on the grain, the new wine, the olive oil and everything else the ground produces, on people and livestock, and on all the labor of your hands."

Then Zerubbabel son of Shealtiel, Joshua son of Jozadak, the high priest, and the whole remnant of the people obeyed the voice of the LORD their God and the message of the prophet Haggai, because the LORD their God had sent him. And the people feared the LORD.

Then Haggai, the LORD's messenger, gave this message of the LORD to the people: "I am with you," declares the LORD. So the LORD stirred up the spirit of Zerubbabel son of Shealtiel, governor of Judah, and the spirit of Joshua son of Jozadak, the high priest, and the spirit of the whole remnant of the people. They came and began to work on the house of the LORD Almighty, their God, on the twenty-fourth day of the sixth month. (Haggai 1:1–15)

While these verses are certainly historical in nature, because they record what actually happened to begin rebuilding the Second Temple, they also point us forward, because again the house of the Lord lies in ruins today. And perhaps, if there was no mention of a last-days temple in Scripture, then there would be a case, for Christians at least, to say that it would be wrong to build it again. But there are actually seven temples mentioned in scripture (a full list is in the Appendix), including two in the last days. First, in addition to the verses already quoted, God has revealed a future temple in Ezekiel 40–45. These events have not yet happened, so clearly God has ordained that another temple will yet be built. This should be a clear indication that the call to build the house of the Lord is still in effect. Admittedly, the Ezekiel temple describes marking off an area surrounding the whole temple complex that is 25,000 cubits (8 miles) by 25,000 cubits as a sacred district, which is difficult to imagine in the current climate in Israel today. But does that mean that the call to begin rebuilding the temple should be ignored until a more convenient time?

What about Daniel 9:24–27? Daniel also prophesies that a temple will be standing in the last days. Some may believe that everything in this passage is past and has been fulfilled, but that is just wishful thinking. These days are certainly yet to come. God has decreed it, and they will come to pass:

Seventy "sevens" are decreed for your people and your holy city to finish transgression, to put an end to sin, to atone for wickedness, to bring in everlasting righteousness, to seal up vision and prophecy and to anoint the Most Holy Place.

Know and understand this: From the time the word goes out to restore and rebuild Jerusalem until the Anointed One, the ruler, comes, there will be seven "sevens," and sixty-two "sevens." It will be rebuilt with streets and a trench, but in times of trouble. After the sixty-two "sevens," the Anointed One will be put to death and will have nothing. The people of the ruler who will come will destroy the city and the sanctuary. The end will come like a flood: War will continue until the end, and desolations have been decreed. He will confirm a covenant with many for one "seven." In the middle of the 'seven' he will put an end to sacrifice and offering. And at the temple he will set up an abomination that causes desolation, until the end that is decreed is poured out on him.

Next, we have the testimony of Micah, who both prophesied the complete destruction of the temple in chapter 3 and described a last-days temple in chapter 4. Together with Daniel's and Ezekiel's prophecies, how can there be any doubt that God has still ordained that a temple will stand before him in the last days?

Therefore because of you, Zion will be plowed like a field, Jerusalem will become a heap of rubble, the temple hill a mound overgrown with thickets. (Micah 3:12)

In the last days the mountain of the LORD's temple will be established as the highest of the mountains; it will be exalted above the hills, and peoples will stream to it. Many nations will come and say, "Come, let us go up to the mountain of the LORD, to the temple of the God of Jacob. He will teach us his ways, so that we may walk in his paths." The law will go out from Zion, the word of the LORD from Jerusalem. He will judge between many peoples and will settle disputes for strong nations far and wide. They will beat their swords into plowshares and their spears into pruning hooks. Nation will not take up sword against nation, nor will they train for war anymore. Everyone will sit under their own vine and under their own fig tree, and no one will make them afraid, for the LORD Almighty has spoken. All the nations may walk in the name of their gods, but we will walk in the name of the LORD our God for ever and ever. (Micah 4:1–5)

We also have the words of Zechariah in chapter 6 (c. 520–518 BC) that tell us of a last-days temple at the same time that the Second Temple is being rebuilt. How do we know that? The temple of Solomon was destroyed in 586 BC, and work rebuilding the Second Temple began about 521 BC and it was completed in 516 BC. So, Zechariah made a messianic reference regarding the rebuilding of the temple by the one called "the Branch" who is a priest-king ("a priest on his throne"), during the same time that the Second Temple was being built. Therefore, he is referring to another future temple, even while the current temple is being built, because the Messiah had not yet been revealed. We know "the Branch" is a messianic reference because it is tied to the priest-king Melchizedek (Genesis 14 and Psalm 110:4). Christians will also recognize the reference to a priest-king from Hebrews 5–7 in reference to Jesus.

Tell him this is what the LORD Almighty says: "Here is the man whose name is the Branch, and he will branch out from his place and build the temple of the LORD. It is he who will build the temple of the LORD, and he will be clothed with majesty and will sit and rule on his throne. And he will be a priest on his throne. And there will be harmony between the two." The crown will be given to Heldai, Tobijah, Jedaiah and Hen son of Zephaniah as a memorial in the temple of the LORD. Those who are far away will come and help to build the temple of the LORD, and you will know that the LORD Almighty has sent me to you. This will happen if you diligently obey the LORD your God. (Zechariah 6:12–15)

The L‍ord has sworn and will not change his mind: "You are a priest forever, in the order of Melchizedek." (Psalm 110:4)

The passage in Zechariah, though, can be referenced to assert that a third temple can only be built by the Messiah, because it says that "he will branch out from his place and build the temple of the L‍ord." But it doesn't exactly say that only the Branch can build the temple. It says that the Messiah will build a temple at that appointed time. In fact, as already mentioned, the Second Temple was even then under construction, and it wasn't the Messiah building it. Hence, the construction of another temple before that cannot be precluded by this verse, either. Not only that, but there is a sense in which everything can logically be attributed to God, even though other people or forces could have been the visible actors. For example, Amos 3:6 implies that God is the one acting behind the scenes bringing events, such as judgment, to pass: "When a trumpet sounds in a city, do not the people tremble? When disaster comes to a city, has not the L‍ord caused it?"

And I would argue that it was God who established the State of Israel in one day, as foretold in Isaiah 66:8, even though it was done through a UN resolution and a declaration by David Ben Gurion and the new State of Israel.

Who has ever heard of such things? Who has ever seen things like this? Can a country be born in a day or a nation be brought forth in a moment? Yet no sooner is Zion in labor than she gives birth to her children. (Isaiah 66:8)

Thus, if a third temple is built, it will still be God who ultimately is behind its building, regardless of the human agents actually involved.

Another biblical reference that tells us that a temple will again be constructed comes from Ezekiel 37. It is clear that a messianic age temple is being referred to because Ezekiel (c. 570 BC) was writing nearly four hundred years after the death of King David, but he still wrote, "My servant David will be king over them." Then, amazingly, we read that all nations will know that the Lord makes Israel holy when

His sanctuary is among them forever. This would be a strange statement if it referred to a temple that won't be built until Jesus returns, because surely the return of the Messiah alone will prove that to the nations. Therefore, I would propose that Ezekiel was prophesying that a temple, which will serve as a sign to the nations, will be constructed before the return of Jesus Christ:

> My servant David will be king over them, and they will all have one shepherd. They will follow my laws and be careful to keep my decrees. They will live in the land I gave to my servant Jacob, the land where your ancestors lived. They and their children and their children's children will live there forever, and David my servant will be their prince forever. I will make a covenant of peace with them; it will be an everlasting covenant. I will establish them and increase their numbers, and I will put my sanctuary among them forever. My dwelling place will be with them; I will be their God, and they will be my people. Then the nations will know that I the LORD make Israel holy, when my sanctuary is among them forever. (vv. 24–28)

A similar account discussing a last-days temple is also found in Isaiah 60, which refers to both the regathering of Israel and the restoration of the temple, complete with sacrifices. We also see in this passage the kings of foreign lands visiting Jerusalem, which has been happening on a regular basis since 1967, as well as a reference to the rebuilding of Jerusalem's walls, which was done by foreigners in the past (Suleiman the Magnificent c. 1537–1541). There is perhaps also an allegorical reference to foreigners helping to increase Israel's defenses.

> Lift up your eyes and look about you: All assemble and come to you; your sons come from afar, and your daughters are carried on the hip. Then you will look and be radiant, your heart will throb and swell with joy; the wealth on the seas will be brought to you, to you the riches of the nations will come. Herds of camels will cover your land, young camels of Midian and Ephah. And all from Sheba will come, bearing gold and incense and proclaiming the praise of the LORD.

All Kedar's flocks will be gathered to you, the rams of Nebaioth will serve you; they will be accepted as offerings on my altar, and I will adorn my glorious temple.

Who are these that fly along like clouds, like doves to their nests? Surely the islands look to me; in the lead are the ships of Tarshish, bringing your children from afar, with their silver and gold, to the honor of the LORD your God, the Holy One of Israel, for he has endowed you with splendor.

Foreigners will rebuild your walls, and their kings will serve you. Though in anger I struck you, in favor I will show you compassion. Your gates will always stand open, they will never be shut, day or night, so that people may bring you the wealth of the nations—their kings led in triumphal procession. For the nation or kingdom that will not serve you will perish; it will be utterly ruined.

The glory of Lebanon will come to you, the juniper, the fir and the cypress together, to adorn my sanctuary; and I will glorify the place for my feet. The children of your oppressors will come bowing before you; all who despise you will bow down at your feet and will call you the City of the LORD, Zion of the Holy One of Israel. (vv. 4–14)

Finally, in the book of Revelation (which is universally believed to have been written after AD 70), John describes a temple in the last days, before the return of Jesus and before the Great Tribulation (or time of Jacob's Trouble) begins. This particular passage also includes an intriguing reference to the outer court, which belongs to "the Gentiles." It is certainly possible that it is a reference to the central and southern portion of the Temple Mount enclosure, which currently holds the Dome of the Rock and al-Aqsa mosque:

I was given a reed like a measuring rod and was told, "Go and measure the temple of God and the altar, with its worshipers. But exclude the outer court; do not measure it, because it has been given to the Gentiles." (11:1–2)

Altogether, I think the scriptural case to affirm that another temple will be rebuilt before the Great Tribulation is clear. Consequently, I think Christians should support, at least ideologically, the rebuilding of the temple, and at the very least refrain from actively opposing or speaking out against efforts to do so, because God has ordained it.

But, when will it happen? When the Spirit of God moves His people to act. But at the same time, God does not force people into action as if they were robots. He gently calls them to heed his voice. It is a matter of the heart. Perhaps if the Jewish people had really understood that the temple location lay open and ready for building, preserved for them by God all this time, they would have already started building. They certainly have made most, if not all, of the other provisions necessary to rebuild the temple. It is my sense, however, that the time is close at hand.

THE SITE IS CLEAR AND READY FOR BUILDING

Now we know the site is ready. In fact, the view on the cover of this book shows exactly what you would see if you stood on the Temple Mount directly in front of the Dome of the Spirits. In Figure 40, you can see the view from even farther west, looking east at the Dome of Spirits.

In the picture, looking through the central columns of the dome you can see a small group of people in the distance, and beyond that, you will see the very top of the Golden Gate directly behind them, partially obscured by trees and barely over the level of the platform. And if you could stand in that spot, you would be standing, as I was, just to the west of the temple site and looking toward the Golden Gate and where someday soon a rebuilt temple will be standing.

This should be exciting from the standpoint that there really is no need to talk about mutually exclusive options; that is, it's not a case of either the Dome of the Rock or the Jewish temple. Clearly, the Jewish temple could be rebuilt now without a significant impact to existing Islamic religious sites. This large open courtyard area is essentially a blank slate where building could begin almost immediately and in earnest (political obstacles notwithstanding).

Figure 40: Photo of the unoccupied northern portion of the Temple Mount platform, looking directly at the Dome of the Spirits in line with the Golden Gate. *[Author's photo]*

PREPARATIONS HAVE BEEN LONG IN THE MAKING

Amazingly, most of the preparations needed for the third temple have already been completed. In fact, in many ways the past seventy years have been like the reign of David preparing the way for his son Solomon to begin the building project:

> Then King David said to the whole assembly: "My son Solomon, the one whom God has chosen, is young and inexperienced. The task is great, because this palatial structure is not for man but for the LORD God. With all my resources I have provided for the temple of my God—gold for the gold work, silver for the silver, bronze for the bronze, iron for the iron and wood for the wood, as well as onyx for the settings, turquoise, stones of various colors, and all kinds of fine stone and marble—all of these in large quantities. Besides, in my devotion to the temple of my God I now give my personal treasures of gold and silver for the temple of my God, over and above every-thing I have provided for this holy temple: three thousand talents of gold (gold of Ophir) and seven thousand talents of refined silver, for the overlaying of the walls of the buildings, for the gold work and the silver work, and for all the work to be done by the craftsmen. Now, who is willing to consecrate themselves to the Lord today?" (1 Chronicles 29:1–5)

One of the first things that was needed was to reestablish a Sanhedrin. The Sanhedrin disappeared almost sixteen hundred years ago when it was abolished by the order of Emperor Theodosius II. He passed a law to end the Jewish patriarchate on May 30, 429, after the death of Gamaliel VI, the Sanhedrin's last president.[4] Over the years there have been numerous attempts to reinstate the Sanhedrin, but not until 2004 did they succeed.[5] Since 2007, the new Sanhedrin has been conducting fully kosher practice sacrifices with blemish-free lambs and petitioning the Israeli Supreme Court to reinitiate sacrifices on the Temple Mount, and they have continued to make those petitions regularly since then.[6] The practice sacrifice was made in cooperation with the Temple Institute, founded in 1987, which has been remaking most of the temple arti-facts and priestly garments needed to reinstate the priesthood and the sacrifices, and to rebuild the temple.[7] One of the most striking temple artifacts that have been remade is the golden menorah, shown in Figure 41. But the golden menorah is not all that has been prepared. All of the priestly garments and vessels needed to begin the priestly service have also been prepared, and there is even now a school in Israel training the first generation of priests.[8] A portable altar, constructed in full compliance with both biblical regulations and the instructions found in the Mishnah, has also been built and made ready for the future temple.[9]

Figure 41: The golden menorah intended for use in a future third temple, on display in Jerusalem. *[Author's photo]*

Finally, there have been efforts for decades to breed completely blemish-free red heifers, and one has now finally been produced.[10] This is exciting news for all who would like to see these prophetic events unfolding before their eyes. Detailed architectural plans have also been made for the entire temple complex, including a building that would house the new Sanhedrin.[11] The Sanhedrin also has officially called "upon the Jewish people to contribute towards the acquisition of materials for the purpose of rebuilding the Holy Temple."[12] What remains now is really just building it, which should depend solely on the decision of the collective will of the people of Israel and the blessing of God.

THE LAST ROADBLOCKS

There are still two major roadblocks that are currently preventing the rebuilding of the temple. I have already addressed the first, having a place to build it. Of course, any rebuilding effort also requires the understanding and acceptance of the people of Israel, the scholarly community, and to some extent the world at large. I am not naive about how difficult that is to achieve. It's not as bad as convincing the world that the earth is round instead of flat, or that slavery should be abolished, or that women should have the right to vote. Nevertheless, convincing the world that the Jews should be able to build another temple on the Temple Mount and that the correct place has been identified still seems pretty tough. Fortunately, I think God will do that heavy lifting. I'm just trying to do a small part and make the information available.

The other roadblock is the fact that Israel does not really have control of the Temple Mount, for two main reasons. The first and primary reason is that the site is controlled by the Islamic Waqf of Jordan.[13] It is very unlikely that they will support rebuilding a temple anywhere on the site. Second, any move to rebuild the temple could cause violent resistance from the Arab Palestinians living in Israel. I don't believe the second reason is actually as insurmountable as it seems. Israel has the ability to maintain security within her borders, if they need to. It's actually managing the relationship with Jordan that could prove to be the most difficult. Israel needs to have the political will to risk jeopardizing peace with Jordan over rebuilding the Temple.

However, the political situation in Jordan is at risk from elements emerging from its more volatile neighbors. In November 2018, the *Arab Weekly* reported that Jordan remains vulnerable to ISIS because as U.S. and international forces combat radicalized fighters in Iraq and Syria, they are being driven into Jordan.[14] The newspaper quoted retired CIA officer Emile Nakhleh: "The situation in Jordan is unsustainable and if it continues along this path, we should expect to see more terrorist attacks in Jordan, which could undermine [King Abdullah II] and his regime." If Jordan became unstable, then taking away control of the Temple Mount from the Islamic Waqf of Jordan would be one of the likely Israeli responses. Tragically, the prophet Obadiah, in his prophecy about Edom, may have been warning about this very scenario.

> The vision of Obadiah.
> This is what the Sovereign LORD says about Edom—
> We have heard a message from the LORD:
> An envoy was sent to the nations to say,
> "Rise, let us go against her for battle"—
> "See, I will make you small among the nations;
>   you will be utterly despised.
> The pride of your heart has deceived you,
>   you who live in the clefts of the rocks
>   and make your home on the heights, you who say to yourself,
> 'Who can bring me down to the ground?'
> Though you soar like the eagle
>   and make your nest among the stars,
>   from there I will bring you down," declares the LORD.
>   "If thieves came to you, if robbers in the night—
>   oh, what a disaster awaits you!—
>   would they not steal only as much as they wanted?
> If grape pickers came to you,
>   would they not leave a few grapes?

But how Esau will be ransacked,
    his hidden treasures pillaged!
All your allies will force you to the border;
    your friends will deceive and overpower you;
    those who eat your bread will set a trap for you,
    but you will not detect it.
"In that day," declares the LORD,
    "will I not destroy the wise men of Edom,
    those of understanding in the mountains of Esau?
Your warriors, Teman, will be terrified,
    and everyone in Esau's mountains
    will be cut down in the slaughter.
Because of the violence against your brother Jacob,
    you will be covered with shame;
    you will be destroyed forever.
On the day you stood aloof
    while strangers carried off his wealth and foreigners
        entered his gates
    and cast lots for Jerusalem,
    you were like one of them.
You should not gloat over your brother
    in the day of his misfortune,
    nor rejoice over the people of Judah
    in the day of their destruction,
    nor boast so much in the day of their trouble.
You should not march through the gates of my people
    in the day of their disaster,
    nor gloat over them in their calamity
    in the day of their disaster,
    nor seize their wealth
    in the day of their disaster.
You should not wait at the crossroads
    to cut down their fugitives,

nor hand over their survivors
in the day of their trouble.
The day of the LORD is near
for all nations.
As you have done, it will be done to you;
your deeds will return upon your own head.
Just as you drank on my holy hill,
so all the nations will drink continually; they will drink and drink
and be as if they had never been.
But on Mount Zion will be deliverance;
it will be holy, and Jacob will possess his inheritance.
(Obadiah 1–17)

While some may feel that the above passage is as clear as mud, there are several key statements that I think connect this passage with modern events. It describes the people of Edom (1) doing violence against their brother Jacob, (2) gloating over his misfortune, (3) marching through their gates (Jerusalem), (4) ambushing the Israelites on the roadways, and (5) drinking on (occupying) God's holy hill. To better understand how this passage reflects modern events, it is helpful to review the history of the conflict between Israel and Jordan from 1948 to 1967, and their relationship post-1967. I will have to leave most of that as homework for you, but there are a couple of key points to know. First, the Kingdom of Jordan today occupies much of what was called the land of Edom. Furthermore, Jordan was an enemy of Israel from 1948 to 1967 and has controlled God's "holy hill" (the Temple Mount) since 1948, with only a short interruption following the Six-Day War.[15] Not only that, but while they have had a successful peace treaty since that time, Jordan remains critical of Israel on almost all issues related to the Temple Mount and their politics regarding the Palestinians. The final line, however, may be understood to be saying that Israel will get back the Temple Mount when Edom faces the troubles foretold by Obadiah, because it ends with "Jacob will possess his inheritance."

I would much rather see Jordan change its posture toward Jewish access to the Temple Mount and move toward a plan like the one described in the next chapter, but that may be too much to hope for, considering that Jordan was among the first nations to invade Israel in 1948. As a result of that initial invasion, they occupied the eastern half of Jerusalem from 1949 to 1967.

In fact, I see Jordan's invasion of Israel in 1948, along with other Arab nations, as a fulfillment of another prophecy, found in Zechariah 14. Most people probably view this as a yet-future event, and perhaps it will happen again, but the events described in verse 2 actually occurred in 1948–49. Furthermore, verse 3 could describe very well the military victories that Israel has experienced since that time:

> 2 For I will gather all the nations against Jerusalem to battle, and the city will be captured, the houses plundered, the women ravished and half of the city exiled, but the rest of the people will not be cut off from the city. 3 Then the LORD will go forth and fight against those nations, as when He fights on a day of battle. 4 In that day His feet will stand on the Mount of Olives, which is in front of Jerusalem on the east; and the Mount of Olives will be split in its middle from east to west by a very large valley, so that half of the mountain will move toward the north and the other half toward the south. 5 You will flee by the valley of My mountains, for the valley of the mountains will reach to Azel; yes, you will flee just as you fled before the earthquake in the days of Uzziah king of Judah. Then the Lord, my God, will come, and all the holy ones with Him! (Zechariah 14:2–5 NASB)

The fiercest battle in the Israeli war of independence was fought over Jerusalem. At the end of it, the armistice line divided the city in half between the Old City and the New City. When the Jewish Quarter in the Old City fell, many were killed, others were taken into Jordanian captivity, and the rest were deported to the New City. Their homes were pillaged and set ablaze, and the synagogues were destroyed.[16] And as one might expect, some of the women taken captive were also ravaged.[17]

Since Israel's founding as a nation, God has been fighting for them, as described in verse 3. This has been evidenced by Israel's survival in the war of independence and in all of the wars since that time, most notably the Six-Day War in 1967 and the Yom Kippur War in 1973, when the odds were certainly not in their favor. Consequently, we should consider the possibility that these particular events have already been fulfilled in modern history and we are living in the days between verses 3 and 4 because the events from verse 4 on are obviously still to come. The phrase "in that day" in verse 4 can sound as though it is talking about the very same day as verse 2, but the reference could easily be applied to the final of a series wars that are the subject of verse 3. In either case, it seems unlikely that everything happens in just one day, so the reference is probably best understood as taking place at that general time, rather than everything taking place in twenty-four hours. Therefore, since the city really was divided in half, for the first time in Jerusalem's four-thousand-year history, I think it is reasonable to conclude that 1948–49 already saw the fulfilment of that portion of the prophecy.

A FINAL QUESTION . . .

So, the big question is, in spite of the obstacles, when will it begin? How long will the people of Israel let the place on which God said he would place the soles of his feet, where he stopped the avenging angel at Araunah's threshing floor, and where Abraham offered Isaac, to be left desolate?

The Gate of the Tribes, Temple Mount entrance near the Lion's Gate. Currently admission through this gate is for Muslims only. [*Author's photo*]

8

A JOINT-USE PLAN FOR
THE TEMPLE MOUNT

THERE IS NOW OVERWHELMING EVIDENCE that the true location of the Jewish temple was just north of the Dome of the Rock in line with the Golden Gate. But knowing the true location has never been the only problem for rebuilding the temple. The main problem has been how to do it, peacefully.

One solution to the Temple Mount dilemma could be to define an Israeli-controlled portion that contains the temple on the north end, and an Islamic Waqf–controlled portion that maintains the status quo in the area that contains the Dome of the Rock and Al-Aqsa Mosque on the southern end. This could be similar to the way the Tomb of the Patriarchs in Hebron is currently managed, but with improvements based on lessons learned. The other solution would be to exert full sovereign control over the site and enforce the rule of law and maintain peace and free access for all to the Temple Mount, but I think that may be more vigorously opposed than a dual-zone option. In either instance,

Israel exerting any control of the Temple Mount area will be met by objections from Jordan; however, the relationship with Israel is arguably even more beneficial for Jordan than it is for Israel and Jordan has many potential external threats that would make losing Israel as an ally very undesirable. Furthermore, if Jordan ever became destabilized then they may no longer be in a position to properly manage the Waqf, in which case Israel would likely assume control for security reasons. If a dual-zone plan was pursued, I would also suggest that some archaeological exploration zones be established to begin to explore the southeast corner and better elucidate that part of Temple Mount history.

To that end, I am suggesting an option for designating two main areas on the Temple Mount, with different control authorities. The benefit of such a plan is that it would supply sufficient space for the temple, which could be separated from the al-Aqsa mosque and the Dome of the Rock. There would, of course, still be objections based on Islamic historical connections to the Dome of the Spirits and the Golden Gate. However, the Golden Gate building would be made accessible to all, and the cupola of the Dome of the Spirits would be preserved and relocated to prepare the area for the new holy temple.

Obviously, any change to the status quo will have its challenges and will probably be met with resistance; however, the current status quo has been disrupted repeatedly and is not really in a tenable situation as it is anyway. A more mutually acceptable solution needs to be found, if there is to be a chance for a lasting agreement. This dual-zone proposal is perhaps one way that a more lasting peace between Jewish and Muslim interests could be achieved.

ESTABLISHMENT OF AN ISRAELI-CONTROLLED ZONE ON THE TEMPLE MOUNT

One of the relatively unknown injustices that is openly tolerated in Jerusalem is ultra-limited access to the Temple Mount for all non-Muslims, and free and open access anytime for Muslims, year-round. This is done not to intentionally discriminate but as an appeasement to avoid violence. But haven't we seen enough of what appeasement has won in regard to religious freedom and tolerance on the Temple Mount (or anywhere else in the world, for that matter)?

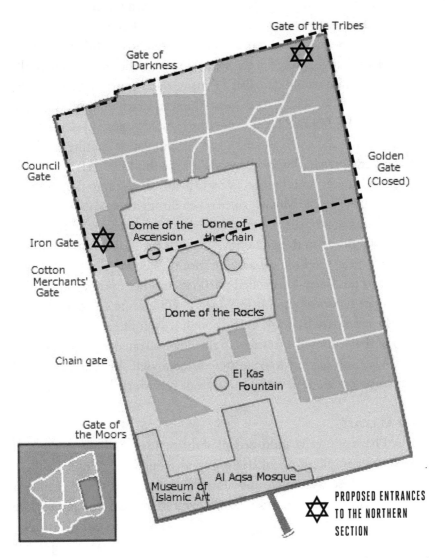

Figure 42: Proposed shared-use plan with separate Jewish/Non-Muslim Temple Mount, with author additions for a temple area and access points/gates (white dashed line and white stars).[1]

Therefore, as a compromise, I believe it would be possible to use the northern approximate one-third of the temple complex to house an Israeli-controlled area (similar to how the Western Wall area is controlled today), as shown in Figure 42. The southern portion would then be mostly a separate Muslim zone including the Dome of the Rock and Al-Aqsa Mosque that would remain under status quo conditions, with the exception of changing some of the access points for the area. Prophetically, this configuration would establish a massive outer court, or Court of the Gentiles (Revelation 11:2). After establishing an Israeli-controlled zone in the top one-third of the Temple Mount complex, more in-depth investigations of the site could establish precise foundation footing locations and allow site preparations to be made for the third temple.

The next question is how to safely provide for access to the northern portion of the Temple Mount, since travel through the Muslim Quarter for Jews can sometimes present challenges. A relatively straightforward solution would be to designate the "Gate of the Tribes" on the northeast corner near the Lion's Gate entrance to the Old City as the main entrance to the Israeli-controlled portion. Another option is the "Iron Gate," since it is near the Little Western Wall, a site currently visited regularly and safely by Jews, even though it is in the Muslim Quarter. A map of the proposed entrances to the newly created zone is shown in Figure 42. After having walked these areas myself, I think this would present a practical, defensible, and overall very workable solution.

THE FALLOUT

I know I have not really addressed all of the political, military, economic, and religious implications of beginning to rebuild the temple in these few pages. These issues will undoubtedly surface, and it will require a significant effort from the Israeli government to manage for a project like this. So, it's not hard to understand why it has been put off. In a similar way, the United States delayed acknowledging Jerusalem as the capital of Israel for almost twenty years. And when it was done, the world was up in arms over it! But in the end, what happened? Not that much compared to what was feared. Donald Trump thought about it, decided it was the right thing to do, and then signed the proclamation that had been ordered by Congress two decades earlier. It was a historic event!

Because of the complex issues facing Israel over the controversy of the Temple Mount, some authors have sought to find alternate locations that would be less controversial, and in their haste have tried to look outside the Temple Mount.[2] But the flaws of the reasoning behind those views have been thoroughly debunked in chapter 6. Nevertheless, these issues must be dealt with. The Jews, who have been praying for a rebuilt temple for two thousand years, are not going to just decide to forget about it forever because it's too controversial.

Surprisingly, there is also at least some support for rebuilding the temple within the Israeli Palestinian community. For example, Tuvia Sagiv (who believes the temple was located on the southern end of the Temple Mount, near the al-Kas fountain) wrote to both Palestinians and the Israeli prime minister and Knesset in 2000 that a cooperative use of the Temple Mount is needed to achieve true peace.[3] He even outlined a strong Islamic argument for allowing the Jews to pray on the Temple Mount and rebuild their temple next to other Muslim sites. His reasons were based on the Quran, the Hadith, and on arguments made by Sheikh Abdul Hadi Palazzi, who supports a tolerant view toward allowing the Jews to continue in their practices while Muslims continue in their own.[4] While I clearly think his argument for a location in the southern portion of the Temple Mount is untenable, his work demonstrates that there is a real desire from at least some parties on the Muslim side to see this happen in a reasonable way.

However, just like the Jerusalem embassy issue, if done carefully but decisively, a joint-use plan could avoid the cataclysms that have been foretold. But we have to avoid the kind of double speak that has marked U.S. policy in the past. In 1995, under the administration of President Bill Clinton, Congress passed a law recognizing Jerusalem as the capital of Israel,[5] but it was never enacted by the president. Later presidents, for twenty years, supported Israel in their own ways, but each of them signed a petition delaying the recognition of Israel's capital every six months.[6] Twice a year, they had to think about whether to honor the congressional decree and support Israel, or delay it another six months, for a total of eight times each term. Donald Trump signed it once, but only to allow the time needed for a smoother transition, and then he kept his campaign promise to recognize Jerusalem as the capital of the State of Israel. His predecessors also made similar campaign promises, but none of them honored those promises once they were elected.

For my part, I hope the United States will continue to support Israel. History will certainly record that the administration under President Donald Trump was a great supporter of Israel. I suspect, though, that the weight of world opinion will be against Israel rebuilding the temple, if the voting trend against the State of Israel in the United Nations is any indication.[7] But God does not ask the United Nations what they think before he makes his plans. Lest the nations forget, setting themselves against Israel is not a good idea, because God has said repeatedly that he will take up her cause.

> On that day, when all the nations of the earth are gathered against her, I will make Jerusalem an immovable rock for all the nations. All who try to move it will injure themselves. (Zechariah 12:3)

> I will bless those who bless you, and whoever curses you I will curse; and all peoples on earth will be blessed through you. (Genesis 12:3)

However, I am encouraged by the United States' nearly unwavering supportive stance toward Israel. When there is a champion for Israel sitting in the White House, the support of the United States can do a lot to help ensure peace in the region while moving to a more tenable status quo condition. Consequently, U.S. support would make it much easier for the Israeli's to make serious steps towards actually rebuilding the temple. The U.S. has been involved in every attempt to achieve peace between Israel and the Palestinians. Trump's Deal of the Century, released in January of 2020, is no exception.[8] Whether or not the final plan is actually led by the U.S., peace will someday be achieved. May God grant that lasting peace comes quickly to Jerusalem.

Pray for the peace of Jerusalem: "May those who love you be secure." (Psalm 122:6).

ACHIEVING LASTING PEACE

I think that one of the missing pieces for real peace between the Israelis and the Palestinians has been the lack of a peaceful solution regarding the Temple Mount, and specifically, a workable solution regarding the rebuilding of a temple. There is just no way that long-term peace can be achieved while the Jews are not allowed to pray on the Temple Mount or rebuild the holy temple. Many have been hoping that the Jews would just forget about it and accept that they have lost the Temple Mount. But that is just not ever going to happen . . .

So why is the issue still being avoided? For one, because everyone really thought that it would have to mean two things: (1) The destruction of the Dome of the Rock and probably the al-Aqsa Mosque, and (2) a global intifada and World War III. When those are the dreaded consequences, it is no wonder that everyone is "kicking the can down the road" on the temple.

And yet, it can now be seen that there is reliable evidence to support a northern location for the temple. So, doesn't this mean there is now a chance to have a permanent solution for the Temple Mount, without all of that? I think it does. It will still take some incredible bravery on the part of leaders in Israel, and probably the support of moderate Islamic nations and the United States. But irrespective of how it is accomplished, the temple should be a part of any comprehensive peace plan.

Finally, whatever the solution, the Palestinians have been demonstrating that they probably won't accept any peace deal, no matter what they are offered, unless 100 percent of their demands are met. Therefore, they should be given a reasonable solution, but also be required to accept it, just as a plaintiff in a bitter divorce case is forced to accept the decision of the judge. No one wants it to be that way. It should be by mutual consent, but hasn't the last fifty years proven that just isn't going to happen either? This of course means that there are really only a couple of possible options. I think the best option for the Palestinians was the one was proposed by President Donald Trump. This is the only plan where the Palestinians have any kind of a self-governing future, and it avoids making them part of the Jewish state. It's a good plan. Nevertheless, it failed to address rebuilding the temple, as already mentioned. It did, however, declare that all faiths should have open and available access to the Temple Mount and should be allowed to pray there according to their religion. It represented an enormous step forward from the status quo situation and could lead to the initiation of sacrifices on the Temple Mount.[9] Historically, as recorded in Ezra 3, the sacrifices should start first and the rebuilding of the temple would begin after that.

> Jerusalem's holy sites should remain open and available for peaceful worshippers and tourists of all faiths. People of every faith should be permitted to pray on the Temple Mount/Haram al-Sharif, in a manner that is fully respectful to their religion, taking into account the times of each religion's prayers and holidays, as well as other religious factors.[10]

Another option is not a two-state solution, but a full one-state solution, where Israel abolishes the Palestinian Authority, expels Hamas from Gaza, takes over and controls the curriculum in Arab schools to eliminate anti-Semitism and false historical narratives, roots out terrorist dogma from the mosques, makes all Arabs at least permanent residents, engages in a massive economic development effort, and exerts full sovereignty over the entire land of Israel. While this last option would eventually work, it could precipitate a massive conflict and significant loss of life. I don't think either side really wants to see that happen. Finally, there could perhaps be a third compromise solution, where religious Jews are allowed to set up a temporary tabernacle and the portable altar that they have constructed during defined Jewish holidays for prayer and sacrifices. For example, a tabernacle and altar could be set up during Passover, Shavuot, and the High Holy Days, and then taken down again after those days are over.

There really aren't any other viable options, besides the status quo, which is no solution at all. The current status quo is like the Cold War between the United States and the USSR; it just isn't a good long-term situation to be in. However, the White House has signaled that they will support Israel implementing the provisions of the peace plan with or without the participation of the Palestinian Authority.[11] In that case, the world could be closer to a peaceful solution than most realize. But whether or not that really happens, I think moving forward with one of the above solutions will be the only way to ultimately achieve peace.

SUMMARY

The key issue may not really be knowing where the temple should be located, but rather whether or not the desire and political will exist to see the Jewish presence in Israel fully reestablished. Will Israel get the support it needs to exert at least partial control over the Temple Mount, the holiest place on earth, in order to rebuild the temple? Then maybe we could finally see the restoration of the holy temple, as a house of prayer for all nations, sitting in its rightful place on the Temple Mount, as shown in Figure 43.

I for one believe it can be done. And like the declaration of Jerusalem as the capital of the State of Israel and the annexation of the Golan Heights, it will likely not be as bad as everyone fears. The time to rebuild the temple is at hand. May it be soon! And as so many Jews say every year at the end of the Passover Seder,[12] "Next year in Jerusalem, the rebuilt!"

Maranatha!

Figure 43: Composite image showing a rebuilt temple in line with the East Gate. *[Photo-edited composite of Figure 26 and the Second Temple model in the Israel Museum]*

Blessed is he who comes in the name of the Lord.
From the house of the Lord we bless you.

Current view of the Temple Mount platform that covers the area where the holy temple once stood. The view is from standing in front of the Dome of the Spirits and looking east toward the Golden Gate. [*Author's photo*]

EPILOGUE

AT FIRST, I was hesitant to presume that I could add anything to this discussion where so many have labored before me. But as I studied the issue, I saw how I could help people better understand the available information and arrive at a definitive conclusion. If I didn't think this evidence really proved the case, I wouldn't have written the book. There would have been no value in adding one more opinion to the pile. But the evidence is now in; the case has been heard. I am grateful for the opportunity God has given me to write this book, and I pray that he will bless it and cause it to have the effect that he desires. I hope that you have enjoyed reading it and will consider even more the reliability of the Word of God, and endeavor to read it daily and to put it into practice in your life.

Albert Einstein once said, "I have no special talent. I am only passionately curious."[1] I love this quote, because it expresses very well how I feel. I just kept chipping away at the question of the temple until I felt that all of the big questions could be answered. The quote also speaks to me about the fact that I did so little of the real work of solving this enigma. I am indebted to the diligent work of so many who did the toilsome job of translation, excavation, and transmission of their findings. In this book I am mostly just collecting the data and pointing out what was for some inexplicable reason still hidden. Another saying I really like is, "If you can't explain it simply, you don't understand it well enough." I hope that the explanations presented in this book have been clear and sufficient to communicate the truth about the former location of the temple. It's hard to say that an entire book to make a point is ever a simple explanation. However, with such a sensitive, controversial, and well-studied subject, using fewer than 230 pages to tell this story is probably about as short as it could have been.

Also, I hope you will forgive any minor mistakes or scholarly errors, which generally occur in a work this size. There will be mistakes, despite my best efforts. In fact, it is easy to find mistakes in any human work. But not in the Bible. That is why it is a holy book. In Hebrew, the word for holy is *qodesh*. It means "apartness, separateness, otherness, transcendent, and totally other than." We say "Holy Bible" because "Holy" means that we believe it is wholly separate from all other works of men. The Bible was written by men, but it was guided by and it proceeded from God's Holy Spirit, and was transferred to men through his prophets, who were attested by signs and miracles.

> So we have the prophetic word made more sure, to which you do well to pay attention as to a lamp shining in a dark place, until the day dawns and the morning star arises in your hearts. But know this first of all, that no prophecy of Scripture is a matter of one's own interpretation, for no prophecy was ever made by an act of human will, but men moved by the Holy Spirit spoke from God. (2 Peter 1:19–21 NASB)

If it is hard to accept that the Word of God is absolutely true, consider this: There either exists revelation from God to humanity, or there does not. Without it, what other authority do we have? Some would say science. But anyone in science knows that even there, there are precious few unchanging "facts." Scientific knowledge is subject to constant revision, and only the things that can be tested and proven by repeated experiments qualify as true facts. The rest of science is described by endless theories in a continual state of revision. Furthermore, science also lacks the ability to truly say anything about morality, ethics, meaning, and purpose, or how we got here . . . despite the many theories that propose to do so. Therefore, humanity is left with only their own minds and hearts to determine those things, which is then just a matter of personal opinion or consensus opinion. As a result, we are left with total relativism, and are thrust back into the darkness of a never-ending sea of changing public opinion. We can replace relativism with totalitarianism, which is in many ways already underway, but it is still a human-derived and relative truth claim. There can be no reliable truth outside of an externally given revelation from the Creator of the universe. We need God. God does not need us, and he could certainly leave us to our own devices—except that he loves us. It is all perfectly explained in the pages of Scripture, where not only do we find truth about the way things happened in the past, but also about why things are the way they are, what God's plan is, and what his intentions are for the future. As for why the Bible and not any other religious book . . . this is for each reader to determine after his or her own study, but I can affirm that exclusivity is the claim of God as revealed in the Bible. It's not my personal claim; it is the claim that God made about himself in the words that he revealed and inspired to be written in the Bible.

In this book, we have covered a lot of prophetic scripture. Many of the things foretold regarding the final days before the return of Jesus Christ have already happened. Likewise, we can be sure that everything else written will happen as well, perhaps sooner than later. It was the inspiration of Scripture, describing a temple in Jerusalem in the last days, that provided the impetus for this book. Faith in that truth gave me the motivation to look beyond consensus and discover what was buried underneath. As a consequence, the historic facts about the existence of the Jewish temple on the Temple Mount in Jerusalem have been sustained, and its location precisely determined. What happens next is still up to the people of Israel, but I feel the force of history and the prophetic words of Scripture moving me to support their efforts to reestablish the temple, which has lain in ruins for nearly two thousand years. Will you add your voice of support for the Jewish people to finally rebuild the temple in this incredibly historic and significant time?

Soli Deo Gloria

ENDNOTES

Preface

1.   Lexico, s.v. "relativism," accessed April 24, 2020, https://www.lexico.com/definition/relativism.

Introduction

1.   Donald J. Trump, "Presidential Proclamation Recognizing Jerusalem as the Capital of the State of Israel and Relocating the United States Embassy to Israel to Jerusalem," December 6, 2017, https://www.whitehouse.gov/presidential-actions/presidential-proclamation-recognizing-jerusalem-capital-state-israel-relocating-united-states-embassy-israel-jerusalem/.

2.   Lawrence D. Sporty, "The Location of the Holy House of Herod's Temple: Evidence from the Post-Destruction Period," Biblical Archaeologist 54, no. 1 (1991): 28–35.

3.   Robin Ngo, "Contested Temple Mount History?" Biblical Archaeology Society Bible History Daily, October 13, 2015, https://www.biblicalarchaeology.org/daily/news/contested-temple-mount-history/.

4.   F. M. Loewenberg, "Did Jews Abandon the Temple Mount?" Middle East Quarterly (2013).

5.   Yaron Z. Eliav, God's Mountain: The Temple Mount in Time, Place, and Memory (Baltimore: Johns Hopkins University Press, 2005).

6.   Mazar, Discovering the Solomonic Wall in Jerusalem, 10.

7.   Mike Mason, Jesus: His Story in Stone (Victoria, BC: FriesenPress, 2017), 105.

8.   Anna Laura Lepschy, Viaggio in Terrasanta di Santo Brasca 1480: Con l'Itinerario di Gabriele Capodilista, 1458 (Milan: Longanesi, 1966), 68.

9.   Robert D. Kaplan, Eastward to Tartary: Travels in the Balkans, the Middle East, and the Caucasus (New York: Random House, 2000), 205.

10. "List of former monarchies," Wikipedia, accessed April 27, 2020, https://en.wikipedia.org/wiki/List_of_former_monarchies.

Chapter 1: Hidden in Plain Sight

1.   Andrew Shiva, Wikipedia, CC BY-SA 4.0, accessed on 11-1-19, https://commons.wikimedia.org/wiki/File:Jerusalem-2013-Aerial-Temple_Mount_02.jpg.

2.   Merriam-Webster.com, s.v. "hidden," accessed April 27, 2020, https://www.merriam-webster.com/dictionary/hidden.

3.   See Encyclopedia Britannica, s.v. "Humpty Dumpty," accessed April 28, 2020, https://www.britannica.com/topic/Humpty-Dumpty.

4. Supported by (1) G. Williams (1849); (2) M. de Vogüé (1864)—*north of al-Sakhra, but not on the Dome of the Spirits*; (3) J. E. Hanauer (1926); (4) A. S. Kaufmann (1983); (5) L. Sporty (1990); (6) E. H. Skolfield (2001); (7) G. R. Grant (2007); (8) Watchman Bible Study (2017); (9) D. Goldstein (2018); and (10) C. A. Widener (2020).

5. Supported by (1) J. Lightfoot (1664); (2) Menke (1868); (3) K. Furrer (1876); (4) C. R. Conder (1884); (5) J. Porter (1886); (6) C. Schick (1896); (7) C. M. Watson (1896); (8) C. Mommert (1903); (9) J. L. Leeper (1903); (10) G. Dalman (1909); (11) F. Hollis (1934); (12) L. Vincent (1954); (13) L. Ritmeyer (1985); (14) D. Jacobson (1990); (15) D. Bahat (1990); (16) A. Yisrael (1993); and (17) C. Richman (1997).

6. Supported by (1) J. Barclay (1858); (2) J. Fergusson (1878); (3) C. Warren (1880); (4) J. L. Porter (1886); (5) H. Moskoff (2019); (6) N. Robertson (2014); and (7) T. Sagiv (2004).

7. Supported by (1) E. Martin (1994); (2) B. Cornuke (2014); (3) M. Sams (2019).

Chapter 2: The Threshing Floor Is the Datum

1. "About the Project," The Temple Mount Sifting Project website, accessed April 29, 2020, http://tmsifting.org/en/brief-introduction-to-the-project/.

2. Katharina Galor, *Finding Jerusalem: Archaeology between Science and Ideology* (Oakland: University of California Press, 2017), 162.

3. Asher Selig Kaufman, *The Temple Mount: Where Is the Holy of Holies?* (Jerusalem: Har Yéra'eh Press, 2004).

4. Leen Ritmeyer, *The Quest: Revealing the Temple Mount in Jerusalem* (Jerusalem: Carta, 2006), 162–63.

5. Jaime L. Waters, Threshing Floors in Ancient Israel: Their Ritual and Symbolic Significance (Minneapolis: Fortress Press, 2015), 9.

6. Ruth Shahack-Grass, Mor Gafri, and Israel Finkelstein, "Identifying Threshing Floors in the Archaeological Record: A Test Case at Iron Age Tel Megiddo, Israel," *Journal of Field Archaeology* 34, no. 2 (2009): 181.

7. G. Eric and Edith Matson, "Galilee Trip. General view of the Saffourie(h) Threshing Floors," Library of Congress, accessed April 29, 2020, https://commons.wikimedia.org/wiki/File:Galilee_trip._Saffourieh_(near_Nazareth)._Saforis_(Sepphoris)._General_view_of_the_Saffourie(h)_threshing_floors_below_the_village_with_watchman%27s_booth_LOC_matpc.20757.jpg.

8. "Notes (1) on Two Tribula, or Threshing-Sledges," *Society of Antiquaries of Scotland* 38 (1903–1904): 506–19.

9. Yizhar Hirschfeld, "Ancient Wine Presses in the Park of Aijalon," *Israel Exploration Journal* (1983): 207–18.

10. S. Avitsur, *Man and His Work, Historical Atlas of Tools and Workshops in the Holy Land* [in Hebrew] (Jerusalem, 1976), 28, in Ritmeyer, The Quest, 245.

11. Charles William Wilson and Charles Warren, *The Recovery of Jerusalem: A Narrative of Exploration and Discovery in the City and the Holy Land*, vol. 1.(London: R. Bentley, 1871).

12. "Deir Samaan," BibleWalks.com, accessed April 29, 2020, https://www.biblewalks.com/DeirSamaan.

13. Yizhar Hirschfeld and Rivka Birger-Calderon, "Early Roman and Byzantine Estates Near Caesarea," *Israel Exploration Journal* (1991): 81–111.

14. Patricia C. Anderson et al., "Insights from a Tribological Analysis of the Tribulum," *Journal of Archaeological Science* 33, no. 11 (2006): 1559–68; Gurova, Maria. "Tribulum inserts in ethnographic and archaeological perspective: Case studies from Bulgaria and Israel." *Lithic Technology* 38, no. 3 (2013): 179-201.

15. Groman-Yaroslavski, Iris, Mark Iserlis, and Michael Eisenberg. "Potters' Canaanean Flint Blades During the Early Bronze Age." *Mediterranean Archaeology & Archaeometry* 13, no. 1 (2013).

16. James Edward Hanauer, *Walks in and around Jerusalem* (Jerusalem: Church Missions to the Jews, 1926), 260.

17. Sir Charles William Wilson, contrib., *Itinerary from Bordeaux to Jerusalem: The Bordeaux Pilgrim (333 A.D.),* trans. Aubrey Stewart (London: Palestine Pilgrim's Text Society, 1887), 21.

18. Ritmeyer, *The Quest,* 163.

19. Ritmeyer, 163.

20. Capt. [Charles] Wilson, RE, and Capt. [Charles] Warren, RE, *The Recovery of Jerusalem. A Narrative of Exploration and Discovery in the City and the Holy Land* (London: R. Bentley & Son, 1871), 315.

21. Ritmeyer, *The Quest,* 245.

22. Y. Baruch, R. Reich, and D. Sandhaus, "A Decade of Archaeological Exploration on the Temple Mount," *Tel Aviv* 45, no. 1 (2018): 4.

23. Kaufman, *The Temple Mount,* 60.

24. Ritmeyer, *The Quest,* 251–68.

25. Yusuf Natsheh, *Ottoman Jerusalem: The Living City: 1517–1917,* ed. Sylvia Auld and Robert Hillenbrand (London: Altajir World of Islam Trust, 2000), 888.

26. Mukaddasi (c. 985), *Description of Syria, Including Palestine,* trans. Guy Le Strange (London: Palestine Pilgrim's Text Society, 1886), 42.

27. Ritmeyer, *The Quest,* 241–77.

Chapter 3: The East Gate Points the Way

1. "The Location of the Temple and the Holy of Holies on the Temple Mount," Temple Mount & Land of Israel Faithful Movement website, accessed April 29, 2020, http://www.templemountfaithful.org/articles/temple-location.php.

2. Solomon H. Steckoll, *The Gates of Jerusalem* (n.p.: Praeger, 1968), 18–19.

3. A portion of the video is posted on YouTube, although the entire ninety-minute video is no longer online. See Temple Institute, "Exclusive Video Footage: The Temple Mount," 8:56, February 1, 2008, https://www.youtube.com/watch?v=sh27UWmCd7E.

4. Randall Price, *Rose Guide to the Temple* (Torrance, CA: Rose, 2012), 135.

5. Flavius Josephus, *The Antiquities of the Jews,* bk. 15, chap. 11, in William Whiston, *The Works of Josephus* (Peabody, MA: Hendrickson, 1987), 417–20.

6. Francis E. Peters, *Jerusalem: The Holy City in the Eyes of Chroniclers, Visitors, Pilgrims, and Prophets from the Days of Abraham to the Beginnings of Modern Times* (Princeton, NJ: Princeton University Press, 1985).

7. Al-Muqadassi, *Description of Syria, Including Palestine*, Palestine Pilgrims' Text Society vol. 3, trans. Guy Le Strange (London: 24 Hanover Square, W., 1896).

8. Nāṣir-i Khusraw, *Naser-e Khosraw's Book of Travels*, trans. W. M. Thackston Jr. (New York: Bibliotheca Persica, 1986).

9. Niccolò (da Poggibonsi), *A Voyage beyond the Seas (1346–1350)*, trans. Theophilus Bellorini and Eugene A. Hoade (Jerusalem: Franciscan Pres, 1945).

10. 'Ulaimî, Mujîr al-Dîn 'Abd al-Raḥmân b. Muḥammad, *Histoire de Jérusalem et d'Hébron, Fragments de la Chronique*, ed. Ernest Leroux, trans. Henry Sauvaire (n.p.: Paris, 1876), emphasis added.

11. Flavius Josephus, *The Wars of the Jews*, bk. 6, chap. 5, in William Whiston, *The Works of Josephus* (Peabody, MA: Hendrickson, 1987), 316, emphasis added.

12. Josephus, *The Wars of the Jews*, bk. 7, chap. 1, from Whiston, *The Works of Josephus*, 1, 17.

13. G. Williams, *The Holy City*, vol. 2 (London: J. W. Parker, 1849), 338, 355-57.

14. John Wilkinson, *Jerusalem Pilgrims before the Crusades: Translation of "The Piacenza Pilgrim: Travels (c. 570 A.D.)"* (n.p., 2015), 138.

15. Palestine Pilgrims' Text Society, *The Pilgrimage of Arculfus in the Holy Land (About the Year A.D. 670)*, trans. Rev. James Rose Machpherson, BD (London, 1895), emphasis added.

16. Mason, *Jesus: His* Story *in Stone*, 105 (see intro., n. 6).

17. There are other ways to translate "facing the Temple," but the Hebrew word here is *mehabbayit* (מֵהַבַּיִת), a combination of *mah* (a modifying word) and *bayith* (a house, or in this case, the temple), so the more literal rendering is preferred here.

18. Josh McDowell and Sean McDowell. *Evidence That Demands a Verdict: Life-Changing Truth for a Skeptical World* (Nashville: Thomas Nelson, 2017), 92–99.

19. McDowell and McDowell, 100–9.

20. Josephus, *Wars of the Jews*, bk. 5, chap. 4, from Whiston, *Works of Josephus*, 703–4.

21. Bahat. *The Carta Jerusalem Atlas*, 87.

22. Borgehammar, Stephan (2009): "Heraclius Learns Humility: Two Early Latin Accounts. Composed for the Celebration of Exaltatio Crucis," Millennium, vol. 6, 145-201.

23. Pseudo-Hrabanus in Borgehammar (2009): 186-89.

24. Williams, *The Holy City*, 2:355–58.

25. (Left): Maison Bonfils. *Intérieur de la porte dorée Interior of the golden gate*. From the Library of Congress. https://www.loc.gov/pictures/item/2004669846/ (accessed on 7-22-20), with author notations. (Right): Melchior de Vogüé, *Le Temple de Jerusalem* (Paris, 1864) 12, fig. 10.

26. Leen Ritmeyer, "The Golden Gate of the Temple Mount in Jerusalem," Ritmeyer.com, March 11, 2019, https://www.ritmeyer.com/2019/03/11/the-golden-gate-of-the-temple-mount-in-jerusalem/?fbclid=IwAR3W-G2nR_q4HTIBu3zO8QkDtvlGHMBoG806tGjD3DOddpgr4Gz5TSLSdgo.

27. Ritmeyer, *The Quest*, 109, 178, emphasis added (see chap. 2, n. 4).

28. Doron Chen, "On the Golden Gate in Jerusalem and the Baptistery at Emmaus—Nicopolis," *Zeitschrift Des Deutschen Palästina-Vereins (1953–)* 97, no. 2 (1981): 171–77.

29. James Fleming, "The Undiscovered Gate Beneath Jerusalem's Golden Gate," *Biblical Archaeology Review* 9, no. 1 (1983): 24–27.

30. Josias Leslie Porter, *Jerusalem, Bethany and Bethlehem* (Jerusalem: Ariel, 1886), 28.

31. Ritmeyer, *The Quest*, 110.

32. Leen Ritmeyer, "The Eastern Gate of the Temple Mount in Jerusalem," Ritmeyer Archaeological Design, May 8, 2013, https://www.ritmeyer.com/2013/05/08/the-eastern-gate-of-the-temple-mount-in-jerusalem/.

33. Charles Warren and Claude R. Conder, *The Survey of Western Palestine: Jerusalem* (Committee of the Palestine Exploration Fund, 1884), 13, 22.

34. Peters, *Jerusalem*, 203.

35. James Fergusson, *The Temples of the Jews and the Other Buildings in the Haram Area at Jerusalem* (London: J. Murray, 1878), 145.

36. Joe Zias and Émile Puech, "The Tomb of Absalom Reconsidered," *Near Eastern Archaeology* 68, no. 4 (2005): 148–65.

37. Natsheh, *Ottoman Jerusalem*, 490 (see chap. 2, n. 24).

38. This image is available from the United States Library of Congress's Prints and Photographs division under the digital ID matpc.05874.

39. Rivka Gonen. Contested Holiness: Jewish, Muslim and Christian Perspectives on the Temple Mount in Jerusalem (Jersey City, NJ: KTAV, 2003), 120–22.

40. See "Golden Gate: Fifth in the 'Gates of Jerusalem' Numismatic Bullion Series," The Holy Land Mint, 41.

41. Gonen. *Contested Holiness*, 122.

42. Kaufman, *The Temple Mount*, 110 (see chap. 2, n. 3).

43. Gabriel Barkay and Amos Kloner, "Jerusalem Tombs from the Days of the First Temple." *Biblical Archaeology Review* 12, no. 2 (1986): 22–39; Ritmeyer, *The Quest*, 129 (see chap. 2, n. 4).

44. Williams, *The Holy City*, 2:353–54 (see chap. 3, n.13); William Henry Bartlett, *Walks about the City and Environs of Jerusalem* (UK: A. Hall, Virtue, 1844), 175–76.

45. Main Photo by Andrew Shiva, Wikipedia, CC BY-SA 4.0, retrieved from https://commons.wikimedia.org/wiki/File:Temple_Mount_(Aerial_view,_2007)_07.jpg; the overlaid photo of the temple was taken by the author at the Israel National Museum, using the temple model designed by M. Avi-Yonah.

Chapter 4: Why the Temple Wasn't at the Dome of the Rock

1. Ritmeyer, *The Quest* (see chap. 2, n. 4).

2. Cristian Chirita, Wikipedia, CC BY-SA 3.0, accessed May 1, 2020, https://commons.wikimedia.org/wiki/File:CrossPatheeDome.jpg.

3. Flavius Josephus, *The Wars of the Jews*, bk. 7, ch. 1, in Whiston, *The Works of Josephus*, 751 (see chap. 3, n. 12).

4. *Dio's Roman History*, trans. Earnest Cary, vol. 8 (New York: G. P. Putnam's Sons, 1917), 447.

5. Martin Goodman, *Rome and Jerusalem: The Clash of Ancient Civilizations* (New York: Alfred A. Knopf, 2007), 462.

6. Ludwig August Dindorf, vol. 1, *Chronicon Paschale: Ad Exemplar Vaticanum* (n.p.: Garnier, 1865), 474.

7. Peters, *Jerusalem*, 129 (see chap. 3, n. 6).

8. *The Scriptores Historiae Augustae,* vol. 1, trans. David Magie (London: W. Heinemann, 1921), 42–43.

9. *The Scriptores Historiae Augustae,* vol. 2, trans. David Magie (London: W. Heinemann, 1924), 267.

10. Sir Charles William Wilson, contrib., *Itinerary from Bordeaux to Jerusalem*, emphasis added (see chap. 2, n. 16).

11. Admittedly, the idea of this statue being an original artifact in Israel from the second century has been challenged. Richard A. Gergel, "The Tel Shalem Hadrian Reconsidered," *American Journal of Archaeology* (1991): 231–51. However, while some interesting questions are raised, they are far from enough to discredit the find for purely subjective and stylistic questions. Furthermore, what they claim are likely modifications to the statue could just as easily be repairs.

12. Hershel Shanks, *Jerusalem's Temple Mount: from Solomon to the Golden Dome* (New York: Continuum, 2007), 48–51.

13. Charles Warren, *The Temple or the Tomb: Giving Further Evidence in Favour of the Authenticity of the Present Site of the Holy Sepulchre, and Pointing Out Some of the Principal Misconceptions Contained in Fergusson's "Holy Sepulchre" and "The Temples of the Jews."* (London: Richard Bentley and Son, 1880), 43.

14. "Plan of the Haram Area at the Present Time (1899)," accessed May 1, 2020, https://commons.wikimedia.org/wiki/File:MACCOUN(1899)_p221_PLAN_OF_THE_HARAM_AREA_AT_THE_PRESENT_TIME.jpg.

15. Averil Cameron and Stuart G. Hall, trans. *Eusebius' Life of Constantine* (Oxford, UK: Clarendon, 1999), bk. 3, chaps. 26–28.

16. Peters, *Jerusalem*, 131–40.

17. Williams, *The Holy City*, 2:333 (see chap. 3, n.13).

18. Williams, 338.

19. Fergusson, *The Temples of the Jews and the Other Buildings in the Haram Area at Jerusalem*, 197–98.

20. Peters, *Jerusalem*, 145–47.

21. Sozomen (c. AD 324–440), *A History of the Church in Nine Books* (n.p.: Aeterna, 2014), bk. 5, 196–98, emphasis added.

22. Mujir al-Din in A. S., Marmadji, *Textes Geographiques Arabes Sur la Palestine* (Paris: J. Gabalda et Cie), quoted in Peters, *Jerusalem*, 195.

23. *The History of al-Tabari*, vol. 12, trans. Yohanan Friedman (Albany: State University of New York Press, 2007), 193–96.

24. Fergusson, *The Temples of the Jews and the Other Buildings in the Haram Area at Jerusalem*, 225, emphasis added.

25. G. Le Strange, quoted in Peters, *Jerusalem*, 189.

26. Rina Avner, "The Initial Tradition of the Theotokos at the Kathisma: Earliest Celebrations and the Calendar," in *The Cult of the Mother of God in Byzantium: Text and Images*, ed. Leslie Brubaker and Mary B. Cunningham (n.p.: Routledge, 2016), 31–52.

27. Fergusson, *The Temples of the Jews and the Other Buildings in the Haram Area at Jerusalem*, 221–22.

28. Fergusson, 223–24.

29. Natsheh, *Ottoman Jerusalem*, 87–93 (see chap. 2, n. 24).

30. Peters, *Jerusalem*, 184.

31. Le Strange, in Peters, *Jerusalem*, 197.

32. Baldi, quoted in Peters, *Jerusalem*, 189–90.

33. Photius, quoted in John Wilkinson, *Jerusalem Pilgrims: Before the Crusades* (Havertown, PA: Oxbow Books, 2002), 258.

34. Benjamin de Tudèle, *The Itinerary of Benjamin of Tudela: Critical Text, Translation and Commentary*, trans. Marcus Nathan Adler (n.p.: Henry Frowde, 1907), 23.

35. de Tudèle, *The Itinerary of Benjamin of Tudela*, 22–23.

36. Peters, *Jerusalem*, 227.

37. Peters, 329.

38. Joseph ben Isaac (c. AD 1334), quoted in Peters, *Jerusalem*, 191–92.

39. Some may argue that "the Gate of Mercy" is an esoteric reference to the Western Wall. But based on the fact that "gate" is used, and there are no gates in that immediate part of the Western Wall, this seems unlikely.

40. Ritmeyer, *The Quest*, 265–77.

41. Ritmeyer, 258.

42. Ritmeyer, 246.

43. "Dome of the Rock," Library of Congress, Matson Photograph Collection, accessed May 4, 2020, https://commons.wikimedia.org/wiki/File:The_rock_of_the_Dome_of_the_Rock_Corrected.jpg.

44. Kaufman, *The Temple Mount*, 58.

45. Yuval Baruch, Ronny Reich, and Débora Sandhaus, "A Decade of Archaeological Exploration on the Temple Mount," *Tel Aviv* 45, no. 1 (2018): 4.

46. Ritmeyer, *The Quest*, 262–63.

47. *Indiana Jones and the Last Crusade*, directed by Steven Spielberg (Paramount Pictures, 1989).

48. This point is detailed in the article by Asher Kaufman, "Where the Ancient Temple of Jerusalem Stood." *Biblical Archaeology Review* 9, no. 2 (1983): 40-59.

49. Ritmeyer, *The Quest*, 168–69.

50. Josephus, *Wars of the Jews*, bk. 5, chap. 4, from Whiston, *The Works of Josephus*, 704, emphasis added.

51. Edward Robinson and Eli Smith, et al., *Biblical Researches in Palestine and the Adjacent Regions: A Journal of Travels in the Years 1838 & 1852*. In Three Volumes (London: John Murray, 1856), 293; Williams, *The Holy City*, 2:349–53 (see chap. 3, n.13).

52. Sir Charles William Wilson, contrib., *Itinerary from Bordeaux to Jerusalem*, 45–55.

53. Kaufman, *The Temple Mount*, 30-55.

54. Baruch, Reich, and Sandhaus, "A Decade of Archaeological Exploration on the Temple Mount," 3–22.

Chapter 5: Why the Temple Wasn't to the South

1. Andrew Shiva, Wikipedia, CC BY-SA 4.0, accessed May 4, 2020, https://commons.wikimedia.org/wiki/File:Jerusalem-2013(2)-Aerial-Temple_Mount-(south_exposure).jpg.

2. Warren, *The Temple or the Tomb* (see chap. 4, n. 13).

3. Norma Robertson, *Locating Solomon's Temple* (updated June 2014), accessed May 4, 2020, http://templemountlocation.com/chapterOne.html.

4. Fergusson, *The Temples of the Jews and the Other Buildings in the Haram Area at Jerusalem* (see chap. 3, n.35).

5. Ferguson, plate 7.

6. Price, *Rose Guide to the Temple*, 70 (see chap. 3, n. 4).
7. Warren, *The Temple or the Tomb*.
8. Warren, 82, 84.
9. Wilson and Warren, *The Recovery of Jerusalem*, vol. 1 (see chap. 2, n. 11).
10. Ritmeyer, *The Quest*, 110–13 (see chap. 2, n. 4).
11. Wilson and Warren, *The Recovery of Jerusalem*, 159–69.
12. Ritmeyer, *The Quest*, 105–7.
13. Wilson and Warren, *The Recovery of Jerusalem*, 151.
14. Berthold Werner, "Madaba Map," CC BY 3.0, accessed May 5, 2020, https://commons.wikimedia.org/wiki/File:Madaba_BW_8.JPG.
15. Ritmeyer, *The Quest*, 198–200.
16. Tuvia Sagiv, The Location of the Temple on the Temple Mount Based on the Aqueduct and Rock Levels at Mount Moriah in Jerusalem (2008), accessed May 5, 2020, http://www.templemount.org/tuviatemple.pdf.
17. Tuvia Sagiv, "Determination of the Location of the Temple Based on the Angle of Sight of Agrippa II," April 4, 2004, http://www.templemount.org/sagiv2/index.html.

Chapter 6: Why the Temple Wasn't at the City of David

1. Andrew Shiva, Wikipedia, CC BY-SA 4.0, accessed May 5, 2020, https://commons.wikimedia.org/wiki/File:Jerusalem-2013(2)-Temple_Mount-Southern_Wall_(south_exposure).jpg.
2. Ernest L. Martin, *The Temples That Jerusalem Forgot* (Portland: ASK Publications, 2000).
3. Marilyn Sams, *The Jerusalem Temple Mount Myth* (Marilyn Sams, 2014); Robert Cornuke, *Temple: Amazing New Discoveries that Change Everything about the Location of Solomon's Temple* (Charlotte: LifeBridge Books, 2014).
4. The grammatical distinction is just as clear in Greek as it is in English.
5. The Temple Mount is on average 300 meters wide and 475 meters long and at its tallest point is about 47 meters tall. Using an average wall height of 25 meters, the volume encompassed by the Temple Mount is 3,562,500m³. To put that in perspective, the volume of the Great Pyramid at Giza is approximately 2,650,000m³.
6. Josephus, *Antiquities of the Jews*, bk. 15, chap. 11, from Whiston, *The Works of Josephus*, 423–24.
7. Martin, *The Temples That Jerusalem Forgot*, 58, 163–67.
8. Yaakov Katz, "New Discovery in Jerusalem's City of David: 2,000-Year-Old Pilgrimage Road," *Jerusalem Post*, June 30, 2019, https://www.jpost.com/Magazine/Ascending-a-2000-year-old-Pilgrimage-Road-593766.
9. Josephus, *The Wars of the Jews*, bk. 7, chap. 1, in Whiston, *The Works of Josephus*, 750–51.
10. Eilat Mazar, "The Temple Mount Excavations in Jerusalem 1968–1978 Directed by Benjamin Mazar: Final Reports Volume IV: The Tenth Legion in Aelia Capitolina." *Qedem* 52, no. 3 (2011): 348.
11. Gabriel Barkay and Zachi Dvira, "Relics in Rubble: The Temple Mount Sifting Project," *Biblical Archaeology Review* 42, no. 6 (2016): 44–55.
12. Martin, *The Temples That Jerusalem Forgot*, 82–84.
13. Martin, 85–87.
14. Martin, 88–92, 135–36.

15. The historic accounts are found in chapter 4 (see notes 23 and 25).
16. Martin, *The Temples Jerusalem Forgot*, 134.
17. Martin, 159.
18. The historic account is found in chapter 4 (see note 23).
19. Cornuke, *Temple*, 65-80.
20. "Bob Cornuke - Temple Defense," Prophecy in the News, https://www.youtube.com/watch?v=yxnJW2LWSOw, accessed on May 16, 2020.
21. Stewart, *Extracts from Aristeas, Hecataeus, Origen and Other Early Writers*, 9. [referenced online at: https://www.youtube.com/watch?v=4oBWNp6Rq9s]
22. There are objections to the accuracy of Hecataeus' account in any case, and in the introduction to the translation it is noted that Origen declared the account spurious, but nevertheless, rather than confirming a City of David hypothesis it presents better evidence for rejecting the idea.
23. Cornuke, *Temple*, 85.
24. Martin, *The Temples That Jerusalem Forgot*, 288–92.
25. Martin, 284.
26. Tacitus, *History*, ix.
27. *Ibid*, bk. 5, par. 12.
28. "Eusebius' Recording of Aristeas," in Martin, *The Temples That Jerusalem Forgot*, 289.
29. Ruth Shahack-Grass, Mor Gafri, and Israel Finkelstein, "Identifying Threshing Floors in the Archaeological Record: A Test Case at Iron Age Tel Megiddo, Israel," *Journal of Field Archaeology* 34, no. 2 (2009): 171–84.
30. Israel *Antiquities Authority*, "Excavation Reveals Ancient Aqueduct in Jerusalem," Israel Ministry of Foreign Affairs (website), June 16, 2009, https://mfa.gov.il/mfa/israelexperience/history/pages/excavation%20reveals%20ancient%20aqueduct%20in%20jerusalem16-jun-2009.aspx.
31. Leen Ritmeyer, "Trumpeting on the Temple Mount: How a Hebrew Inscription Blasts the Temple Mount Deniers," Ritmeyer.com, January 24, 2018, https://www.ritmeyer.com/2018/01/24/trumpeting-on-the-temple-mount/
32. *Ibid*.
33. James King. *Recent Discoveries on the Temple Hill at Jerusalem*, 36.

Chapter 7: Time to Rebuild the Temple

1. Hillel Fendel, "49% Want Holy Temple Rebuilt," Arutz Sheva, July 18, 2010, http://www.israelnationalnews.com/News/News.aspx/138655.
2. Lahav Harkov, "Poll: 68% of Israeli Jews Want Prayer on Temple Mount," *Jerusalem Post*, November 3, 2017, https://www.jpost.com/Israel-News/68-percent-of-Israeli-Jews-want-Jewish-prayer-on-Temple-Mount-poll-513227.
3. Donald J. Trump, "Proclamation on Recognizing the Golan Heights as Part of the State of Israel," March 25, 2019, https://www.whitehouse.gov/presidential-actions/proclamation-recognizing-golan-heights-part-state-israel/.
4. Peter Schäfer, *The History of the Jews in the Greco-Roman World* (London: Routledge, 2003), 187.
5. "Sanhedrin Launched in Tiberias," Arutz Sheva, January 20, 2005, http://www.israelnationalnews.com/News/News.aspx/70349.

ENDNOTES

6. "Sacrifice of the Paschal Lamb Returns to Jerusalem after Millennia," Breaking Israel News, April 19, 2016, https://www.breakingisraelnews.com/66076/passover-sacrifice-makes-comeback-overlooking-temple-mount-photos/.

7. See the Temple Institute website, https://www.templeinstitute.org/main.htm.

8. "Temple Institute Announces School to Train Levitical Priests," Jewish Telegraphic Agency, August 2, 2016, https://www.jta.org/2016/08/02/israel/temple-institute-announces-school-to-train-levitical-priests.

9. Ahuva Balofsky, "Jewish Temple Altar Rebuilt, Ready for Use," Israel National News, March 9, 2015, https://www.breakingisraelnews.com/32009/altar-jewish-holy-temple-rebuilt-jewish-world/.

10. Red Heifer Birth, Paves Way for Renewed Temple Service," Breaking Israel News, September 8, 2018, https://www.breakingisraelnews.com/113476/temple-institute-certifies-red-heifer/.

11. "Blueprints for the Holy Temple," Olive Press, February 12, 2011, https://olivepress.wordpress.com/2011/02/12/blueprints-for-the-holy-temple/.

12. Hillel Weiss and R. Chaim Richman, "The Sanhedrin's Decision Regarding the Holy Temple, the Temple Mount, and Jerusalem," cached on the Sanhedrin Court Activity page at JewishRoots.net, June 6, 2005, https://www.jewishroots.net/library/end-times/sanhedrin-activity.html.

13. Israel relinquished control back to Jordan in 1967, as part of the peace agreement with the country.

14. Mamoon Alabasi, "Jordan Remains Vulnerable to ISIS but the Fight Is On," *Arab Weekly*, November 18, 2018, https://thearabweekly.com/jordan-remains-vulnerable-isis-fight.

15. Yossi Klein Halevi, "The Astonishing Israeli Concession of 1967," *The Atlantic*, June 7, 2017, https://www.theatlantic.com/international/archive/2017/06/israel-paratroopers-temple-mount-1967/529365/

16. Teddy Kollek and Moshe Pearlman, *Jerusalem: A History of Forty Centuries* (New York: Random House, 1968), 250–52.

17. Shimon Re'em, Female Prisoners of War in Israel's War of Independence (Haifa: National Midrasha for Underground and Zionism Studies, 2010).

Chapter 8: A Joint-Use Plan for the Temple Mount

1. "Map of Temple Mount," CC BY-SA 1.0, accessed May 11, 2020, https://commons.wikimedia.org/w/index.php?curid=63360961.

2. Norman H. Anderson, *Jerusalem's Temple Now! Political, Military, Economic, and Religious Implications* (n.p.: Lifebridge, 2015).

3. Tuvia Sagiv, "Where Is the Temple?" Passover 1996,, http://www.templemount.org/sagiv00.html.

4. Abdul Hadi Palazzi, *The Jewish-Moslem Dialogue and the Question of Jerusalem* (Israel: Institute of the World Jewish Congress, 1997).

5. "Jerusalem Embassy Act of 1995," Public Law 104-45, Nov. 8, 1995, https://www.congress.gov/104/plaws/publ45/PLAW-104publ45.pdf

6. "Statement by President Trump on Jerusalem," White House Press Release, Dec. 6, 2017, https://www.whitehouse.gov/briefings-statements/statement-president-trump-jerusalem/

7. "UN Resolutions Singling Out Israel," UN Watch, November 15, 2018, https://unwatch.org/2018-un-general-assembly-resolutions-singling-israel-texts-votes-analysis/.

8. See *Peace to Prosperity: A Vision to Improve the Lives of the Palestinian and Israeli People*, January 2020, https://www.whitehouse.gov/wp-content/uploads/2020/01/Peace-to-Prosperity-0120.pdf.

9. Adam Eliyahu Berkowitz, "Thanks to Trump: Pascal Lamb Could Be Sacrificed on Temple Mount for First Time in 2,000 Years," *Breaking Israel News*, February 27, 2020, https://www.breakingisrael-news.com/145899/thanks-to-trump-pascal-lamb-could-be-sacrificed-on-temple-mount-for-first-time-in-2000-years/.

10. *Peace to Prosperity*, 16.

11. Aaron Reich, "Kushner: US to Approve Annexation If Palestinians Don't Negotiate," *Jerusalem Post*, March 8, 2020, https://www.jpost.com/Middle-East/Kushner-US-to-approve-Israeli-annexation-if-Palestinians-dont-negotiate-620135.

12. Dara Linddara, "Why are you supposed to say 'next year in Jerusalem'?" Vox, Aug 5, 2014, https://www.vox.com/2014/8/5/18002034/why-are-you-supposed-to-say-next-year-in-jerusalem.

Epilogue

1. Alice Calaprice and Trevor Lipscombe, *Einstein: A Biography* (Westport, CT: Greenwood, 2005), front matter.

BIBLIOGRAPHY

Adler, Marcus Nathan. *The Itinerary of Benjamin of Tudela: Critical Text, Translation and Commentary.* Henry Frowde, 1907.

Al-Tabari. *History of al-Tabari, The.* Vol. 12, *The Battle of al-Qadisiyyah and the Conquest of Syria and Palestine AD 635–637/AH 14–15.* SUNY Press, 2015.

Anderson, Norman H. *Jerusalem's Temple Now: Political, Military, Economic and Religious Implications.* Charlotte: LifeBridge Books, 2015.

Arculf, A. *The Pilgrimage of Arculfus in the Holy Land (670 AD).* London: Library of the Palestine Pilgrims Pilgrim's Text Society, 1895.

Ariel, Yisrael. *The Odyssey of the Third Temple.* Translated by Chaim Richman. G. Israel Publications & Productions/Temple Institute, 1993.

Bahat, Dan, Hayim Rubinstein, and Rami Yizre'el. *The Carta Jerusalem Atlas.* Carta Jerusalem, 2011.

Bartlett, William Henry. *Walks about the City and Environs of Jerusalem.* London: George Virtue, 1846.

Bar-Yosef, Ofer, A. Nigel Goring-Morris, and Avi Gophner, eds. *Gilgal: Early Neolithic Occupations in the Lower Jordan Valley, the Excavations of Tamar Noy.* Oxford, UK: Oxbow Books, 2010.

Bauer, Susan Wise. *The History of the Medieval World: From the Conversion of Constantine to the First Crusade.* New York: W. W. Norton, 2010.

Ben-Dov, Meir, Mordecai Naor, and Zeev Aner. (1983). *The Western Wall.* Translated by Raphael Posner. Jerusalem: Ministry of Defense Publishing House.

Ben-Tor, Amnon. *The Archaeology of Ancient Israel.* New Haven, CT: Yale University Press and the Open University of Israel, 1992.

Bildersee, Adele. *Jewish Post-Biblical History through Great Personalities.* Cincinnati: The Union of American Hebrew Congregations, 1918.

Bordeaux Pilgrim. *Itinerary from Bordeaux to Jerusalem: The Bordeaux Pilgrim (333 A.D.).* Translated by Aubrey Stewart. London: Palestine Pilgrim's Text Society, 1887.

Cameron, Averil, and Stuart Hall, eds. *Eusebius' Life of Constantine.* Oxford, UK: Clarendon Press, 1999.

Cary, Earnest, trans. *Dio's Roman History,* New York: G. P. Putnam's Sons, 1917.

Chareyron, Nicole. *Pilgrims to Jerusalem in the Middle Ages.* Translated by W. Donald Wilson. New York: Columbia University Press, 2000.

Cornuke, Robert. *Temple: Amazing New Discoveries That Change Everything about the Location of Solomon's Temple.* Charlotte: LifeBridge Books, 2014.

Davidson, William. *The William Davidson Digital Edition of the Koren Noé Talmud, with Commentary by Rabbi Adin Even-Israel Steinsaltz,* Koren Publishers, online at: http://sefaria.org.

De Vogüé, Melchior. *Le temple de Jérusalem: Monographie du Haram-ech-Chérif: suivive d'un essai sur la topographie de la Ville-Sainte.* Paris : Noblet & Baudry, 1864.

Fergusson, James *The Temples of the Jews and the Other Buildings in the Haram Area at Jerusalem.* London: J. Murray, 1878.

Finkelstein, Israel, and Neil Asher Silberman. *The Bible Unearthed: Archaeology's New Vision of Ancient Israel and the Origin of Its Sacred Texts.* New York: Free Press, 2001.

Galor, Katharina. *Finding Jerusalem: Archaeology between Science and Ideology.* Oakland: University of California Press, 2017.

Garfinkel, Yosef, Saar Ganor, and Michael G. Hasel. *In the Footsteps of King David: Revelations from an Ancient Biblical City*. London: Thames & Hudson, 2018.

Garfinkel, Yosef, and Madeleine Mumcuoglu. *Solomon's Temple and Palace: New Archaeological Discoveries*. Translated by Miriam Feinberg Vamosh. Jerusalem: Bible Lands Museum Jerusalem, 2016.

Geva, Hillel, ed. *Ancient Jerusalem Revealed: Archaeological Discoveries, 1998–2018*. Israel Exploration Society, 2019.

———. *Ancient Jerusalem Revealed*. Israel Exploration Society, 1994.

Gonen, Rivka. *Contested Holiness: Jewish, Muslim, and Christian Perspectives on the Temple Mount in Jerusalem*. Jersey City: KTAV, 2003.

Goodman, Martin. *Rome and Jerusalem: The Clash of Ancient Civilizations*. New York: Alfred A. Knopf, 2007.

Goldstein, Daniel. *The Third Temple: A Sign of the Coming Messiah*. Jerusalem: Jewels of Judaism, 2018,

Gower, Ralph. *The New Manners and Customs of the Bible*. Chicago: Moody Press, 1987.

Grant, Michael. *Herod the Great*. New York: American Heritage Press, 1971.

Gutmann, Joseph. *The Temple of Solomon: Archaeological Fact and Medieval Tradition in Christian, Islamic and Jewish Art*. Missoula, MT: Scholars Press, 1976.

Holum, Kenneth G., Robert L. Hohlfelder, Robert J. Bull, and Avner Raban. *King Herod's Dream: Caesarea on the Sea*. New York: W. W. Norton, 1988.

Horowitz, Ahron. *Discovering the City of David: A Journey to the Source*. Jerusalem: Koren, 2015.

James, Peter, and Peter G. van der Veen, eds. *Solomon and Shishak: Current Perspectives from Archaeology, Epigraphy, History and Chronology, Proceedings of the Third BICANE Colloquium held at Sidney Sussex College, Cambridge, 26–27 March 2011*. Oxford: BAR, 2015.

Jeffrey, Grant R. *The New Temple and the Second Coming.* Waterbrook Press, 2007.

Jeremias, Joachim. *Jerusalem in the Time of Jesus: An Investigation into Economic and Social Conditions During the New Testament Period.* Translated by F. H. and C. H. Cave. Philadelphia: Fortress Press, 1969.

Jones, Melanie S., and Rachael D. Wakefield, eds. *Aspects of Stone Weathering, Decay and Conservation. Proceedings of the 1997 Stone Weathering and Atmospheric Pollution Network Conference (SWAPNET '97).* London: Imperial College Press, 1999.

Kaufmann, Asher Selig. *The Temple Mount: Where Is the Holy of Holies?* Jerusalem: Har Yeraeh Press, 2004.

Kennedy, David, and Robert Bewley. *Ancient Jordan from the Air.* London: Council for British Research in the Levant, 2004.

King, James. *Recent Discoveries on the Temple Hill at Jerusalem.* Religious Tract Society, 1884.

Kollek, Teddy, and Moshe Pearlman. *Jerusalem: A History of Forty Centuries.* New York: Random House, 1968.

Landay, Jerry M. *Dome of the Rock.* Edited by Joseph L. Gardener. New York: Newsweek, 1972.

Le Strange, G., ed. *Description of Syria: Including Palestine.* Vol. 3. London: Palestine Pilgrim's Text Society, 1896.

Levy, Thomas E. *Journey to the Copper Age: Archaeology in the Holy Land.* San Diego: San Diego Museum of Man, 2007.

Lustig, Michael. *Gate of Heaven: The Holy Mountain of Jerusalem.* Lexington, KY, 2018.

Magie, David, trans. *The Scriptores Historiae Augustae.* Vol. 1, London: W. Heinemann, 1921.

———. *The Scriptores Historiae Augustae.* Vol. 2, London: W. Heinemann, 1924.

Magness, Jodi. *The Archaeology of the Holy Land: From the Destruction of Solomon's Temple to the Muslim Conquest.* Cambridge, UK: Cambridge University Press, 2012.

Martin, Ernest L. *The Temples That Jerusalem Forgot.* Portland: ASK Publications, 2000.

Mazar, Amihai. *Archaeology of the Land of the Bible 10,000–586 B.C.E.* New York: Doubleday, 1992.

Mazar, Eilat. *Discovering the Solomonic Wall in Jerusalem: A Remarkable Archaeological Adventure.* Jerusalem: Shoham Academic Research and Publication, 2011.

McDowell, Josh, and Sean McDowell. *Evidence That Demands a Verdict: Life-Changing Truth for a Skeptical World.* Nashville: Thomas Nelson, 2017.

McKitterick, Rosamond. *Atlas of the Medieval World.* Oxford: Oxford University Press, 2004.

Millgram, Abraham E. *Jerusalem Curiosities.* New York: Jewish Publication Society, 1990.

The Misnah. Translated from the Hebrew by H. Danby, Oxford, 1933.

Natsheh, Yusuf. *Ottoman Jerusalem: The Living City: 1517–1917.* Edited by Sylvia Auld and Robert Hillenbrand. London: Altajir World of Islam Trust, 2000.

Netzer, Ehud. *The Architecture of Herod, the Great Builder.* Tubingen, DEU: Mohr Siebeck, 2006.

O'Connor, Jerome Murphy. *The Holy Land: An Archaeological Guide from Earliest Times to 1700.* Oxford: Oxford University Press, 1980.

Paschale. *Chronicon Paschale 284–628 AD.* Trans. with a commentary by M. Whitby and M. Whitby. Liverpool: Liverpool University Press, 1989.

Peters, Francis E. *Jerusalem: The Holy City in the Eyes of Chroniclers, Visitors, Pilgrims, and Prophets from the Days of Abraham to the Beginnings of Modern Times.* Princeton, NJ: Princeton University Press, 1985.

Poggibonsi, Fra. Nicollo. *A Voyage Beyond the Seas (1346–1350)*. Translated by Fr. T. Bellorini O.F.Am. and Fr. E. Hoade O.F.M. on the Occasion of the Sixth, Centenary. Jerusalem: Franciscan Press, 1945.

Price, Ira Maurice. *The Monuments and the Old Testament: Oriental Light on Holy Writ*. Philadelphia: American Baptist Publication Society, 1907.

Price, Randall. *The Stones Cry Out*. Harvest House Publishers, 1997.

Price, Randall. *Rose Guide to the Temple*. Edited by Jessica Curiel. Peabody, MA: Rose Publishing, 2012.

Pritchard, J. B., ed. *Everyday Life in Bible Times*. National Geographic Society Book Service, 1967.

Procopius. *Buildings*. Translation by H. B. Dewing with the collaboration of G. Downey, Loeb Classical Library, 1971.

Richardson, Peter. *Herod: King of the Jews and Friend of the Romans*. Columbia: University of South Carolina Press, 1996.

Richman, Chaim. *The Holy Temple of Jerusalem*. Jerusalem: Temple Institute, 1997.

Ritmeyer, Leen. *The Quest: Revealing the Temple Mount in Jerusalem*. Jerusalem: Carta, 2006.

Rodkinson, M., ed. *The Babylonian Talmud*. Talmud Society, 1918.

Roller, Duane W. *The Building Program of Herod the Great*. Berkeley: University of California Press, 1998.

Sams, Marilyn. *The Jerusalem Temple Mount Myth*. Marilyn Sams, 2015.

Schäfer, Peter. *The History of the Jews in the Greco-Roman World: The Jews of Palestine from Alexander the Great to the Arab Conquest*. London: Routledge, 2003.

Seely, David Rolf, and William J. Hamblin. *Solomon's Temple: Myth and History*. London: Thames & Hudson, 2007.

Shanks, Hershel. *Jerusalem's Temple Mount: From Solomon to the Golden Dome*. New York: Continuum International, 2007.

Skolfield, Ellis H. *The False Prophet.* Fish House Publishing, 2001.

Slemming, Charles W. *Made According to the Pattern.* Fort Washington, PA: Christian Literature Crusade, 1971.

Stewart, Aubrey, Hecataeus (Abderita), and Origen. *Extracts from Aristeas, Hecataeus, Origen and Other Early Writers:* Trans. by Aubrey Stewart. Palestine Pilgrims' Text Society, 1895.

Tacitus, Cornelius. *The Complete Works of Tacitus.* Translated by Alfred John Church and William J. Brodribb. Edited by Moses Hadas. New York: Modern Library, 1942.

Turtledove, H., ed. *The Chronicle of Theophanes: Anni Mundi 6095–6305 (AD 602–813).* Philadelphia: University of Pennsylvania Press, 1982.

Warren, Charles. *The Temple or the Tomb: Giving Further Evidence in Favour of the Authenticity of the Present Site of the Holy Sepulchre and Pointing Out Some of the Principal Misconceptions Contained in Fergusson's "Holy Sepulchre" and "The Temples of the Jews."* London: Richard Bentley, 1880.

Warren, Charles, and Claude Reignier Conder. *The Survey of Western Palestine: Jerusalem.* London: The Committee of the Palestine Exploration Fund, 1889.

Waters, Jamie L. *Threshing Floors in Ancient Israel: Their Ritual and Symbolic Significance.* Minneapolis: Fortress Press, 2015.

Whiston, William. *The Works of Josephus: Complete and Unabridged.* Peabody, MA: Hendrickson, 1987.

Wilkinson, John, trans. *Jerusalem Pilgrims: Before the Crusades.* Oxford, UK: Oxbow Books, 2002.

Williams, George. *The Holy City.* Vols. 1 and 2, London, 1849.

Willibaldus. *The Hodoeporicon of Saint Willibald (754 A.D.).* Translated by Reverend Canon Brownlow. London: Palestine Pilgrims' Text Society, 1895.

Wilson, Charles W., and Charles Warren. *The Recovery of Jerusalem: A Narrative of Exploration & Discovery in the Holy Land.* Vol. 1. London: Richard Bentley and Son, 1871.

Wolff, Odilo. *Der Tempel von Jerusalem: Und Seine Maasse.* Graz, AT: Verlags-Buchhandlung Styria, 1887.

Wright, George Ernest, and Floyd Vivian Filson, eds. *The Westminster Historical Atlas of the Bible.* Philadelphia: Westminster Press, 1956.

Wright, Thomas. *Early Travels in Palestine.* N.p.: Courier Corporation, 2003.

APPENDIX

TEMPLE MOUNT PLACEMENT VIEWS

This chronological list is an attempt to capture all of the principal published views on the subject. It may still be missing some, particularly if they are published in languages other than English. No published view has been intentionally omitted.

1. Lightfoot, Rev. John, DD. *The Works of the Reverend and Learned John Lightfoot D.D. Late Master of Katherine Hall in Cambridge; Such as Were, and Such as Never before Were Printed*. Two vols. London, 1664.
2. Kiepert, Heinrich, and E. G. Schultz. *Jerusalem: Eine Vorlesung*. Berlin: S. Schropp, 1845.
3. Williams, George. *The Holy City*, Two vols. London: John W. Parker, 1849.
4. Tobler, Titus. *Denkblatter aus Jerusalem*. St. Gallen-Konstanz, 1852.
5. Thrupp, Joseph Francis. *Antient Jerusalem: A New Investigation into the History, Topography and Plan of the City, Environs, and Temple, Designed Principally to Illustrate the Records and Prophecies of Scripture*. Cambridge, UK: Macmillan, 1855.

6. Robinson, Edward, and Eli Smith, et al. *Biblical Researches in Palestine and the Adjacent Regions: A Journal of Travels in the Years 1838 and 1852. In Three Volumes.* London: John Murray, 1856.

7. Barclay, James Turner. *The City of the Great King; Jerusalem as It Was, as It Is, and as It Is to Be.* Philadelphia: Challen and Sons, 1858.

8. Lewin, Thomas. *Jerusalem: A Sketch of the City and Temple from the Earliest Times to the Siege by Titus.* London: Longman, Green, Longman and Roberts, 1861.

9. de Vogüé, Melchior. *Le Temple de Jerusalem.* Paris, 1864.

10. Rosen, Georg. *Das Haram von Jerusalem und der Tempelplatz des Moria.* Gotha, DEU: Verlag von Rud. Busser, 1866.

11. de Saulcy, Louis Félicien Joseph Caignart. *Mémoire sur la Nature et l'âge Respectif des Divers Appareils de Maçonnerie Employés Dans L'enceinte Extérieure du Haram-ech-Chérif de Jérusalem.* Paris : Imprimerie Impériale, 1866.

12. Fergusson, James. *The Temples of the Jews and the Other Buildings in the Haram Area at Jerusalem*, London: J. Murray, 1878.

13. Warren, Charles. *The Temple or the Tomb.* London, 1880.

14. Warren Charles, and Claude R. Conder, *The Survey of Western Palestine: Jerusalem.* London, 1884.

15. Porter, Josias Leslie. *Jerusalem, Bethany, and Bethlehem.* Jerusalem: Ariel, 1886.

16. Wolff, P. Odilo. *Der Tempel von Jerusalem: Und Seine Maasse.* Graz, AT: Verlags-Buchhandlung Styria, 1887.

17. Schick, Conrad. *Die Stiftshutte, der Tempel in Jerusalem und der Tempelplatz der Jetztzeit.* Berlin, 1896.

18. Watson, Charles M. "The Site of the Temple," *Palestine Exploration Fund Quarterly* (1896): 47–60 and 226–28.

19. Leeper, J.L. "Remains of the Temple at Jerusalem." *The Biblical World* 22, no. 5 (1903): 329-41.

20. Mommert, Carl. *Topographie des alten Jerusalem, Zweiter Tell: Das Salomonische Tempel—und Palast—quartier auf Moriah.* Leipzig, DEU, 1903.

21. Dalman, Gustaf. "Der zweite Tempel zu Jerusalem," *Palastina-Jahrbuch* 5 (1909): 29-57.

22. Hanauer, J. E. *Walks in and around Jerusalem*. Jerusalem: Church Missions to the Jews, 1926.

23. Hollis, Frederick. *The Archaeology of Herod's Temple: With a Commentary on the Tractate Middoth*, London, 1934.

24. Simons, Jan. *Jerusalem in the Old Testament*, Leiden, NL, 1952.

25. Vincent, Louis-Hughes. *Jerusalem de l'Ancien Testament*, 3 vols., Paris, 1954.

26. Avi-Yonah, Michael. "The Facade of Herod's Temple, an Attempted Reconstruction," *Religions in Antiquity* (1968): 327–35.

27. Jacobson, David M. "Ideas Concerning the Plan of Herod's Temple," *Palestine Exploration Quarterly* 112, no. 1 (1980): 33–40, DOI: 10.1179/peq.1980.112.1.33.

28. Kaufman, Asher S. "Where the Ancient Temple of Jerusalem Stood." *Biblical Archaeology Review* 9, no. 2 (1983): 40-59.

29. Sporty, Lawrence D. "The Location of the Holy House of Herod's Temple: Evidence from the Pre-Destruction Period." *Biblical Archaeologist* 53, no. 4 (1990): 194–204.

30. Bahat, Dan and Hayim Rubinstein. *The Illustrated Atlas of Jerusalem*. Jerusalem: Carta, 1990.

31. Jacobson, David. "The Plan of Herod's Temple." *Bulletin of the Anglo-Israel Archaeological Society* 10 (1990): 36–66.

32. Ariel, Israel. *The Odyssey of the Third Temple*. G. Israel Publications & Productions/ Temple Institute, 1993.

33. Ritmeyer, Leen. "Locating the Original Temple Mount," *Biblical Archaeology Review* 18, no. 2 (1992): 24–45, 64–65.

34. Richman, Chaim. *The Holy Temple of Jerusalem*. Jerusalem: Temple Institute, 1997.

35. Jacobson, David. "Sacred Geometry: Unlocking the Secrets of the Temple Mount, Parts 1 & 2." *Biblical Archaeology Review* (Jul/Aug & Sep/Oct 1999).

36. Martin, Ernest L. *The Temples That Jerusalem Forgot*. ASK Publications, 2000.

37. Skolfield, Ellis H. *The False Prophet*. Fish House Publishing, 2001.

38. Kaufmann, Asher Selig. *The Temple Mount: Where Is the Holy of Holies?* Jerusalem: Har Yéra'eh Press, 2004.

39. Ritmeyer, Leen. *The Quest: Revealing the Temple Mount in Jerusalem*.

Jerusalem: Carta, 2006.

40. Jeffrey, Grant R. *The New Temple and the Second Coming.* Waterbrook Press, 2007.

41. Sagiv, Tuvia. *The Location of the Temple on the Temple Mount Based on the Aqueduct and Rock Levels at Mount Moriah in Jerusalem* (Online, 2008), http://www.templemount.org/tuviatemple.pdf.

42. Robertson, Norma. *Locating Solomon's Temple* (Online, 2014), chap. 1, http://templemountlocation.com/chapterOne.html.

43. Sams, Marilyn. *The Jerusalem Temple Mount Myth.* Marilyn Sams, 2014.

44. Cornuke, Robert. *Temple: Amazing New Discoveries That Change Everything ABOUT the Location of Solomon's Temple.* Charlotte: LifeBridge Books, 2014.

45. Goldstein, Daniel. *The Third Temple: A Sign of the Coming Messiah.* Jerusalem: Jewels of Judaism, 2018,

46. Dolphin, Lambert, and Michael Kollen. "On the Location of the First and Second Temples in Jerusalem," last updated August 24, 2018, http://www.templemount.org/

47. theories.html.

48. Moskoff. Rabbi Harry. "Expert: Gold Dome of the Rock Not Where Jewish Temples Stood," Breaking Israel News, January 9, 2019, https://www.breakingisraelnews.com/120064/gold-dome-rock-jewish-temples-stood.

49. Baruch, Yuval, and Ronny Reich, "The Herodian Temple Mount in Jerusalem: A Few Remarks on Its Construction and Appearance." *CORNUCOPIA* (2019): 157–69.

50. Watchman Bible Study. "The Temple at the Dome of the Spirits/Tablets," last updated April 28, 2020, http://www.watchmanbiblestudy.com/BibleStudies/Temple/NorthernMount.html.

51. Widener, Christian. *The Temple Revealed: The True Location of the Jewish Temple Hidden in Plain Sight,* End Times Berean, 2020.

MORE SCRIPTURES REGARDING THE TEMPLE

While I wasn't able to include and discuss all of these scriptures in the book, they provide additional context for understanding God's plan for the temple throughout the ages.

You will bring them in and plant them on the mountain of your inheritance—the place, LORD, you made for your dwelling, the sanctuary, Lord, your hands established.

EXODUS 15:17

Then have them make a sanctuary for me, and I will dwell among them.

EXODUS 25:8

Observe my Sabbaths and have reverence for my sanctuary. I am the LORD.

LEVITICUS 19:30 AND 26:2

You must not sacrifice the Passover in any town the LORD your God gives you except in the place he will choose as a dwelling for his Name. There you must sacrifice the Passover in the evening, when the sun goes down, on the anniversary of your departure from Egypt.

DEUTERONOMY 16:5-6

Do not be stiff-necked, as your ancestors were; submit to the LORD. <u>Come to his sanctuary, which he has consecrated forever</u>. Serve the LORD your God, so that his fierce anger will turn away from you.

2 CHRONICLES 30:8

Although most of the many people who came from Ephraim, Manasseh, Issachar and Zebulun had not purified themselves, yet they ate the Passover, contrary to what was written. But Hezekiah prayed for them, saying, "<u>May the LORD, who is good, pardon everyone who sets their heart on seeking</u>

*God—the L*ORD*, the God of their ancestors—even if they are not clean according to the rules of the sanctuary.*"

2 CHRONICLES 30:18-19

But now, for a brief moment, the LORD *our God has been gracious in leaving us a remnant and giving us a firm place in his sanctuary, and so our God gives light to our eyes and a little relief in our bondage. Though we are slaves, our God has not forsaken us in our bondage. He has shown us kindness in the sight of the kings of Persia: He has granted us new life to rebuild the house of our God and repair its ruins, and he has given us a wall of protection in Judah and Jerusalem.*

EZRA 9:8-9

Mount Bashan, majestic mountain, Mount Bashan, rugged mountain, why gaze in envy, you rugged mountain, at the mountain where God chooses to reign, where the LORD *himself will dwell forever? The chariots of God are tens of thousands and thousands of thousands; the* LORD *has come from Sinai into his sanctuary. When you ascended on high, you took many captives; you received gifts from people, even from the rebellious—that you,* LORD *God, might dwell there.*

PSALM 68:15-18

Your procession, God, has come into view, the procession of my God and King into the sanctuary. In front are the singers, after them the musicians; with them are the young women playing the timbrels. Praise God in the great congregation; praise the LORD *in the assembly of Israel. There is the little tribe of Benjamin, leading them, there the great throng of Judah's princes, and there the princes of Zebulun and of Naphtali.*

PSALM 68:24-29

Because of your temple at Jerusalem kings will bring you gifts.

PSALM 68:29

Remember the nation you purchased long ago, the people of your inheritance, whom you redeemed — Mount Zion, where you dwelt. <u>Turn your steps toward these everlasting ruins, all this destruction the enemy has brought on the sanctuary.</u>

Your foes roared in the place where you met with us; they set up their standards as signs. They behaved like men wielding axes to cut through a thicket of trees. They smashed all the carved paneling with their axes and hatchets. <u>They burned your sanctuary to the ground; they defiled the dwelling place of your Name.</u> They said in their hearts, "We will crush them completely!" <u>They burned every place where God was worshiped in the land.</u>

PSALM 74:2-8

Open for me the gates of the righteous; I will enter and give thanks to the LORD.

This is the gate of the Lord through which the righteous may enter.

I will give you thanks, for you answered me; you have become my salvation.

The stone the builders rejected has become the cornerstone; the LORD has done this, and it is marvelous in our eyes. The LORD has done it this very day; let us rejoice today and be glad.

LORD, save us! LORD, grant us success!

Blessed is he who comes in the name of the LORD. From the house of the LORD we bless you.

The LORD is God, and he has made his light shine on us. With boughs in hand, join in the festal procession up to the horns of the altar.

You are my God, and I will praise you; you are my God, and I will exalt you.

Give thanks to the LORD, for he is good; his love endures forever.

PSALM 118:19-29

For the LORD has chosen Zion, he has desired it for his dwelling, saying, "This is my resting place for ever and ever; here I will sit enthroned, for I have desired it."

PSALM 132:13-14

In the last days, the mountain of the LORD's temple will be established as the highest of the mountains; it will be exalted above the hills, and all nations will stream to it.

Many peoples will come and say, "Come, let us go up to the mountain of the LORD, to the temple of the God of Jacob. He will teach us his ways, so that we may walk in his paths."

ISAIAH 2:2–3

All Kedar's flocks will be gathered to you, the rams of Nebaioth will serve you; they will be accepted as offerings on my altar, and I will adorn my glorious temple.

Who are these that fly along like clouds, like doves to their nests? Surely the islands look to me; in the lead are the ships of Tarshish, bringing your children from afar, with their silver and gold, to the honor of the LORD your God, the Holy One of Israel, for he has endowed you with splendor.

Foreigners will rebuild your walls, and their kings will serve you. Though in anger I struck you, in favor I will show you compassion. Your gates will always stand open, they will never be shut, day or night, so that people may bring you the wealth of the nations—their kings led in triumphal procession. For the nation or kingdom that will not serve you will perish; it will be utterly ruined.

The glory of Lebanon will come to you, the juniper, the fir and the cypress together, to adorn my sanctuary; and I will glorify the place for my feet. The children of your oppressors will come bowing before you; all who despise you will bow down at your feet and will call you the City of the LORD, Zion of the Holy One of Israel.

ISAIAH 60:7–14

Thus says the LORD of hosts, the God of Israel, "Once again they will speak this word in the land of Judah and in its cities when I restore their fortunes,
  'The LORD bless you, O abode of righteousness,
  O holy hill!'"

JEREMIAH 31:23 (NASB)

APPENDIX

*"This is what the Lord says: 'You say about this place, "It is a desolate waste, without people or animals." Yet in the towns of Judah and the streets of Jerusalem that are deserted, inhabited by neither people nor animals, there will be heard once more the sounds of joy and gladness, the voices of bride and bridegroom, **and the voices of those who bring thank offerings to the <u>house of the Lord</u>**, saying,*

"Give thanks to the Lord Almighty,
for the Lord is good; his love endures forever."

For I will restore the fortunes of the land as they were before,' says the Lord.

"This is what the Lord Almighty says: 'In this place, desolate and without people or animals—in all its towns there will again be pastures for shepherds to rest their flocks. In the towns of the hill country, of the western foothills and of the Negev, in the territory of Benjamin, in the villages around Jerusalem and in the towns of Judah, flocks will again pass under the hand of the one who counts them,' says the Lord.

"'The days are coming,' declares the Lord, 'when I will fulfill the good promise I made to the people of Israel and Judah.

"'In those days and at that time
I will make a righteous Branch sprout from David's line;
he will do what is just and right in the land.
In those days Judah will be saved
and Jerusalem will live in safety.
This is the name by which it will be called:
The Lord Our Righteous Savior.'

For this is what the Lord says: 'David will never fail to have a man to sit on the throne of Israel, nor will the Levitical priests ever fail to have a man to stand before me continually to offer burnt offerings, to burn grain offerings and to present sacrifices.'"

JEREMIAH 33:10-18 (EMPHASIS ADDED)

For zeal for your house consumes me, and the insults of those who insult you fall on me.

PSALM 69:9

On the twenty-first day of the seventh month, the word of the Lord came through the prophet Haggai: "Speak to Zerubbabel son of Shealtiel, governor of Judah, to Joshua son of Jozadak, [a] the high priest, and to the remnant of the people. Ask them, 'Who of you is left who saw this house in its former glory? How does it look to you now? Does it not seem to you like nothing? But now be strong, Zerubbabel,' declares the Lord. 'Be strong, Joshua son of Jozadak, the high priest. Be strong, all you people of the land,' declares the Lord, 'and work. For I am with you,' declares the Lord Almighty. 'This is what I covenanted with you when you came out of Egypt. And my Spirit remains among you. Do not fear.'

"This is what the Lord Almighty says: 'In a little while I will once more shake the heavens and the earth, the sea and the dry land. I will shake all nations, and what is desired by all nations will come, and I will fill this house with glory,' says the Lord Almighty. 'The silver is mine and the gold is mine,' declares the Lord Almighty. 'The glory of this present house will be greater than the glory of the former house,' says the Lord Almighty. 'And in this place I will grant peace,' declares the Lord Almighty."

HAGGAI 2:1-9

Solomon's Prayer of Dedication

Then Solomon stood before the altar of the LORD in front of the whole assembly of Israel and spread out his hands. Now he had made a bronze platform, five cubits long, five cubits wide and three cubits high, and had placed it in the center of the outer court. He stood on the platform and then knelt down before the whole assembly of Israel and spread out his hands toward heaven. He said:

"LORD, the God of Israel, there is no God like you in heaven or on earth—you who keep your covenant of love with your servants who continue wholeheartedly in your way. You have kept your promise to your servant David my father; with your mouth you have promised and with your hand you have fulfilled it—as it is today.

"Now, LORD, the God of Israel, keep for your servant David my father the promises you made to him when you said, 'You shall never fail to have

a successor to sit before me on the throne of Israel, if only your descendants are careful in all they do to walk before me according to my law, as you have done.' And now, LORD, the God of Israel, let your word that you promised your servant David come true.

"But will God really dwell on earth with humans? The heavens, even the highest heavens, cannot contain you. How much less this temple I have built! Yet, LORD my God, give attention to your servant's prayer and his plea for mercy. Hear the cry and the prayer that your servant is praying in your presence. May your eyes be open toward this temple day and night, this place of which you said you would put your Name there. May you hear the prayer your servant prays toward this place. Hear the supplications of your servant and of your people Israel when they pray toward this place. Hear from heaven, your dwelling place; and when you hear, forgive.

"When anyone wrongs their neighbor and is required to take an oath and they come and swear the oath before your altar in this temple, then hear from heaven and act. Judge between your servants, condemning the guilty and bringing down on their heads what they have done, and vindicating the innocent by treating them in accordance with their innocence.

"When your people Israel have been defeated by an enemy because they have sinned against you and when they turn back and give praise to your name, praying and making supplication before you in this temple, then hear from heaven and forgive the sin of your people Israel and bring them back to the land you gave to them and their ancestors.

"When the heavens are shut up and there is no rain because your people have sinned against you, and when they pray toward this place and give praise to your name and turn from their sin because you have afflicted them, then hear from heaven and forgive the sin of your servants, your people Israel. Teach them the right way to live, and send rain on the land you gave your people for an inheritance.

"When famine or plague comes to the land, or blight or mildew, locusts or grasshoppers, or when enemies besiege them in any of their cities, whatever disaster or disease may come, and when a prayer or plea is made by anyone among your people Israel—being aware of their afflictions and pains, and

spreading out their hands toward this temple—then hear from heaven, your dwelling place. Forgive, and deal with everyone according to all they do, since you know their hearts (for you alone know the human heart), so that they will fear you and walk in obedience to you all the time they live in the land you gave our ancestors.

"As for the foreigner who does not belong to your people Israel but has come from a distant land because of your great name and your mighty hand and your outstretched arm—when they come and pray toward this temple, then hear from heaven, your dwelling place. Do whatever the foreigner asks of you, so that all the peoples of the earth may know your name and fear you, as do your own people Israel, and may know that this house I have built bears your Name.

"When your people go to war against their enemies, wherever you send them, and when they pray to you toward this city you have chosen and the temple I have built for your Name, then hear from heaven their prayer and their plea, and uphold their cause.

"When they sin against you—for there is no one who does not sin—and you become angry with them and give them over to the enemy, who takes them captive to a land far away or near; and if they have a change of heart in the land where they are held captive, and repent and plead with you in the land of their captivity and say, 'We have sinned, we have done wrong and acted wickedly'; and if they turn back to you with all their heart and soul in the land of their captivity where they were taken, and pray toward the land you gave their ancestors, toward the city you have chosen and toward the temple I have built for your Name; then from heaven, your dwelling place, hear their prayer and their pleas, and uphold their cause. And forgive your people, who have sinned against you.

"Now, my God, may your eyes be open and your ears attentive to the prayers offered in this place.

Now arise, LORD God, and come to your resting place, you and the ark of your might. May your priests, LORD God, be clothed with salvation, may your faithful people rejoice in your goodness. LORD God, do not reject your anointed one. Remember the great love promised to David your servant."

2 CHRONICLES 6:12–42

THE SEVEN TEMPLES FOUND IN SCRIPTURE

1. God's eternal temple in Heaven—We see this several places in scripture (Isaiah 6:1-4, 2 Corinthians 5:1, Revelation 7:15 & 11:19). This is the place where God dwells in Heaven in unapproachable light, but after the Great White Throne judgment, it will come down to the new heaven and a new earth where believers will dwell with God as his children forevermore.

2. Solomon's temple—The temple first built by Solomon found in 1 Kings chapters 5-9, which was built on the location shown to his father David—the threshing floor of Araunah.

3. Zerubbabel's temple—A rebuilt temple, which was only a shadow of its former glory and is described in the book of Ezra.

4. Herod's temple—The reconstructed and beautified temple built by Herod the Great around the time of Christ, which replaced Zerubbabel's temple and is mentioned in Luke 21:5, John 2:20, Mark 13:1 and was also described in great detail by Flavius Josephus.

5. The Church—A temple made of living stones not built by human hands. The spiritual temple that Paul and others described in 1 Corinthians 3:16-17 & 6:19, 2 Corinthians 6:16, Ephesians 2:19-22, 1 Peter 2:5, 2 Corinthians 5:1, and Revelation 3:12, 21:9-14 & 21:22.

6. The Tribulation temple—Daniel 9:27, 11:31 & 12:11, Jeremiah 33:11, Ezekiel 37:24-28 & 43:1-4, Mathew 24:15, 2 Thessalonians 2:4, Revelation 11:1. The Bible describes that there will be a temple and sacrificial service and offerings during the time before Jesus returns to defeat the Antichrist, in accordance with the prophecy pronounced by Daniel.

7. Ezekiel's temple/millennial temple—Ezekiel chapters 40-45, Micah 4:1-5, Isaiah 2:2-3, 60:4-14 & 66:20, Zechariah 6:12-15. After the devastation and destruction of the Tribulation, the tribulation temple will be either damaged or totally destroyed and will then be purified and repaired/rebuilt and expanded under the reign of Christ (which may also be another and final fulfillment of the 2300 mornings and evenings in Daniel 8:13-14).

ACKNOWLEDGMENTS

I WANT TO THANK GOD for being able to write this book to reveal what he has hidden for so long in plain sight. This book has been written for his glory.

I must again acknowledge the invaluable work of Dr. Asher Kaufmann and Dr. Leen Ritmeyer, who each identified a key landmark of the temple, which together make the case for its location so clear. I also want to thank renowned Israeli archaeologist Dr. Dan Bahat for his willingness to engage in discussions regarding his temple placement views and objections to a northern location.

I am also incredibly grateful for the advice and support of Josh McDowell and for his willingness to write the foreword for this book. Without his friendship and encouragement, I would have been hesitant to write a book on such a momentous and controversial subject. I am deeply grateful for the help of another well-known Christian author whom I have had the pleasure of knowing, Joel Richardson. His support and assistance navigating the world of Christian publishing was invaluable. As a consequence, I can also thank Geoff Stone for his excellent editing work and for guiding me through the publishing process, as well as Mark Karis for his outstanding design skills. This book wouldn't be what it is without them.

I would additionally like to thank some friends—Paul Simpson, Michael McCormick, Haiping Hong, Pastor David Greenhood, Pastor Russ Ryherd, Pastor Tom Yount, Andrew Jones, L. A. Marzulli, Shane Heilman, Chad Burns, Maury Carlisle, Ryan Tidrick, Dalton Thomas, Marc Ash, and Pastor Oleg Reutki—for their advice and encouragement. I owe a special thanks to my former pastor Mike Andrus for reviewing my draft manuscript and giving me valuable feedback to improve the text. I also need to thank Dr. Kyle Caudle, an associate professor of mathematics at the South Dakota School of Mines and Technology for his consultation and verification of my methods regarding the probability calculations discussed in the book.

I want to thank Moshe Bronstein, who led my family and me around Israel for three weeks during the High Holy Days in 2017 and again in the fall of 2019, visiting archaeological sites. Without those trips, this book could not have been written.

I would be remiss without thanking my parents, Russ and Maggie Widener, who have been godly parents, constant encouragers, and my prayer warriors, for helping me with edits and useful comments for the book.

I also have to thank my wonderful wife, Consuelo, who is the sounding board for all of my best and worst notions and ideas, and who has been a true partner in this task as well.

Finally, I want to acknowledge my four most treasured possessions in the world, my "gold bricks": Elena, Corban, Noah, and Eva. It is to them that I most want to pass on a legacy of faith and deep study in the inspired Word of God to help guide them to become all God has made them to be as the next generation of Christ followers in our family.

ABOUT THE AUTHOR

Dr. Christian Widener is a biblical scholar, researcher, and engineer. His interest in biblical archaeology stems from a passion for apologetics and the reliability of the literal and historic accounts of the Bible, as well as its prophetic predictions for the coming Tribulation, the last-days temple, and the return of Jesus Christ to bring "all things in heaven and on earth together under one head" (Ephesians 1:10). While the Scriptures include many things that may be hard to believe or understand, Dr. Widener believes that the Bible is trustworthy, and that it can be tested scientifically and reasoned out logically, providing one separates facts from their interpretations. He believes that the Bible—not external sources or modern secular speculations based on naturalistic assumptions—is the preeminent testimony about the past. The precise location of the temple has been a subject of his private interest and study for more than a decade.

Dr. Widener earned his PhD in mechanical engineering, with an emphasis in materials and manufacturing from Wichita State University and was a tenured associate professor at the South Dakota School of Mines and Technology. In his professional career, Dr. Widener is a successful entrepreneur and an internationally recognized expert in the fields of solid-state metals deposition and processing, additive manufacturing, and repair.

Dr. Widener lives in the Black Hills of South Dakota, with his wife and their four children.

FURTHER ENGAGEMENT

Are you interested in ways to help support this work and Israel rebuilding the temple? Here's how you can help:

1. Please leave an honest and unbiased review for this book on Amazon and other retailer websites to help encourage people to read it.

2. Please tell others what you thought about my book and share a link to it on your social media accounts so that others in your network can also learn what you now know.

3. Follow my blog and find out the latest updates at my website: EndTimesBerean.com.

 End Times Berean

4. Watch for updates on my next book: *Finding Solomon: Rediscovering the Works of Israel's Greatest Builder.*

Thank you so much for reading my book! I hope it was a real encouragement to you and that you have your extra oil ready and the wick of your lamp trimmed, because the bridegroom is coming soon! Maranatha!

— CHRISTIAN WIDENER

INDEX

SCRIPTURE INDEX

Printed in the USA
CPSIA information can be obtained
at www.ICGtesting.com
LVHW021945220324
775262LV00005B/371/J

9 780578 748825